Journeys to
Professional Excellence
Lessons From Leading
Counselor Educators and Practitioners

Edited by
Robert K. Conyne and Fred Bemak

AMERICAN COUNSELING ASSOCIATION
5999 Stevenson Avenue
Alexandria, VA 22304
www.counseling.org

Journeys to
Professional Excellence
• •
Lessons From Leading
Counselor Educators and Practitioners

10   9   8   7   6   5   4   3   2   1

American Counseling Association
  5999 Stevenson Avenue
  Alexandria, VA 22304

Director of Publications
  Carolyn C. Baker

Production Manager
  Bonny E. Gaston

Copy Editor
  Christine Calorusso

Cover design by Martha Woolsey

Library of Congress Cataloging-in-Publication Data
Journeys to professional excellence: lessons from leading counselor educators and practitioners / Robert K. Conyne and Fred Bemak, editors.
    p. cm.
  Includes bibliographical references.
  ISBN 1-55620-242-3 (alk. paper)
  1. Counselors—United States—Biography. I. Conyne, Robert K. II. Bemak, Fred.

  BF637.C6J69 2005
  158'.3'092273—dc22   2004019722

Contents

Acknowledgments

· ·

I am moved by the deeply personal and meaningful nature of the sharing exhibited by the authors in this book. Thank you for your openness! And, for all those (too numerous to mention) who have helped me along the path of my own professional journey, I am profoundly grateful. A special acknowledgment goes to my coeditor, Fred, who is always great to work with and who advised me, "Go to the Simon and Garfunkel concert, Bob. You only live once!" Of course, in a personal vein, I would be remiss if I did not single out Lynn Rapin, with whom I have been traveling our life's journey; our children, Suzanne and Zack; and the memories of my parents.

—*Bob Conyne*

· · ·

This book was a gift to edit. The contributing authors are exceptional people and skilled writers who are established leaders in the field of counseling. My coeditor, Bob Conyne, is a wonderful friend and colleague and a dream to work with. The stories of my colleagues and friends in this book are deeply personal and moving, and inspirational for us all. My deep thanks to the contributors and my coeditor, as well as to my lifelong companion Rita Chi-Ying Chung; my children, Amber and Lani; and my parents, Walter and Ruth, who have all made my journey that much richer and more meaningful.

—*Fred Bemak*

Preface

• •

People often work with colleagues about whom they really know very little, sometimes for years and even decades. Likewise, we hear about famous individuals, read their writings in books and journals, and hear them speak. Yet we may know precious little about their personal lives, how they go about their work, or how their ideas originated and evolved. This book is an attempt to get a closer look at some of the leading people in our field: those who are renowned for their work and have made an impact in the field of counseling. All of us are on our own journey, trekking along paths that have taken us to various destinations and are destined to take us to still different places in the future. Yet much of this journey is privately held. Some people know about our trials and tribulations and our ups and downs, but typically this knowledge is limited to those who are most intimately involved with our personal lives, such as life partners, family members, and close friends and colleagues. Our time is short and the pressure of modern-day living is ever present, leaving us little time to sit, reflect, and share our unique experiences and pathways. A famous colleague lamented to me (Fred) several years ago that she felt sorry for my generation of professionals. "Why?" I asked. Her response was poignant: "Because you don't have time to sit and reflect on your experience, to enjoy and think about what you are doing and where you came from to get where you are."

Both of us (Bob and Fred) are regularly reminded of the perceptiveness of this colleague's observation. People regularly ask us in the hallways at work, "How are you?" Frequently, we are rushing ahead to our next task, scurrying down the hallway to another meeting or to a waiting computer to finish the last touches on an article or book. Our replies are always similar: "Kind of frantic, actually," or "Okay, but really swamped," or "Fine, fine, but on the move." Our colleagues, who most often have the same response, nod their heads in acknowledgment and frequently comment, "I know what you mean," and move on to their waiting meetings and tasks. We all expect this kind of encounter and might feel quite put out if people regularly stopped us to explain how they really felt, share their experiences from earlier that morning or the night before, or talk about some of the existential questions they were wrestling with at the time. The point is that these kinds of social exchanges, which occur frequently during the course of any workday, do little to help any of us become known to or know about our colleagues. We find out about the death of a colleague's parent, the illness of a child or partner, the new theory they are developing, or the grant they submitted only sometimes and, then, frequently after the fact.

Just today, before passing someone in the hallway with the typical rushed greeting, I (Bob) got a call from our college development officer, who said he had something to give me. It turned out to be three small gifts, each acknowledging that I annually give a small amount of money to the college. One of the gifts was an empty, bound notebook intended to be a journal. I appreciated this gift, because it provided a means for recording life events and encouraging reflection on their meaning. It offered a way to examine one's journey, whether or not that was the conscious intention of the giver. Gifts like these are less frequent in our rushed professional lives but symbolize a different side of us that is regularly ignored in our fast-paced lives.

This book chronicles the self-described professional journeys of 15 highly regarded counselor educators and practitioners. It was created with the "journal" metaphor in mind, not the "passing in the hallway" one. The idea was born of informal discussions we had at a conference with some well-known colleagues about aspects of their professional lives (see chapter 1 for more detail). We discovered four very important points during those conversations: (a) Each of these individuals had a tremendous number of important personal things to say (which was no surprise), (b) they had found little opportunity to share these things with colleagues over the years (which was disappointing), (c) they became very engaged as they talked about their life experiences (which was exciting), and (d) we and everyone at the table became fascinated by what others were saying.

We then realized that these tales needed telling. We thought about the need for others to hear about the journeys of these renowned professionals and decided that a book could be beneficial to all levels of our profession: the younger, up-and-coming professionals already in the field; students in training and just beginning their professional journeys; and middle- and senior-level professionals who can compare and contrast the stories in the book with their own journeys. We saw this book as a way to provide some examples, in very personal and moving prose, of how some of the well-known people in our field have grown, developed, and become the individuals and professionals they are today.

The more we thought about it, the more exuberant we became about the idea of this book. We began shaping guidelines for authors, trying to provide some order to the personal narratives of our contributors. Selecting authors (from so many wonderful choices) was very difficult: There are so many terrific colleagues, and we only had room for 15. We asked 15 very busy people each to write a chapter in the book, and they all agreed (see the list of contributors and table of contents). As each chapter arrived, we were profoundly moved by our colleagues' stories without exception. What a joy to read such a wealth of personal journeys. The content was deep, revealing, and compelling. We were so moved by what the authors had written that we sent Carolyn Baker (director of publications at the American Counseling Association) this gushing e-mail:

> Fred and I just want you to know that we are absolutely bowled over by the powerful chapters we have been receiving from the authors of the *Professional Journeys* book! The level of personal disclosure as it relates to career paths has far exceeded anything we could have hoped for, and the quality of writing (as we would all expect) has been high!

We went on to add:

> We read these chapters and think something like this: "How fortunate we are to be in this profession with these terrific people." And, further, we can't help but think that readers will find the book's contents to be inspiring and important. (R. K. Conyne, personal communication, March 11, 2004)

Of course, we could be wrong, swept up in the rapture of the moment and having lost all objectivity. We must leave it to you, the reader, to judge. Our hope is that you will find the descriptions of these professional journeys to be as exciting, instructive, and inspiring as we have found them. And we hope that they help each of you on your wonderful journey.

About the Editors

Robert K. Conyne, PhD, is a professor and director of the Counseling Program at the University of Cincinnati. Bob has authored or coauthored 10 books and more than 200 scholarly articles, all focused on group work, prevention, and ecological approaches to counseling. He is married to Lynn S. Rapin, PhD, and they have two children, Suzanne and Zachary. The family lives in Cincinnati, Ohio, and spends rare special moments at their cottage in St. Joseph Island, Ontario.

• • •

Fred Bemak, EdD, is a professor and program coordinator of the Counseling and Human Development Program at George Mason University. Fred has written extensively about working with at-risk youth and families, cross-cultural counseling, group counseling, the transformation of school counseling, and refugee mental health. He has provided consultation and training and offered seminars and lectures throughout the United States and in 30 other countries, and is a former Fulbright Scholar, Kellogg International Fellow, and World Rehabilitation Fund International Exchange of Experts Fellow. Fred enjoys traveling, hiking, theater, and music with his wife and two children.

About the Contributors
● ●

Patricia Arredondo, EdD, is a professor in the Division of Psychology in Education at Arizona State University.

Madonna G. Constantine, PhD, is a professor in the Department of Counseling and Clinical Psychology at Teachers College, Columbia University.

Gerald Corey, PhD, is a professor emeritus of human services at California State University, Fullerton.

George M. Gazda, EdD, is a research professor emeritus at the University of Georgia and a clinical professor in the Department of Psychiatry at the Medical College of Georgia.

Samuel T. Gladding, PhD, is an associate provost and chair of the Department of Counseling at Wake Forest University.

Jane Goodman, PhD, is a professor in the Department of Counseling at Oakland University.

A. Michael Hutchins, PhD, is in private practice in Tucson, Arizona, and on staff at Cottonwood de Tucson Treatment Center.

Allen E. Ivey, PhD, is a distinguished university professor emeritus at the University of Massachusetts, Amherst.

Jeffrey A. Kottler, PhD, is a professor and chair of the Department of Counseling at California State University, Fullerton.

Courtland C. Lee, PhD, is a professor of counselor education at the University of Maryland.

Judy Lewis, PhD, is a university professor and chair of the Department of Addictions Studies at Governors State University.

Marianne H. Mitchell, PhD, is a professor emerita of education at Indiana University.

Mark Pope, EdD, is an associate professor in the Division of Counseling, Counseling Psychology, and Family Therapy at the University of Missouri—St. Louis.

Derald Wing Sue, PhD, is a professor of psychology and education at Teachers College, Columbia University.

Clemmont E. Vontress, PhD, is a professor emeritus of counseling at George Washington University.

Chapter 1

Introduction to the Journeys
●●

Robert K. Conyne and Fred Bemak

The idea for this book began innocuously enough. Spending some down-time during an Association for Counselor Education and Supervision national conference (October 2002), we (Bob and Fred) started talking about how each of us goes about the task of scholarly writing. Quickly, we discovered quite different styles. For instance, Fred tends to mass his writing in set-aside chunks of time, whereas Bob tries to write a little bit every day, around the "edges" of work time. Although both styles have been productive, we were struck with how differently we approached our writing. We then began to reflect on the history of our experience and training that influenced who we are today as professionals and how we work.

As we talked, we realized that this kind of conversation—revealing and comparing writing styles—was very interesting and exciting. This led us to wonder how other scholars in our field approached the task of writing, and we began to consider the possibility of researching this question and, perhaps, writing about it if we found anything of substance. We became quite enthusiastic about this prospect and began asking other scholars at the conference about their writing styles. People were very open to discussing this question, but it was difficult for them to restrict their answers to the issue of writing style only. Ultimately, the conversation expanded to an exploration of individuals' working styles in general and their emergence developmentally.

At our luncheon table that day, we (Bob and Fred) participated in perhaps the most involving table discussion either of us had ever experienced at a conference. We simply observed that talking that morning with some attendees (all well-known professionals) had led to lots of interesting material about how they went about their work and how they had gotten to the present point in their professional lives. Others around the table began to connect with this issue, and soon there was a lively and in-depth interaction occurring. One person talked about how growing up in poverty had led to a certain set of values that had informed her work style; another, about how a childhood of international travel had shaped him in specific ways. The energy level was high, and the connections being made were palpable.

We were amazed and invigorated! Asking simple questions of accomplished individuals about their professional lives seemed to tap an immediate reservoir of memories and personally meaningful material. Moreover, it seemed that there was almost a kind of hunger to share these stories.

We processed these experiences later in the day and hypothesized that busy, successful counselor educators and counseling practitioners not only have much to convey about their professional lives that could benefit others but also may have taken little opportunity to share these things with others. Talking about one's own professional life course may just be something that is outside the realm of typical conversation.

Looking Inward

After returning home, we (Bob and Fred) decided to test this hypothesis through some self-examination. That is, we each spent some time looking inward, asking ourselves if we shared much with others about our own professional journeys and if others did so with us. The answer, clearly, was not often. Recently, on a long plane trip back from consulting work in Northern Ireland, we took some time to share with each other some of our own professional journeys. This process of sharing was both liberating and meaningful (we are counselors, after all!).

For instance, we discovered that not only were our writing styles different but we had grown up quite differently as well. Bob's family, for example, lived in a small, barren, and isolated rural town near the Canadian border and had no history of college attendance, experienced economic hardship, and had little orientation to cultural events and experiences. On the other hand, Fred grew up near a large metropolitan city that offered access to cultural diversity and the arts and encouraged a strong emphasis on education.

And yet, both of us seemingly have progressed well in our respective careers, with a considerable amount of overlap in terms of professional values and commitment. The counseling programs that we direct, for example, have been written about in *Counseling Today* as highly innovative and unique, focusing on themes of social justice (George Mason University with Fred) and ecological approaches (University of Cincinnati with Bob).

We decided, then, to formally explore this whole issue through a book. Over a few weeks of e-mail and phone conversations, we developed a book proposal centered on the concept of the "professional journey." We wanted famous professionals to trace their steps and look to the future in a way that would guide and inspire readers.

Selecting the authors was a difficult task. We were interested in well-known professionals that readers would be intrigued by and want to learn more about. We also wanted to represent some diversity among those authors in terms of race, gender, sexual orientation, specialty area, counselor educator versus practitioner, and other variables. Because of space limitations, we were forced to select 15 authors. Those who have written about their professional journeys in this book are all at the top of the profession and have provided us with exceptional travelogues. Unfortunately, many other wonderful role models and colleagues could not be included simply because of page limits.

We developed a set of guiding questions over time (see below), that emerged from our own curiosity and related literature (e.g., Krumboltz, 1998; Magnuson, Wilcoxon, & Norem, 2003; West, Osborn, & Bubenzer, 2003). General categories of questions emerged to guide our instructions to authors: (a) past influences, (b) the experience of the journey, (c) the connection between theory and practice, (d) development as a multicultural counselor, (e) style of working and accomplishments, (f) predictions about the future journey, and (g) advice for younger professionals. Including references was optional.

By providing such a guiding structure, we intended for readers to be exposed to a consistency of approach that often is lacking in edited books. In addition, we thought that this kind of consistency might lead to the possibility of identifying themes and divergence across the journeys. We will leave it to readers and reviewers to judge whether the first goal was met. We can say that the second one was, and we were able to draw from those themes in producing the final chapter of this book.

What follows are the general guiding questions that the authors were asked to consider as they wrote their chapters:

Questions That Guided Authors' Exploration and Writing

We asked each contributing author to be guided generally by the questions below as they wrote their chapters. Authors were asked to address all seven categories by selecting from each the questions that were most relevant to them.

Past Influences on Your Journey

- How did your journey take you to the counseling field?
- What happened in your life that caused you to become a professor?
- What event or events from your childhood relate to where you are today?
- What values or family influences contributed to you being who and where you are today?

Experiencing Your Professional Journey

- How has the journey been for you?
- What were your most fulfilling moments?
- What were your scariest moments?
- What have you valued over the years?
- What has been burdensome for you?
- How have you kept your focus in the midst of daily events and challenges?
- What were your challenges?

- From what sources have you gathered strength?
- How have you been able to balance work and personal life?

Connection Between Theory and Practice

- What do you believe about people and change (e.g., the philosophy that is the foundation for your work in the counseling field)?
- How has your practice as a counselor (define role and function and elaborate implementation) influenced your development as a professor or practitioner?
- How have you been able to balance practice and theory in your role?
- What advice do you have for newcomers to the field?
- What advice do you have for people who are at a mid-career point in counseling?

Development as a Multicultural Counselor

- When did you learn about or become aware of cultural diversity?
- How did you learn about cultural diversity?
- Were there any key moments in your life that heightened your awareness and sensitivity beyond your own culture?
- What significant personal or professional experiences did you have that helped you integrate cultural diversity into your work?
- What advice or suggestions do you have from your own experience for up-and-coming colleagues in the field regarding the development of multiculturalism as a line of research, practice, or service?

Style of Working and Accomplishments

- What is your work style?
- Given your accomplishments, how have you approached combining work and personal life?
- What do you consider your biggest accomplishments, and how were you able to do these things?
- What were some of your biggest challenges?
- What is the "secret" of your success?
- Where do you get your new ideas from?
- Looking back, what have you learned?

Predictions About Your Future Journey

- What more do you want to do?
- Realistically, what's next for you?
- Where do you see the profession going?

Advice for Younger Professionals

- What's your advice for how graduate students can best prepare for becoming a faculty member or future professional?

- What tips might you give to younger faculty members?
- Any final thoughts and reflections?

There were many surprises and new information as we read about the journeys of our colleagues. Each journey is captivating in its own way and helps us understand the individual in a far deeper and more profound way. We hope you will enjoy reading these stories as much as we have.

References

Krumboltz, J. (1998). Serendipity is not serendipitous. *Journal of Counseling Psychology, 45*, 390–392.

Magnuson, S., Wilcoxon, S. A., & Norem, K. (2003). Career paths of professional leaders in counseling: Plans, opportunities, and happenstance. *The Journal of Humanistic Counseling, Education and Development, 42*, 42–52.

West, J., Osborn, C., & Bubenzer, D. (Eds.). (2003). *Leaders and legacies: Contributions to the profession of counseling.* New York: Brunner-Routledge.

Uncharted Waters:
Autobiographical Notes
• •

Clemmont E. Vontress

My life has not been easy. At times, I have felt as if I were afloat on a turbulent sea, buffeted by gigantic waves and headed toward an unknown destination. Despite such intermittent feelings, I have been a counselor educator and psychologist for more than 40 years. If I have been successful in either role, it is only because I am a wounded healer. Despite my imperfection, I have taught and helped others to live a richer life than I have lived. The purpose of this chapter is to indicate briefly some of the people, places, events, and conditions that have shaped my existence. Finally, I mention some of my professional contributions of which I am most proud.

People Who Influenced My Life

Many people have influenced my life in ways that were not always obvious to me then and there. Primary among them was my father, the repository of our family history. He told my siblings and me that our ancestors were European immigrants from Germanic Alsace who arrived in the New World in the 18th century and settled in Kentucky. During the Civil War, the men on the Vontress plantation went off to fight for or against the Union. Children, women, and slaves stayed behind to manage the farm. One of these children was a 14-year-old boy who cohabited with a mulatto slave girl who worked in the big house. According to my father, that boy fathered three children by the girl, who was only 13 years old when the relationship began. One of the children was my grandfather.

The Civil War ended in 1865, and the period between 1867 and 1877 became known as the Reconstruction. Although Kentucky had not been part of the Confederacy, sentiments for and against the Union ran high there. It was during that period that Night Riders, later known as the Ku Klux Klan (KKK), began to terrorize newly emancipated Blacks in order to keep them "in their place" at the bottom of the social, political, and economic scales. They also punished Whites for openly associating with Blacks. My great-grandfather had violated a racial taboo by marrying a slave, and the KKK killed him for the violation. My grandfather stayed on the farm to work the land. He "married colored." His two sisters went to live with an aunt and "married White." When the children became adults, each got one third of the plantation. When my father inherited the land, he married a Black woman and fathered 10 children. I am one of them. He and my older siblings farmed the land uneventfully until I was born in 1929, the year of the Great Depression.

When the American economy collapsed, things changed rapidly and drastically for the Vontress family. My father had to sell the farm for what he could get for it. We became sharecroppers, working as semi-slaves for White landowners. I remember moving from one dilapidated farmhouse to another. Obliged to work the fields alongside my father, my siblings and I attended elementary school only intermittently. However, during the off-season, we walked to the one-room schoolhouse located about two miles down a dirt road. Sometimes we stayed home for want of warm clothes to wear. The lack of shoes was a real problem. In the fall and spring we could go barefoot, but in the winter we often stuffed newspaper in our shoes to cover the holes in the soles to protect our feet from the cold and snow. Of the 10 children, only three of us attended high school. My oldest sister, 12 years my senior, finished college, obtained a master's degree in English, and taught school for more than 30 years. I finished college and obtained a master's degree and a doctorate. To this day, I do not know how my sister and I managed to obtain higher education.

My mother was the family's Rock of Gibraltar. She did everything for her 10 children (eight boys and two girls) and husband. Her daily routine was to rise before daybreak to prepare breakfast so that the "men folk" could be in the fields by sunup. After serving a hardy breakfast, clearing the long kitchen table, and washing the dishes, she would start "dinner" (lunch). During the growing season, she usually went out back to pick some "greens" or other wild vegetables that she knew were edible. Once the lunch pots had begun to simmer on the wood-burning kitchen stove, she would boil and wash by hand the work clothes that my father and brothers had worn days before. She wanted to keep her family clean. In addition to performing these chores, she was also seamstress, nursemaid, housekeeper, and hostess for visitors. Regardless of when friends, relatives, or strangers came "a-calling" unannounced, my mother would rush to the henhouse to collect fresh eggs and chase down two or three chickens in the barnyard to "cook up a meal" for the guests.

Whenever my mother gave birth to a child, she was usually up and about the next day to look after her family. After all, she insisted that she was not sick. She only had a baby. My mother was also the one who heated the water to bathe us in the big round tin tub in front of the fireplace in the living room when we were too young to bathe ourselves. I never heard her complain about all the work she did to care for 11 family members. She died of old age at 96.

When I started making fieldtrips to Africa in the 1980s to study traditional healing, I met women who reminded me of my mother, especially housewives in the villages. The supportive role that they play at home is indispensable to the welfare and survival of the family. Their parents, friends, and neighbors usually criticize severely any woman who fails to look after her family. Nobody could criticize my mother for that reason. She executed her perceived duties in a calm, caring, and efficient manner. I do not recall that she ever whipped any of us. She recognized that each of us had a role to play and that each of us tried to perform our chores as well as she performed hers. She always said, "Whatever you do, do it right!" I will never forget her. She influenced my life mostly by her example of caring, empathy, perfection, perseverance, quietude, stoic endurance, and unselfishness.

My sister, the English teacher, also influenced my life. After finishing college in 1940, she married and moved to Indiana, where she and her husband obtained employment. She encouraged me to enroll in the high school where she graduated. I escaped the fields and attended that school, the only one for Blacks in the county. Located in Bowling Green, Kentucky, it was far from where we lived in the country. At 14, I found an after-school job in the city and stayed at a boarding house. I graduated with honors in 1948. To pave the way for her young brother, my sister told the teachers about me before I matriculated. Upon my arrival, they constantly compared me unfavorably with her. She had graduated with high honors.

When I completed high school, I attended Kentucky State University, just as my sister had earlier. In 1952, I obtained a BA degree in French and English. That fall, I entered graduate school on a fellowship at the University of Iowa. Although my first major was French language and literature, I took a graduate course in American literature. I was the only Black in a class of 60 students. Mark Twain was the focus of the class. In lecturing, the professor used many negative racial slurs, such as "nigger in the woodpile." Apparently, he did not notice my presence or did not care that he might offend me. In evaluating my term paper for the course, he told me that my writing skills were inadequate. At the end of the semester, I received a C. That was the only C that I ever got in graduate school. Since that experience, I have tried to prove that professor wrong. My encounter with him, although negative at the time, has turned out to be a positive influence. I have published over 100 articles, chapters, and books on a variety of subjects related to counseling.

I took a minor in sociology at Indiana University in Bloomington, where I received my PhD in counseling in 1965. One of my professors talked a great deal about people being "culturally deprived," "culturally disadvantaged," or "disadvantaged." Although he never used the words "Negro" or "colored" (terms used to refer to African Americans at the time), I knew he was talking euphemistically about my race. I suppressed my anger and declared to myself that one day I would look into the matter more deeply. I had done enough reading in my undergraduate sociology classes to know that culture is a human necessity. Everybody has a culture. That is why I have devoted most of my professional career to studying and writing about culture and its effect on counseling.

There was another professor at Indiana University who influenced me negatively. He taught organization and administration of guidance services. Unfortunately, he did not do the teaching. Instead, he let students give reports. Of course, we knew nothing about the topic. We had enrolled in the class to learn what we did not know. Although I got an *A* in the course, I vowed that if I ever became a university professor, I would not use him as a model. When I became a university professor years later, I developed a course called Organization and Administration of Counseling Services. Of course, I had spent 7 years as director of counseling in a large high school before I became a university professor. I felt that experience as a counselor and administrator was a prerequisite for teaching.

Perry J. Rockwell Jr., my major professor at Indiana University, was a positive influence on my career. A kind and supportive advisor, he came to the university when I was midway through my degree program. I remember showing him an article that I had published in a leading refereed journal. He praised it and said that he wished that he could write like that. That statement meant a great deal to me, especially since the professor at the University of Iowa had said that I could not write. Dr. Rockwell invited me to his home for dinner. Years later, at the American Counseling Association conventions, there he was, sitting in the front row at my presentations, as if he wanted to cheer me on. I felt that he was proud of me. Otherwise, why would he continue to show up year after year to hear my presentations?

While I was at Indiana University, Carl Rogers, then guru of counseling, came to the campus to keynote a statewide conference. I was one of the doctoral students selected to share the dais with him, in order to ask him questions after his speech. It was the 1960s, during the Civil Rights Movement. Client-centered counseling, as compared to the directive or Williamsonian approach, was the preferred psychotherapeutic method. During his presentation, Dr. Rogers talked about the therapeutic importance of rapport, congruence, and unconditional positive regard. He considered these to be prerequisites for effective counseling. When my time came to ask him a question, I wanted to know how his approach could be effective in counseling angry African American clients. He responded that it was effective with all clients, if they perceived the aforementioned qualities in the counselor. Uncomfortable with his response, I wanted to study the matter further. That is what I have done for most of my career. I have taken the best of the Rogerian approach and added to it existential ideas from many parts of the world to develop an existential cross-cultural counseling model.

Two years before I retired in 1997 from George Washington University, where I was professor of counseling and director of the counseling program, I invited Peter Breggin to speak at a seminar at the university. An internationally known psychiatrist and founder and former director of the International Center for the Study of Psychiatry and Psychology, he posits that biopsychiatry is dangerous to adults and children. It is especially dangerous for young children to take antidepressants and other such medicines to reduce their energy and activity, because their brains are still developing. Research has yet to show the possible long-range effects of psychotropic drugs on their bodies. Peter and his wife, Ginger, maintain that as long as we respond to the signals of conflicts and distress in our children by subduing them with drugs, we will never address their genuine needs. As parents, teachers, therapists, and physicians, we need to retake responsibility for children. They need love and attention, not psychiatric medication. Indeed, I found a philosophical soul mate in Peter Breggin. Human life is unimaginable without pain, suffering, and sorrow. This is a theme that I posit often in my writings on existential counseling.

Places That Keep Coming Back

There are many places that I think about for various reasons. Perhaps I still visualize something about them because they affected me significantly in a way that I cannot know. I recall the farms where we lived when I was a child. The barnyard was full of animals. I saw them "doing the natural," as my father called animal intercourse. He explained that the action was necessary to produce little animals. He said that sex was related to life and death. Without sex there would be no life, and without life there would be no death. My father taught me that lesson when I was five, and I have never forgotten it. In one form or another, it has been reflected in my existential essays.

I think about Europe a lot, especially France. Although I lived in Germany most of the time I served in the military in Europe, I spent a great deal of time in France. It was there that I saw Josephine Baker, the African American entertainer who left this country in the early 1920s to seek her fortunes in France. She became a French citizen and fought in the Resistance during the Nazi occupation. In 1953, I went to see her perform at a large music hall in Paris. Playing to a packed house, she apologized for being "chocolate." The men in the audience responded, "It's better that way!" I had never seen Whites express such great appreciation for a Black person. I recognized what could be someday in the United States. I also knew what was missing in my own life: acceptance and respect. Henceforth, I read a great deal, especially books on psychology. I wanted to understand what I had become, living in a racist society.

In Paris, I saw Jean-Paul Sartre and his constant companion Simone de Beauvoir sitting in a bar, which I later learned was their usual hangout. The only reason I know that it was them is because I kept a leaflet that they were handing out one day when I stopped there with a French friend. At the time, I did not associate them with European existentialism. However, years later when I started reading works of existential writers, I read what they had written back then.

I have been to Kuwait twice, once before the Persian Gulf War (1987) and once after the war (1992). The first time there, I was engaged as a consultant to help a group of psychology professors develop a university counseling center. The second time, the university invited my former student Dr. Morris

L. Jackson and me there to teach Kuwaiti social workers counseling techniques designed to help clients who had been traumatized by the Gulf War. Although my experiences surrounding these responsibilities were interesting, they are not what I remember most about Kuwait. The near-death experience I had during my last trip to that country sticks most in my mind. As we entered Kuwaiti airspace, the plane encountered the turbulence of a sandstorm and fell more than a thousand feet. The passengers were praying and screaming loudly in several languages, because they expected immediate death. However, I sat unmoved, observing the panic surrounding me. After the pilot pulled the airplane out of the fall, we landed in nearby Qatar, where we remained until we finally returned to Kuwait. In retrospect, I learned something about myself: I was not afraid of death. In life, change the things you can; but when you cannot alter the inevitable, take it stoically. That recognition is a theme in much of my writing related to existential counseling.

During the last 25 years, I have made six trips to Africa. I went to North Africa (Morocco) once and West Africa (Burkina Faso, Côte d'Ivoire, and Senegal) five times. In these countries I talked with people about whom they consulted when they had physical, psychological, spiritual, and social problems. I also interviewed traditional healers in order to learn how they helped patients with presenting problems. Although I have published several articles highlighting findings of these fieldtrips to Africa, the thing I remember most is how much of what I learned there was what my father taught us when we were young. For example, he told us that God is everywhere and that He exists in each of us. He advised us to love God but to beware of self-appointed people and institutions pretending to represent Him. I am sure he felt that way because the people who killed his grandfather were the local preacher and his deacons dressed in white sheets. In Africa, I heard the same view expressed by people who called themselves animists. God is. It is everywhere. It resides in us. It resides in everything in nature. I understood more clearly what my father taught me when I was a child. I was happy to encounter his message again. I was spiritually revitalized. I have tried to communicate some of that revitalization in my writings about traditional healing and existential counseling.

Memorable Life Events

There are some life events that I think about often. Even though I cannot always recall their precise time or place, they are tucked away in the back of my mind, emerging from time to time. For example, I remember the radio shows that our whole family used to listen to every night after supper. Huddled around the Philco tabletop radio in the living room, we anxiously waited for the beating hoof sounds and the "Hi Yo Silver, away!" signature of the "Lone Ranger," the squeaking door of "I Love a Mystery," or the Saturday night guitar and banjo playing of the Grand Ole Opry. Since there were no images to view, the announcer for each program helped us to visualize what we could not see. A comfortable feeling comes over me when I think of those evenings on the farm when our family enjoyed the only entertainment available to us.

Pearl Harbor is another unforgettable event. It was December 7, 1941. A bulletin came on the radio announcing that American ships had been attacked at Pearl Harbor. Because my family had never heard of the faraway place, we did not believe the event would affect us. We were wrong. A few days later, a representative from the county draft board came to our house to tell us that at least one person from our family would have to go to war. That person was my second oldest brother. He went into the Navy and traveled throughout the world. Although we had never been out of the county where we were born, my brother brought the outside world to us through the letters and pictures he sent home. On one of his leaves, he brought home a young woman from a distant place to visit us. I believe that she was from one of the Pacific islands. In any case, we had never met anybody like her before. As an early adolescent, I was filled with excitement. From then on, I dreamed of seeing the world, and that is what I have done. I have traveled throughout the United States and to more than 20 countries on three continents. My travel has given me a global perspective on human existence. It has helped me to develop a universal existential approach to cross-cultural counseling.

During high school, I worked each day in a print shop from 4 p.m. to late evening to earn money to pay for my room and board. The firm printed professional journals. I cleaned the ink from the huge rollers that were used to print pages from lead slugs that were locked into big plates. At the end of a run, the ink was hard to remove. I sometimes worked until midnight to prepare the rollers for the next day's run. However, that is not what I remember about working there. What I remember most is that the owner of the shop refused to call me by my name. Although I worked for him, an old German American, for four years, he called me John. When I told him that my name was not John, he said, "Well, the last boy who worked here was John. I don't have time to learn another name. Anyway, where did you get a name like Clemmont Vontress?" Even though devastated by that response, I could not do anything about it. I had to tolerate the insult to my dignity, because I needed the job to accomplish a larger goal.

Another significant event in life was marriage to my high school sweetheart. Our relationship started when we were in the ninth grade and continued when I went off to college. She stayed home and went to beauty school. After her graduation, she set up her own salon. I visited her often. Soon my hormones overpowered my reason, and my girl got pregnant during my second year in college. Although I had heard of shotgun weddings, I did not really know what to expect from her parents when they learned that she was expecting. It did not take long for me to find out. A few days after my sweetheart told me about her pregnancy, her father called me into the living room and said, "Son, you have knocked up my daughter. I want to know what you are going to do about it." Even though I had no resources and was working my way through college, I did the honorable thing. We got married. My wife gave birth to a healthy baby boy. I finished college and went on to graduate school at the University of Iowa, where I had received a scholarship to work on a master's degree in the Department of Romance Languages. Little did I realize how poverty and distance between spouses could affect a marriage. We were also immature, and each of us had different dreams. The relationship eventually ended in divorce.

Although I learned a valuable lesson, the insight was too little too late. Certainly, young people ought to think before assuming major adult responsibilities. Happiness in life is usually a product of careful planning. If I could "reshoot" that part of my life, I would have considered the implications of "doing the natural," as my father put it, before marriage. I was not prepared to accept the possible consequences of "going all the way" with someone I liked. Had I been more mature, I would not have taken sexual liberties with my high school sweetheart. Failure to consider the long-range implications of my behavior hurt two other people: my wife and my son. The divorce caused all of us a great deal of pain. Although my former wife eventually remarried, she was troubled most of her life until she died. My son dropped out of high school, became a drug addict, and died of drug-related complications. During his brief and difficult life, he fathered three sons. The youngest, 19, is attending college on a basketball scholarship. I have tried to be the father to my grandsons that I was not able to be to my son.

Restraining Conditions

I attended "separate but equal" schools until I matriculated at the University of Iowa in 1952 to begin graduate studies. Soon I realized how unequal my education had been. Although I had graduated from Kentucky State University with honors, I had to take a remedial course at Iowa State. I was also uncomfortable in classes with White students. I had been socialized to believe that they were superior and that I was inferior. The formative socialization caused me to interact reservedly with my classmates and professors.

I was not supposed to have been drafted into the military while I was in graduate school. When the draft board wrote me inquiring of my educational status, I told them that I was married and still in school, both of which by law should have continued my military exemption. Unfortunately, the tone of my letter was "too uppity," and six weeks after I left the university for summer vacation, I was in basic training at Fort Knox, Kentucky. My White colleagues remained in graduate school. Even so, my induction into the military was a blessing in disguise. When I was discharged two years later, I was able to finish two graduate degrees on the GI Bill of Rights.

I went into the military just when it was beginning to integrate. For the first time in the history of the country, Blacks and Whites were living and working together as equals. During orientation, I took several placement tests. On the basis of the results, I was assigned the military occupational specialty of interpreter. Even so, I was sent to clerk–typing school for eight weeks.

As the only Black in a class of 55 students, I stood out. This may have been why the instructor constantly hovered over my desk. I passed the course with honors and was sent to Germany, where I worked in battalion headquarters as a clerk–typist. As the only Black in my company, I often heard racial jokes and slurs. I got the impression that the White soldiers were not pleased with my presence.

When I was discharged from the army in 1955, I enrolled at Indiana University in Bloomington to work on a master's degree in counseling. In my classes, I was introduced to the views of Carl Rogers and E. G. Williamson, the two main counseling theorists at that time. I completed the program in 1956 but was unable to find a counseling position. I accepted a position as instructor in English at Southern University in Baton Rouge, Louisiana. Apparently, I got the job because I had taught English at an Army education center in Germany for about a year during my tour of duty in that country. In any case, I had never been so far south and was unprepared for the extent of segregation there. As a reaction to lawsuits protesting the inability of Blacks to get legal training in Louisiana, the state had instituted hastily on the Southern University campus a law school consisting of two professors. The Louisiana State University Law School, right across the road, refused to accept Black students. Police stopped students and professors at random, seemingly for no reason at all. White merchants addressed Blacks as "you people," "y'all people," or "you nigras." I left the university after one year to return to Indiana University to work on a PhD in counseling.

Bloomington, Indiana was still segregated in 1957. Local restaurants and pubs reluctantly started serving Blacks only after several weeks of protests in front of their establishments. Although university facilities were integrated, there were few Black students in graduate classes. I was hesitant to participate in class because I did not feel fully accepted. Although I passed the French PhD proficiency test, I had to take 15 hours of German to satisfy the other language requirement. I had taken 11 hours of German at the Indianapolis campus and needed only four more hours. Therefore, I took a two-week, six-day-a-week, all-day summer-intensive German course on campus. I was the only Black student in a class of about 50 doctoral students. The professor called on students to translate orally from randomly selected passages of German. I recall the day he called on me. I translated the designated passage without difficulty. At the end of my translation, the whole class applauded. I did not know how to interpret their reaction, since they did not applaud other students when they translated passages.

While working on my PhD, I took a position at a segregated high school in Indianapolis, Indiana, as director of counseling. There I became aware of the special counseling needs of Blacks. Simultaneously, I discovered that the client-centered counseling that I had learned in school was not effective with this clientele. I began to search for a supplement to it. Gradually, I began to add existential ideas to what I had learned in graduate school. In reading thinkers from many parts of the world over the years, I have formulated what I believe is a universal existential approach to counseling.

I left Crispus Attucks High School in 1965, the year I received my PhD, to take a professorship at Howard University, where I developed the university's first counselor education program. By 1969, predominantly White universities had begun to search for Black faculty members. That year, I accepted an associate professorship at George Washington University and became the second Black professor to be hired at the university. It was a first for most of us involved. I had never taught in a White university. The students there had never had a Black professor. White professors had never had a Black colleague. Understandably, relationships were sometimes racially tense.

I have mixed feelings about my 28 years at George Washington University. At times I felt accepted; at others, I felt rejected and offended. Even so, I received tenure after the required number of years in service, and the School of Education elected me to serve several terms on the university Faculty Senate. While on the senate, I encouraged the university leadership to be more aggressive in recruiting Black faculty members. Recently, the president of the university indicated that the senate resolutions I proposed to address this important matter had helped him promote equal opportunity on campus. I was promoted to full professor and served many years as coordinator of the counseling program. Today, the university provost is an African American man.

Over the years, I learned to respond differently to perceived racism. I used to strike out at people I considered to be overtly or covertly racist. I eventually learned that my defensive response was counterproductive. I began to ignore the racial slurs and rejections. My ignoring the insults seemed to reduce their number and intensity. I got the idea from observing how my African-born friends related to White Americans. Without the burden of the historical baggage of slavery, they were not poised to perceive every act and word as an indication of racism as were many Black Americans in the 1960s and 1970s. Defensive behavior, whatever the basis, tends to poison interpersonal relations. During the peak period of Black militancy in the country, I wrote an article titled "The Black Militant as a Counselor" (Vontress, 1972). I developed the thesis that counselors who force their militancy on their clients were antitherapeutic.

Significant Professional Contributions

I have developed several themes in my writing. The first one has been culture. This one began early in my career, primarily as a reaction to the experiences that I had in my sociology classes at Indiana University. The second theme is cross-cultural counseling. It is related to the first one. It is important to define culture in order to indicate how it affects counseling. I have tried to show that there are five cultural layers: the universal, ecological, national, regional, and racio-ethnic. We are all alike and different at the same time. The third theme is existential counseling. It, too, is related to the others, because it is most useful as a universal counseling model. The fourth theme is traditional healing, which also is related to culture. The fifth and final theme is ethnopsychiatry. I spent several years researching the work of Tobie Nathan at the University of Paris. He combines Western therapy with traditional healing practices in counseling African immigrants in France. Even though all of the themes are interrelated, I have been fulfilled most by my research and writing about existential counseling, because it has been personally psychotherapeutic.

I hold membership in several professional associations. During my professional career, I have been most active in the American Counseling Association. I joined it in 1965, when, on graduation day, my major professor recommended that I join it in order to stay current. Since that time, I have participated in the organization in various ways. From 1969 to 1971, I was a member of the Board of Directors. I served as a member of the association's Human Rights Commission from 1971 to 1975. From 1971 to 1974, I was a trustee and secretary of the association's Insurance Trust. Locally, I have been president of the District of Columbia Counseling Association twice, 1970–1971 and 1988–1989.

I also have served on the editorial boards of several professional journals. Included among them are the *Journal of Mental Health Counseling*, the *Journal of Negro Education*, the *Journal of Multicultural Counseling and Development*, the *Personnel and Guidance Journal* (now the *Journal of Counseling & Development*), and *Ethical Sciences and Services: An International Journal of Critical Inquiry*.

Since 1964, the first year that I attended the American Counseling Association's annual convention, I have presented more than 100 professional papers at 39 conventions. Of course, I also have presented papers at many other conventions. I am most proud of the keynote address, "Cross-Cultural Counseling in the 21st Century," that I gave at the conference of the International Association for Counseling in Tessaloniki, Greece, on May 5, 2000. During my career, I have been consultant to more than 100 groups, institutions, and organizations in this country and abroad. Throughout my professional career, I have taught over 4,000 graduate students and directed over 500 theses and dissertations.

Over the years, I have received countless recognitions. I have been recognized by various Who's Who publications. Three colleagues interviewed me for publication in refereed journals. In 1995, the American Mental Health Counselors Association presented me with the Counselor Educator of the Year Award. In 1997, I received the Counseling Awareness Month Award by the American Counseling Association for distinguished contribution to the counseling profession. In 2002, I was presented with the Lifetime Achievement Award by the International Center for the Study of Psychiatry and Psychology. Currently, I am chairman of the Board of Directors of that association.

During my career, I have been visiting professor at several universities. Included among them are Atlanta University, Johns Hopkins University, Virginia Polytechnic Institute and State University, and Howard University. I have also been consultant to more than a hundred groups, institutions, and organizations. Some of them are the U.S. Civil Service Commission; the U.S.

Defense Department; the U.S. State Department; Yale University; the National Urban League; Headquarters, United States Army, Europe and Seventh Army, Berchtesgaden, Germany; the U.S. Department of Labor; the International Monetary Fund; and the Superior Court of the District of Columbia.

Conclusion

Even though I am a wounded healer, I am a professional warrior. At the beginning, I was uncertain as to the course of my career. Once I got the correct coordinates, I have enjoyed the voyage. Currently professor emeritus of counseling at George Washington University, I continue to do what I was doing before I retired. Unencumbered by teaching and administrative responsibilities, I have more time to research, write, and conduct field trips. I like to let an idea incubate for a long time before I put it on paper. For example, I have been thinking about an article or book on cultural depression. Many of the psychological problems presented by clients today are caused by the nature of our culture. It is something that I have been considering for more than two years. Soon, I will develop it into an article or book. Still active in professional associations, I continue to present at annual conventions. I also try to get to France at least once a year to follow up on my research on counseling immigrants in that country.

As to where the profession is going, who is to say? The counseling profession is part of a larger social order. In our society, helping has become medicalized. When I first became a counselor, it was generally assumed that problems were products of sociocultural factors. Nowadays, many medical helpers believe that unacceptable behavior is a result of the brain gone wrong. Individuals are given pills to correct almost every behavior perceived to be a deviation from the norm. Insurance companies and third-party organizations intrude in the work of psychotherapeutic professionals. Who knows where the present trend will end. It has already changed significantly the work of counselors. In public schools, administrators and teachers want to maintain a quiet learning environment. In order to do so, they are apt to choose medicine over counseling, because they consider it most effective in the short run (their most immediate concern). Medicating people to change their behavior is likely to become more commonplace unless a strong movement emerges to stop the practice. Biopsychiatrists and drug companies are powerful forces to fight.

Reference

Vontress, C.E. (1972). The Black militant as a counselor. *Personnel and Guidance Journal, 50,* 574–580.

Chapter 3

Accentuating the Positives
●●

Samuel T. Gladding

I was born "on the cusp" of the end of World War II and the beginning of the baby boom. My parents were Virginians, as were their parents, grandparents, great-grandparents, and so on, going back on my father's side to the 1640s and on my mother's side to Jamestown. The fact that my birth took place in Atlanta, and that I was raised in the Atlanta suburb of Decatur, was due to my father's being transferred there by his company. The point is that I grew up in a home environment where there was an emphasis on history as well as on the importance of values such as civility, duty, honor, loyalty, work, and faith.

As the youngest of the three children of Russell Burton and Gertrude Templeman Gladding, I was constantly exposed to these principles through verbal and behavioral means. For instance, I frequently heard stories of ancestors who fought as patriots in the American Revolution, volunteered for duty in World War II, and did what they believed to be their patriotic duty as Confederate soldiers. I was taught to say "ma'am" and "sir" to anyone my senior. I grew up immersed in the Protestant work ethic, and every Sunday morning and evening, as well as every Wednesday afternoon and evening, my family went to church. We were Baptist. Having a consistent relationship with God became a strong thread in the fabric of my existence.

A Slow Start

But before that pattern of childhood emerged, there were barriers to overcome. My life from birth through toddlerhood was trying for my parents, siblings, and me. My sister, Peggy, was three years my senior, but my brother, Russell, was only 13 months older. A few months into my life, it was discovered that both Russell and I had dislocated hips as the result of an inherited genetic disorder known today as Brachydactyly Type C. To correct the situation, we each had a number of operations in which our hips were wired into our leg bones, and we wore body casts from our chests down to our toes for months on end. Much of the recovery and rehabilitation, including learning how to walk, took place at Atlanta's Scottish Rite Hospital, where my parents came to visit on Sundays. When we were allowed to go home, my mother propped us up and wheeled us around in wagons because the casts made us too heavy and bulky to carry.

In addition to the dislocated hips, the genetic disorder also left me with a dislocated left elbow, a couple of missing bones in my hands and feet, and shortness of stature. My brother was more fortunate and displayed none of these symptoms. Thus, coming together physically took some time for me, and I was noticeably different from my siblings. My sister grew to be 5'7" and my brother to be 5'10", whereas I reached the height of 5'3" (with shoes). I also had (and still have) what is known as Central Auditory Process Disorder, which manifests as the inability to accurately distinguish the sounds in words. It is a wonder my parents let me go to school, given that I pronounced it "cool" the night before the first day of class. Needless to say, spelling was a nightmare for me throughout my school years (and even today). In addition, I had bad teeth. Water was not fluoridated in the city of Atlanta until I was about 14. Despite brushing, I had more cavities than I could count, and each time I went to the dentist, I usually came back home with a mouthful of pain and fillings.

So life as the youngest Gladding was challenging and often discouraging. I was small and not particularly coordinated, with less than ideal learning abilities and cavity-prone teeth. Therefore, I failed at a lot of the things that were important in the world of boyhood at the time. For instance, I tried out for Little League each year and was immediately cut. Every time there was a spelling test or an in-class essay, my grade was less than the best—much less many times. To give you an example of the difficulty I had in hearing words and transcribing them on paper, I remember my fifth-grade teacher belittling me for writing an in-class essay on the Creek Nation in which I referred to these Native Americans as "Greeks" (I simply could not distinguish sounds). I was given remedial reading as well so I would stay close to the level of the rest of my classmates. And to add insult to injury, at age 11, at 4'7" and 75 pounds, I was teased by people who should have known better as being fat. "Aughh!" as Charlie Brown in the *Peanuts* comic strip would later say.

The Transition

Despite being less than the ideal boy, I came to a realization that still surprises me. For some reason I have yet to ferret out, I began to focus on what I could do rather than what I could not do. It was a quiet transition. I simply remember thinking one day in the sixth grade that I could take more control of much of my life. Therefore, after being called fat one day, I started eating less as well as exercising vigorously. I lost 12 pounds in a matter of a few weeks (yes, I have some empathy and understanding regarding anorexia). In addition, I switched emphasis in regard to athletics. I stopped trying to be competitive in baseball and took up tennis and swimming, which were not flooded with youngsters wanting to be the next Mickey Mantle. (By doing so, I became skilled enough in each sport to make the teams in high school and letter.) As for schoolwork, in the sixth grade, I started on the path of rote memory (which lasted all the way through graduate school). I literally memorized almost everything I read (and the lyrics to every song I heard). The strategy took time, but I was willing to put forth the effort because I did not like the feeling of being a failure or being teased. Therefore, at age 12, I turned a corner and began to be successful in a number of areas. My only setback was losing full rotation in my right elbow after breaking it twice.

Let me quickly add that although I initiated the change process, I did not complete it alone. My maternal grandmother, who lived with us and whom we called "Pal" (because she was our pal), helped me. She was an encourager. She believed in me and offered support. She also inspired me by telling me even more stories than I had heard before about my ancestors, especially my maternal grandfather, her husband, for whom I was named. Story after story seemed to revolve around the theme of overcoming adversity and doing good. For instance, my grandfather once stopped the lynching of an African American man, in what must have been an extremely tense and highly charged atmosphere. I began not only to admire these historical figures that were a part of my family but to believe I could be like them. My parents, although highly demanding, were also often understanding and empathetic when I failed as well as when I triumphed. I never had the slightest doubt that my parents genuinely loved me and wanted the best for me. The leaders of my church youth groups and my Boy Scout troop were positive influences on me as well. From all of these individuals, I learned to be gracious in defeat and modest in success. I had immediate as well as ancestral backing.

And then there was Nancy. She was a pretty, petite girl in my sixth-grade class, and as fate would have it, she liked me as a "boyfriend." I was amazed and extremely pleased, and my self-esteem skyrocketed, at least for the year that we were "a number." I worked hard on my appearance as well as my grades. I had always been social and humorous, but I grew even more so because I became more confident. That confidence helped me address still difficult situations in a manner that was usually constructive.

So with the convergence of people (Pal, my parents, and Nancy), stories, activities (church and Scouts), athletics (tennis and swimming), and a new strategy for being successful in school (rote memory and hard work), my life seemed to come together in a good way. In the idealism of the time, I decided I wanted to emulate my maternal grandfather and become a minister. It was a decision that provided me with a guiding image that gave me hope, resolve, purpose, and determination all through my adolescence and into young adulthood. I was going to serve others in a good and noble way. I was going to give myself to people less fortunate than I. I would live in modern times what my grandfather had lived in the post-Reconstruction period of the South, and maybe, just maybe, in the process I could make a difference—even save a life! I also developed an "inner compass" (i.e., a feeling in the pit of my stomach that basically let me know if I was going in the right direction or not) about this time as well. The compass basically kept me focused on positives and out of trouble.

My Professional Journey

After the sixth-grade decision, my life seemed to go well. High school was fun and rewarding, as was college, where I majored in history. In both environments I was elected or selected for a number of leadership positions and did well academically. It was when I graduated from Wake Forest University and went on to Yale Divinity School that my life hit another crisis. I went to Yale because my grandfather had defied the norms of his time and gone north to divinity school (Colgate Rochester in New York) after finishing at the University of Richmond. His rationale was that he needed to broaden his cultural experience and learn what life was like outside of the South. My rationale was similar, but in New Haven I woke up to another realization. Although I loved Yale, I was not enamored with theology. I thought it was too confining for what I wanted to do with my life. By the first day of the second year, I was ready to give it up, and yet I did not want to just quit. Therefore, I asked the dean what my options were. He suggested finishing the second year and getting a master's of religion instead of staying two more years for a master's of divinity. That made sense, and that's what I did.

In the meantime, I happened to stop by Wake Forest on my way home during a semester break and talked with Dr. Tom Elmore, who had just started a counseling program at my alma mater. After I explained my situation, he suggested I try counseling—which meant I should get personal career counseling. However, I thought he was implying I should enroll in the new counseling program he had created, which I did following graduation from Yale. I immediately loved the courses and the subject area and felt right at home. Thus, serendipitously, I entered the profession of counseling.

The Rockingham County Years

After graduating from Wake Forest, I was offered a job in a rural mental health center in Rockingham County, North Carolina, about 50 miles away. I accepted because it seemed exciting. I was to make the princely salary of $11,000, and I thought I would be close enough to Winston-Salem to continue dating the young woman to whom I was engaged. The job was exciting, but the other two reasons for accepting employment did not pan out. A few days into the job, my director told me he would be able to pay me only $8,500. Then, in a series of events that played out almost like a Shakespearian tragedy, the relationship I was in ended. I was not happy about the salary situation, but the breakup was devastating. I have always been a bit stoic, but the death of the relationship sent me spiraling into depression. It was not immediately apparent to others, however, because I kept functioning.

Nevertheless, I ruminated on what was and what could have been. I naively thought I could figure things out for myself because I was a counselor. That was a mistake, but based on that premise, I did not seek the immediate help I needed at one of the lowest moments in my life. Sadly, I can even remember contemplating many things that would have made the situation worse. Fortunately, one night when I dreamed of lying prone and helpless in a desert, Pal and historical figures from my family, whose faded pictures I had only seen in frames, appeared and lifted me up. "We'll carry you until you're able to walk again," I heard my deceased grandmother say. I awakened, and although still heartbroken, I dismissed the irrational thoughts playing havoc with my mind. The experience, like the weight loss incident, gave me greater insight into life and mental anguish. It also provided me with hope and the ability to continue in the midst of adversity. It gave me insight into dreams and resilience as well. In time, I finally decided not to keep carrying the pain from the termination of the relationship. Thus, I received counseling, which was an excellent and needed move.

However, before that happened, the Army called me up for service in January of 1973. (I had taken ROTC in college and had been commissioned as a 2nd lieutenant but had been assured I would not have to serve because of my dislocated hips.) Rather than fight the orders, I went to Fort Lee, Virginia, for three months for what was known as "active duty for training" to study in the Quartermaster School. When I returned to the mental health center, I was still depressed but determined to overcome it as I had other challenges in life. Thus, besides walking, swimming, biking, and engaging in other physical activities to relieve the mental pain, I moved to Greensboro, joined a church singles group, and started taking night courses in counseling, psychology, and human development at the University of North Carolina at Greensboro. The end result was a 96-semester-hour PhD in human development three years later, at which time I switched jobs from full-time mental health counselor to instructor of psychology at Rockingham Community College, which was right across the street from the mental health center.

I stayed at the community college for five years. While there, I taught five courses a quarter, four quarters a year, and did contract work for the mental health center. My preparations included general psychology, abnormal psychology, personality theories, and developmental psychology. I liked the teaching and counseling–consultation combination and probably would have remained at the college and with the mental health center for life if my father had not humorously reminded me that "you can't be a promising young man forever" (i.e., You have a doctorate and a world of counseling experience. Shouldn't you set your sights on doing more with your life?). Therefore, I began to apply for positions in counselor education programs. In the previous seven years, I had published 10 articles, 23 poems, and two book reviews in refereed journals including what are now the *Journal of Counseling & Development* and *Professional School Counseling*. I had also completed an 18-semester-hour postdoctorate in psychology at the University of North Carolina at Greensboro. Therefore, I did not anticipate that the process of obtaining a counselor education position would be impeded by the circumstances of the times. However, it was 1979, and there was high unemployment and an almost nonexistent market for new assistant professors. Thus, it took 20 months and almost 200 applications for me to finally find a job teaching counseling beginning in the fall of 1981. It was at Fairfield University in Connecticut.

The Fairfield University Years

I had mixed emotions about accepting a position in Connecticut. I had hoped to stay in the South because my family, friends, and feelings of loyalty were there. But I needed to make the most of the opportunity before me. So at 35, I packed my suitcases, sold my small house, hitched up my Sunfish to the back of my car, put my sheltie into the front seat of my Mustang, and left North Carolina. Connecticut the second time around was not as easy as the first. I had to make my way not knowing anyone in my immediate surroundings or having anyone to depend on except myself. It was hard, especially the first year when I realized that my two colleagues in counselor education—both good people—did not seem to like each other much, and that as a new, untenured assistant professor, I had to be both careful and diplomatic so as not to offend either. In addition, I had three new preparations to make each semester and lived in a neighborhood that was not friendly. Then, the long winter came. So, stress, striving, and loneliness became my closest companions that first year.

In order to not just survive but to try to thrive, I came up with a strategy for facing my environmental circumstances. I pretended I was being held captive like the American hostages in Iran, who had been freed some months before. My pretend captors were humane and provided me with books as well as pencils and paper and a lot of free time to write. So I began to structure my days to incorporate times of reading, reflection, and writing. By April, when the president of Rockingham Community College called and said the graduates had voted to ask me to be their commencement speaker, I realized I was going to be okay.

I began to flourish by the second year. My writings in the *Journal of Counseling & Development* and other counseling periodicals picked up because I had a lot of ideas and tons of time on my hands. By the third year, when I went up for promotion to associate professor with tenure, I had published while at Fairfield 19 articles and seven poems in refereed journals, coauthored a monograph chapter, and coedited a monograph. I also had met my future bride Claire, and my spirits were high. Still, I knew my future was not as a Nutmegger, and I began to look for new opportunities.

The University of Alabama at Birmingham

Unlike the first time that I had searched for a university appointment, the process went smoother this time. The University of Alabama at Birmingham

(UAB) offered me a position for the fall of 1984. The arrangement was that I could come with my rank but my salary would be less by about $3,000. I liked what I saw at the university and in the city, so I accepted. Claire drove down with me. She helped me set up my house in Birmingham and then flew back to Connecticut to start her own school year as a middle school librarian. It would be many flights and months before we were married in a small chapel at Wake Forest, which was halfway between Connecticut and Alabama.

Professionally, life was invigorating at UAB. My graduate students were highly motivated and productive, my department chair was supportive, and within the first year I had managed to set up a 60-semester-hour program in marriage and family counseling, become an associate in a private counseling practice, and write a number of manuscripts. The six years at UAB were among the best of my life. In that time I published 22 articles and 13 poems in refereed journals, produced a video, published my first book, become editor of the *Journal for Specialists in Group Work*, and become president of Chi Sigma Iota (international counseling honorary).

I was 38 when I arrived at UAB. Two years later when Claire, who was then 35, and I married, we decided that if we were going to have children, we needed to begin immediately. We did and were blessed with three children in five years—all boys, all joys—Ben, Nate, and Tim. In the meantime, I was promoted to professor. The days were long (I taught from 6 to 10 p.m. two nights a week, four quarters a year, and saw 10 to 15 clients a week in my private practice), but they were wonderful too—full of discoveries. I was energized and thought with everything going so well that we would stay at UAB for the remainder of my career.

Wake Forest Again

My thoughts were interrupted by a phone call in July of 1989 from the president of Wake Forest asking me to come to Winston-Salem to speak to a leadership conference and to consider a potential job offer to be his assistant. I was not sure. I knew it would be great to be back in North Carolina, but I was aware that it would be different too, especially if I was going to be doing some administrative work. However, when the offer came, I talked it over with Claire and we decided to accept because it contained provisions for me to teach in the counselor education program as well as assist the president. So with Claire pregnant for a third and last time, we moved to Winston-Salem in the fall of 1990 and have been here since. In the first seven years, my office was in the president's suite, and I taught a course in counseling each semester. In 1996, with the retirement of Tom Elmore (my original mentor), I became director of the program. With an additional retirement, the creation of a new position, and the converting of adjunct money to a full-time position, I was able to hire new, congenial, and productive colleagues. Then, in the spring of 2002, after the program became accredited by the Council for Accreditation of Counseling and Related Educational Programs for a second time, I joined with my colleagues in requesting that we become the Department of Counseling, which was granted in the fall of 2003. I transitioned at the time from program director to department chair, and since 1998 I have been the associate provost at Wake Forest as well.

These 14 years have been highly productive. I have written 21 books (including revisions), 15 book chapters, and 13 refereed articles, and produced two videos. I have continued to write poetry for pleasure and have included about three dozen of these new poems as "openings" at the beginning of my books. When I first came to Wake Forest, I wrote about two hours at night every day after putting the children to bed. This pattern was just the opposite of my UAB days, when I wrote a couple of hours each morning before going to see clients or attend a university meeting. I am not sure why I have been so productive. One possible reason is that I am passionate about counseling. I love the ideals and realities of the profession! Another reason is that at Fairfield and UAB, I had so many new course preparations to make (a combined total of 25) that I read extensively in all areas of counseling. Finally, there is the matter of owning a computer. Typing (a skill I taught myself after my senior year in high school) is much easier to do on a computer keyboard than on a typewriter—and a computer has spelling programs, too!

Connection Between Theory and Practice

Theories have never been a luxury for me. They have always been a valuable necessity. The reason for this is probably that I started my professional career on the staff of a small mental health center, where five of us served a population of 70,000. I was thrown into the fray almost immediately, and I had to have theories on which I could depend. Initially, I was a Rogerian until I realized that person-centered therapy was not the best approach with a number of clients. Thus, I began to learn behavioral theory because it was practical and worked well with the population I served. Then I branched out to learn other theories—reality therapy, Adlerian therapy, and rational emotive behavior therapy—because I could see my clients benefiting from these approaches. I became deeply immersed in family systems theories, too, when my responsibilities were upgraded at the center to see couples and families. Then there were group theories that I learned at the same time because I had a need to know as well as a desire to grow. In more recent years, I have incorporated existentialism into my repertoire.

I do not think there is anything more useful than a good theory. I also believe that the more theories you learn, the more effective you can be. It is like having the right tools for a job. If all you have is a hammer, everything looks like a nail, and you end up not being constructive. I want to make sure I am as well prepared as possible for the unexpected. Theories give me a conceptual basis, and usually some methods, on which to build a solid rationale and approach to working with clients who come with different needs.

The more I have been in the profession, the more I have realized that for many clients, talk is of limited value. The reasons are varied, but because they are real, I have learned the theories behind how the creative arts (e.g., drama, music, drawing, literature) are used in therapeutic ways. I think that a good theory or a well-thought-out eclectic approach offers clients hope and possibilities. When clients have these two factors as a part of their counseling experience, they appear to get better and change. Regardless of the theory I use, I focus on developing and maintaining good rapport with my clients. I think clients want to know you care deeply about them as individuals rather than how much you know. The relationship is the basis on which change and the effectiveness of any theory takes place. I am convinced Carl Rogers was right about that!

Development as a Multicultural Counselor

The Southern culture of my youth was segregated and stratified. At the top were wealthy, White, Protestant men, followed by those of the middle and lower classes. The hierarchy for women and families followed that of the men. Black people were separated and treated far from being equal. "Yankees," Catholics, and Jews sometimes fit into the mainstream of the White class structure and sometimes maintained their own cultures. Asian Americans, Hispanics, and Native Americans were usually accepted and tolerated because they were few in number and "knew their place" in the social order of the times.

My encounters with people markedly different from me were few. Each spring my father hired an African American man, Will, to plow his garden. Will had a mule and wagon but no phone. Sometimes I rode out with my dad to "colored town," where he went to look for Will. Otherwise, I was sheltered from cultural experiences other than novel events at my church or school. I remember, however, at church, the seeds of living in a multicultural world were at least sown through a song we used to sing in Sunday school. It was called "Chain of Friendship," and I remember the words as these:

> Let's form a chain of friendship to reach the world around
> The links can be the boys and girls wherever they are found
> No matter what their race or creed or what their color may be
> Let's form a chain of friendship to reach the world around.

I liked the song and its message. It seemed exciting. Yet early on, I was aware that the local and state governments, as well as the Ku Klux Klan, would never let the words come to life without a fight. They were there to enforce the boundaries of segregation and White supremacy. I can remember the Klan parading by our house on Church Street for rallies at the Decatur Courthouse Square a few blocks away. It was scary and intimidating.

However, Martin Luther King Jr. and the Civil Rights Movement began to emerge as I entered adolescence. I loved the elegance of King's words. They were profound and poetic, and my heart and head were touched by what he said and did. I was influenced even more by the courage and conviction of another man, Ralph McGill, editor of the *Atlanta Constitution*, which I delivered as a paperboy for four years. McGill spoke out for King and desegregation in his columns. I read them. They helped reinforce what I knew was right in regard to equality in society. I was not old enough to make a difference in the change that occurred, but I remember taking positions regarding desegregation that were not popular with a number of my peers.

Wake Forest and Yale freed me to be more vocal and active. For instance, the summer between my junior and senior years in college, I lived in a lower class, racially mixed neighborhood in Winston-Salem as part of a good neighbor project sponsored by the Baptist Student Union at Wake Forest. It was 1966 and an eye-opener for me because poverty, prejudice, and discrimination were experiences I could see and feel up close. I was called a few choice names that I cannot repeat in writing, but I realized at 20 the names would not hurt me. At Wake Forest and at Yale, I marched in several civil rights and antiwar rallies, and even went to Washington to talk with my senator, Herman Talmadge, without bothering to tell my parents until later. They were cautiously supportive. Slowly but surely, I saw society change and open up, with a parallel process going on within me.

In the counseling world I entered after receiving my master's degree in 1971, there was little emphasis on multicultural counseling. I remember reading Derald Wing Sue's writings in professional journals but not a lot more. However, as I went to counseling conventions, I began to encounter people different from me, and I welcomed the conversations that followed. Nevertheless, the way I really became immersed in multicultural counseling was by working as a counselor in the mental health center I have already described and later as a private practitioner with a group in Birmingham. Clients were all different, and to be effective I had to be able to understand and empathize with them. To do so, I had to know something about their cultures as well as my own. Necessity and a strong moral conviction drove me toward learning all I could, as fast as I could, whenever I could, and from whomever I could.

In more recent years, as president of the Association for Specialists in Group Work and president of the Association for Counselor Education and Supervision, I traveled inside the United States a great deal and visited a number of nations in Europe. At Wake Forest, I taught a Vienna theories course twice in Vienna, Austria, which is a far different experience from teaching a theories course in the United States. During the last decade, I have also made three trips to Japan (one that involved a home stay) and lived three weeks in impoverished conditions in Calcutta, India, working with Wake Forest students and Mother Teresa in trying to serve the poorest of the poor in that society. I also worked with a very diverse client group in New York two weeks following the 9/11 tragedy. I am still learning and changing!

My Style and Accomplishments

As I have indicated, my style of work has changed over the years as my responsibilities or circumstances in different environments have varied. When

I was a full-time clinician in the mental health center, I found I had to be flexible because I shared an office with the rehabilitation specialist and an addiction counselor. Therefore, I often wrote my case notes on the stairs or in a chair by the kitchen window (our mental health center was located in an old house). I also wrote more poetry than prose because the environment was supportive of that style. At the community college, I had my own office and some privacy. I branched out a little more into research but kept penning poems and philosophical articles at times. At Fairfield, as I have mentioned, I used a technique based on pretending to help motivate me to be productive. It worked because of the uniqueness of the situation. At UAB and Wake Forest, my colleagues and graduate students helped spark ideas within me.

However, as I have pointed out, the times in which I have worked have been quite different. At the mental health center and at Wake Forest, my office hours were from 8 a.m. to 5 p.m. each day. At the other settings, I often had night classes and therefore would not go into work most days until early afternoon. On a number of occasions, I used the morning hours at home to write. My style of working has also changed since I married and became a father. Now I live by the motto "family first," and therefore write when it does not interfere with what I need to do with Claire and the children—all teenagers now. I think being a good spouse and parent are the most important things I do, so I stress relationships within my family over writing and service to the profession. I coach, instruct, and attend my children's activities. That is my most important task in life other than making sure Claire and I have enough time together.

I am not sure I can really comment on my accomplishments other than to say I am surprised and pleased in regard to them. I think circumstances in my life, opportunities, persistence, and the values my parents taught me all have contributed to this productivity. In addition, I am well organized. I also am able to let things go and not obsess about them. However, I do not procrastinate and wait until the time is "right" to write. I pen at least a few words a day, and gradually the words become sentences, paragraphs, pages, articles, and books. I am open to criticism, and I think anyone who writes, speaks, or leads needs to be. It helps a lot too that I have patience. I once submitted the same manuscript (slightly revised) to three different editors of a journal over a nine-year period until it was accepted because I thought the article was a good fit for that publication. In the meantime, I worked on other manuscripts. I think it is crucial, if people are to be successful, that they work on multiple projects and revisit these works regularly.

Finally, I think in regard to service, such as being president of the American Counseling Association (ACA), that I have been helped by a number of factors. I am able to interact positively with most individuals because I am good at reading nonverbals and hearing voice tones. I usually listen carefully before speaking, and I try to be reflective and thoughtful when I speak. In addition, I like to work toward solutions and the public or professional good even when these objectives may not initially appear probable. I like to engage in divergent thinking, which is the foundation for creativity. I believe if we are going to work well as leaders in our profession, we must envision what can be as well as implement what is now. That strategy must be coupled with the mundane tasks of answering phone calls, letters, e-mails, and other requests as promptly as possible (i.e., every day if practical).

My Plans for the Future

In the next dozen years or so, I would like to keep contributing to the profession of counseling in whatever ways I can. I do not see myself recycling into leadership positions but rather helping to train and encourage emerging leaders. I think mentoring is important, and I would like to do that. My most influential mentor, Tom Elmore, used to invite me to submit papers with him and go to conventions. He also wrote letters on my behalf. Another mentor, Wes Hood, used to engage me in thought-provoking conversations on our commutes to Rockingham County, and yet a third mentor, Art Lerner, challenged me to be creative and offered me publication outlets for my work. I hope I can do this kind of activity in the future as well as teach full time again. I might also like to write a novel!

I think the future is only going to get better for counseling. We are a young profession compared to other helping specialties. As we grow and become better known, I think the public will be appreciative of what we do and how we work. I really like the emphasis within the profession these days on wellness, prevention, solutions, possibilities, choices, and creativity. I also like the stress within ACA on legislation at state and national levels. It is crucial that we as counselors be included as core providers in federal mental health programs, and I think we will. As each year passes, we are becoming more sophisticated in the way we draft legislation and the manner in which we approach legislatures. I am eager to be a part of ACA and its movement toward acts that will benefit counselors and support the public good.

My Advice for Young Professionals

I usually do not give advice because I think most people do not want it and we are all quite different in our personality makeup and backgrounds. Nevertheless, I also believe that there are some universal aspects to our existence and, therefore, some observations that carry implications for persons just beginning the journey of becoming a counselor. Thus, I think I would say to young professionals:

- Attend state, regional, and national counseling events, especially those conducted by ACA. At such events you will make contacts as well as learn valuable information that can help you as a clinician.
- Organize and present your ideas (whether research based or philosophical) at counseling conferences. The feedback you get will be valuable, and again, you will make contacts and learn valuable information.
- Focus on what you can do rather than what limitations you have.
- Look for opportunities and stretch yourself to take advantage of them.

- Read, discuss, reflect, and integrate. Keep a journal of your growth.
- Get supervision and form a peer supervision group if possible.
- Volunteer to be on or lead a professional committee or to be a candidate for an office in a local, state, regional, or national counseling organization. People will welcome your energy and enthusiasm (and again you will learn much).
- Never focus on compensation. Although necessary, money and fringe benefits (after a certain level) are more distracting than enabling in helping you grow.
- Seek help when you need it, personal and professional.
- Maintain or develop a sense of humor. Situations in counseling are either serious but not hopeless or hopeless but not serious. Humor will help you figure out which is which and assist you in doing something constructive.
- Develop an interest outside of counseling. Otherwise you will burn out.
- Write and present about topics in which you have an interest.
- Make it a point to learn about people from cultures different from your own.
- Stay humble and open. A large ego or a know-it-all attitude is disabling.

Conclusion

I believe that life is a gift and that as recipients of that gift, we should give back to the world, especially to our fellow human beings, as much as we can and whenever we can. In these pages, I have chronicled and highlighted aspects of my life that have been keys to my development. Specific physical and mental factors have impacted me and have helped sensitize me to the plights of others. Values, family stories, personal experiences, professional encounters, happenstance, and the zeitgeist of the times have further influenced my identity, direction, and behavior. I have been most fortunate to play a number of roles: son, brother, student, athlete, counselor, poet, citizen, soldier, writer, editor, presenter, husband, father, professor, association leader, mentor, humorist, armchair theologian, amateur historian, administrator, friend, and colleague. Each has made its own unique contribution to who I am today and where I am going.

I do not know what roles are yet to emerge. Whatever they are, I will try to handle them in a constructive way by seeing what can be done as opposed to what cannot. Likewise, I will try to exemplify the Gladding family motto that my 15-year-old Nate recently created: "Always work hard and never lose hope." Whatever develops, I look forward to having the courage to take the risks and actions necessary so that, ultimately, good may emerge. Since I was an adolescent, I have prayed almost every night for wisdom. That is still my prayer as I anticipate what may yet unfold in accentuating the positives.

Chapter 4

Mis Inspiraciones y Legados
•••

Patricia Arredondo

> *No se apuren, Díos los ayudará.*
> —María Estéfana Morales Zaldívar, mi abuela

My life is full of cross-cutting themes that have evolved throughout my personal and professional life. I used to think that I would become an anthropologist because I was constantly observing people and different situations. At times, I wondered if I had to confess to the priest the thoughts I had about what I witnessed. "It did not make sense," I rationalized. "I was just watching and thinking about what I saw, trying not to judge." From these early processes of observation in my immigrant neighborhood emerged the themes that run throughout my life story: being different; valuing cultural differences; being introspective about my gender, ethnicity, and professional identity; being an educator at heart; using mentors and role models as sources of personal empowerment; seizing opportunities to create necessary change; leading; and of course, emphasizing the love of family and friends. Recollections come pretty easily because I have always reflected on my experiences, kept journals, and noticed what is affecting me and others. For many years, my life involved continuous processes of ethnic, gender, and career identity reexaminations. I processed disquieting thoughts about being different, needing to be twice as good as my peers from the dominant group, and being a late bloomer. Fortunately, at this stage of adulthood, I fully accept who I am and the possibility that I will not accomplish everything in this lifetime. Yet, I know that my parents instilled in me the desire to always do well and to have *orgullo* (pride) in my efforts. I welcome the opportunity to look back a little through this narrative with the hope that my *historia* and *mis inspiraciones* may inspire others.

La Familia and the Roots of My Journey

Growing up in an immigrant, industrial city 15 miles west of Cleveland, Ohio, on Lake Erie initiated my continuous curiosity about cultural differences. Until I finished the 10th grade, our Mexican American family lived in a multiethnic community where Spanish, Hungarian, Greek, Croatian, and

Slovenian were commonly spoken. The Catholic and Protestant churches alike were defined by their ethnic-specific parishioners and schools, picnics, card parties, and neighborhoods. Many Polish families lived on the streets surrounding St. Stanislaus. On the north side of town was St. Mary's, with predominantly Irish parishioners. In south Lorain, near the steel mill, the Thew Shovel heavy equipment factory, and the roads to the farms, were the Mexican, Puerto Rican, Southern White, Serbian, and other smaller ethnic enclaves. I am referring to the 1950s and 1960s primarily. Across the street from my *abuela's* (grandmother's) home was a Black church. I came to realize that in those days, the Black churches (primarily Baptist) were located near public housing projects. Yes, there were different forms of segregation in my community: socioeconomic, religious, ethnic/racial, and occupational.

Our familia, like those of many immigrants, was large by today's standards. There were four girls and three boys, born across a 20-year time span. I was the second oldest daughter but became the designated oldest child because of my older sister's emotional issues. The first home I recall was a duplex, copurchased by my father and my uncle, his oldest brother. Both were immigrants from Salamanca, Guanajuato, in Mexico, which was a source of great pride that was transmitted to all of their children. Neither my *tía* nor my *tío* spoke to us in English, and thus, communicating in Spanish was a home-based practice. I am forever grateful for this early preparation to become bilingual. Another good fortune was having a mother who stayed home to raise the seven of us. Of course, this drove her to exhaustion at times, but we knew she was there with regular meals, clean clothes, and tasks for all of us to do while my father worked different weekly shifts at the steel mill. One thing we could always count on was Sunday dinner together, because he did not work on weekends.

As I mentioned earlier, I was charged very early on with child care and home-based responsibilities. My mother was my role model for everything from changing diapers and burping babies to baking sweets, making flour tortillas (my favorite), and maintaining an organized and clean house. All of these skills have stayed with me, but as a child and adolescent, I often resented the seemingly excessive responsibilities and restrictive rules set by my mother. Unlike other girls, I could not do overnights, visit with friends outside of our Catholic school, or date in high school. As kids, we used to say that my mother judged us guilty before we even thought about what she was accusing us of doing. When it came to education, there was no mistake: My parents made this a priority by spending their limited resources to send the six oldest children to Catholic school through the eighth grade. Indeed, education was a priority. Homework was done immediately after school, and my library card from kindergarten on became a special part of my life, thanks to my mother. I made regular visits to the library during the week and on Saturdays; I loved to read. I remember challenging myself to read beyond my reading level. I could not be an average reader!

Education in My Life

I believe that being an educator at heart began with my thirst for learning and my desire to prove to myself and others that Mexican Americans were capable of academic achievement. In my community there were no Mexicans or Latinos that served as physicians or teachers, nor did they hold public office or other visible roles of authority. When it came to high school graduation, my mother reminded me that very few Mexicans graduated from high school. This became a challenge to me—I knew I was going to make it.

Fortunately, there were significant others who recognized my potential and encouraged and mentored me along the way. The nuns encouraged me, and I did my best to prove that I was as good as or better in school than my non-Mexican classmates. Mine was the only non-Slovenian family in the school, and I was very conscious of this cultural difference. I was darker than my blue-eyed, blond Eastern European peers. Beyond the nuns, I encountered several teachers in public school (Grades 9–12) whom I admired and with whom I developed special connections. My ninth grade and high school counselors took me under their wing and involved me as their aide. They encouraged and praised my performance and became important role models in my career development. It was my high school counselor, Mrs. Mehlow, who guided my college application and scholarship processes. To her I owe enormous gratitude for helping me to become the first member of my extended family to attend college and to appreciate the value of the profession of counseling.

Becoming a college professor had not occurred to me until I met Dr. Pamies during my senior year in college. He was born in Cuba and was my first Latino teacher or professor. I was awed by Dr. Pamies's passion in teaching about Miguel Cervantes, author of *Don Quixote*, the dreamer of the impossible dream. All along, my career goal was to be a teacher; through Dr. Pamies, the image of a college professor began to take form.

Experiencing My Professional Journey

The opportunity for reflection on my professional journey prompts me to recall significant decisions that allowed my career to continue to evolve. Critical points began with my decision to leave Ohio for Boston to begin a new chapter in my life in a place I had idealized from afar through the many books I had read. Although I enjoyed teaching high school Spanish, I became restless and knew that a master's degree would be more stimulating. A degree in school counseling rather than Spanish literature was the path I pursued. Another critical point in my journey was meeting my mentor, Ralph Mosher. Dr. Mosher had observed my work as a high school counselor leading psychoeducational groups with immigrant adolescents. On the basis of his encouragement and my own personal challenge, I embarked on doctoral studies. Often I felt as though my professional life was on automatic pilot; I was in the driver's seat, flowing forward with some sense of predictability, but also charting a great, unknown territory. I simply trusted the process because I had a goal in mind.

I will always remember an interview for my first academic position at the University of New Hampshire (UNH). In the midst of an amiable discussion, one of the professors calmly asked, "What do you have in mind for five years from now?" Because I was just beginning my academic career, I considered this an unfair question and wanted to say, "How should I know? I want to land this job. Then I can think about the future!" This straightforward question as well as a career planning workshop seven years later reminded me of the importance of planning and not staying in my automatic pilot mode.

My academic journey took me from UNH to Boston University (BU) one year later. Because of my interest in bilingual counseling, a former professor included me in a grant that was funded by the Department of Bilingual Education. I faced an important and very difficult career decision: leave UNH, where I was treated as a colleague and had carte blanche to develop courses in multicultural counseling and counseling with women, or head back to Boston, where the need for bilingual counseling in schools and agencies was steadily increasing. My passion for working with immigrants and ethnic minority groups on a regular basis won out. I went back to a city with visible pluralism, both cultural and linguistic.

At BU, I "grew up" quickly. I learned about university politics and prejudices from administrators that unduly burdened academic programs, including ours in counseling. I learned about the different allegiances of my senior colleagues to counselor education and counseling psychology as we slowly changed our program identity to that of counseling psychology. I witnessed the suffering of doctoral students who felt abandoned by their advisors who did not receive tenure, senior professors who felt oppressed because of unfair university policies, and junior professors like me who wanted to trust the system and work toward tenure but felt lost in the sea of change. A divorce in the midst of the chaos at BU was accelerated by a drive for overachievement as well as my oldest-child care-taking tendencies. Students I had admitted and those who were left without advisors became my responsibility. I did not know how to say no at the time. Thus students and their dissertations took center stage in my unbalanced life. I continued to direct the Bilingual Counseling Program, which remained after I left BU. This position allowed me to build valuable networks throughout greater Boston. Outreach became a key strategy in my professional journey and is one that I readily apply in many settings.

When I left BU without tenure in 1985 under my own terms, I had chaired 23 dissertations, mentored numerous students at the master's and doctoral levels, published a few refereed journal articles, and had many new colleagues and friends locally and nationally. During the years 1978–1985, I began my foray into the mainstream of American Counseling Association (ACA) politics and leadership, particularly through the Association of Counselor Education and Supervision (ACES) division.

Developing My Professional Identity

Thanks to my mentor, who took me and fellow graduate students to my first ACA (then the American Personnel and Guidance Association) conference in Chicago, I began to appreciate the importance of professional association involvement. Findings from my dissertation study with immigrant adolescents provided conference program data for both ACA and eventually the American Psychological Association (APA), but I soon learned that few people were interested in the topic of immigrants and cultural awareness, or the other topics that were my passion. It did not take long for me to determine that ethnic minorities were rarely visible at the national professional conferences. I recognized the names Sue and Sue and eventually Padilla, but for me, these were heavy hitters; I was not in their league. However, I plugged along. With colleagues in ACES such as Holly Stadler, I worked on the Human Rights Committee, preparing initial handbooks for creating inclusive curriculum. Our human rights handbook discussed underrepresented groups in counselor education based on age, culture/ethnicity/race, gender, sexual orientation, and physical disability. These were obvious omissions to us, but seemingly not too many of our colleagues thought this was of importance. We had the support of then ACES presidents but few people attended our human rights workshops at national and regional conferences. Thankfully, the tide has changed.

The lack of women in leadership roles was another shortcoming I noted in ACA, and this became a motivator for me to initiate leadership for and with women within ACES. A critical incident was an ACES luncheon in 1982. All of the awardees and officers at the time were White men. The accolades of one man for another, though deserved, made me feel invisible in that room. Was this association merely a club of White men? I learned that until that point, there had been only one woman president, yet there were many women in attendance at the luncheon. Something was wrong with this picture. It seemed unfair, exclusionary, and sexist. Emotions were stirred as I reflected on other groups that were marginalized back in Ohio, at the high school where I had counseled in Brookline, Massachusetts, and in numerous community and school settings. It was time to channel those emotions into action. In the 1980s we did not have e-mail, so long-distance phone calls to women colleagues across the country allowed me to initiate a movement for ACES women to organize ourselves. The end result was the ACES Women's Interest Network, which is alive and well at national and regional levels. Collectively, I saw that we could do much more and become a force in an important ACA division. As a direct result of our shared vision about women's empowerment and leadership abilities, numerous women have served as ACES and ACA division presidents, been promoted and tenured, and completed doctoral studies.

I believe that my professional identity and accomplishments have been activated and shaped through collegial relationships and the willingness to take on tasks in ACA and APA, and through the National Latina/o Psychological

Association. Through the invitation of Courtland Lee, I stepped into a visible role in the Association of Multicultural Counseling and Development (AMCD) in 1989. Courtland needed a local chair for the Boston ACA conference. The rest is history as they say. This volunteerism launched me into AMCD leadership, thanks to many visionaries such as Courtland and Thomas Parham, president in 1991–1992. I had the good fortune of being invited to develop a multicultural competencies document along with Derald Wing Sue and Rod McDavis (Sue, Arredondo, & McDavis, 1992). Little did I know that this document would be a springboard to transforming counseling and psychology and would offer me a new and enriched professional journey. I became involved out of a sense of responsibility and excitement. We had to promulgate statements about the importance of culture in counseling. I was on a new and continuing mission of multiculturalism that has become an important force in the future of counseling and psychology.

A significant chapter of my life came about from a new and unplanned career goal outside of higher education. Upon leaving BU in 1985, I launched Empowerment Workshops, Inc. (EWI) in Boston. This consulting organization became a forum for addressing multiculturalism and diversity in the workplace. Thanks to the career planning workshop I attended with some reluctance back in 1984, I was able to develop a plan for my career and also for my business venture. In reflecting on the EWI journey, I know that I was motivated by several factors: (a) a recognition of the transferability of my clinical, teaching, and research skills from counseling; (b) a desire to take psychoeducational programs into the workplace to promote adult development; (c) a wish not to be controlled by capricious organizational politics that would oppress me and others; and (d) above all, a passion to make culture and multiculturalism the core of my consulting practice. Through EWI, I cut my teeth on innumerable new projects that were not possible had I remained in higher education. I stepped into the corporate and not-for-profit world full force, tenaciously pushing along my plans, making important contacts through networking, and delivering talks for free to help EWI's name recognition. And then I finally landed two fortuitous breaks. As with all consultants, your client organizations become your best references, providing you with name recognition by association.

In the early 1990s, with *Workforce 2000* (Johnson & Packer, 1987) data informing employers about the demographics of the 21st-century workforce, EWI took on a more visible role locally and regionally. My lucky breaks came with a consortium of Boston foundations concerned about the gaps in services to underrepresented ethnic and linguistic minorities. This five-year evaluation project of 64 not-for-profit organizations with a clinical psychologist and law professor led to my first book, *Successful Diversity Management Initiatives* (Arredondo, 1996). My engagements with the Gillette Company, my first corporate client, confirmed my developmental approach to workforce diversity initiatives. This business relationship provided me with innumerable opportunities and invaluable learning experiences that strengthened my competencies as a multicultural-focused consultant.

Double and Triple Tracking

Being a professional Latina has opened the door to many opportunities. I have known for many years that I was privileged to have loving parents and an abuela, to have earned a doctoral degree, and more, and with this good fortune came responsibility and risks. If no one who looks like you has served in visible leadership roles, you run the risk of either ruining it for others or demonstrating that the underrepresented person can also be a leader, professor, and so forth. From the beginning of my academic career at UNH, I have been sought after to fulfill expectations as a woman, Latina, and member of an ethnic minority group. The term *twofer* was often used in reference to ethnic minority women, meaning that we satisfied two Affirmative Action categories for employers. However, it is within ACA and APA that my collective social identities have created more pulls or demands.

Once I became involved as secretary for AMCD and the first vice president of Latino Concerns, it was inevitable, I was told, that I would have to become a candidate for AMCD president. This would be a first for the 24-year-old association, but it happened. In 1996–1997, I became the first Latina/o president. I believe this event opened the door to many firsts in the association: the first presidents of Asian and Native American heritage and at least three more Latina/o presidents to date. I have always felt like a known quantity within ACA thanks to my long-term involvement in ACES, AMCD, and various national committees. All of this involvement has provided me with valuable insights about organizational policies and practices and the importance of having shared visions. This message also served me well in my presidency of APA's Division 45, Society for the Psychological Study of Ethnic Minority Issues. I was able to apply many of my skills of collaboration and facilitation among different cultural groups as Division 45 evolved through the emergence of our journal, the development of multicultural guidelines, and the involvement of new professionals of different cultural backgrounds. During my administration, Allen Ivey became the first White person to serve on the division's Diversity Slate. The other slates in Division 45 are for representatives of the four major ethnic/racial minority groups.

Part of my double- and triple-tracking metaphor has been balancing organizational politics with academic and research endeavors. Following the publication of "Multicultural Counseling Competencies and Standards: A Call to the Profession" (Sue et al., 1992) came the article "Operationalization of Multicultural Counseling Competencies" (Arredondo et al., 1996). Sometimes I wonder how I was able to stick with these projects and the complications that ensued while I was managing my business. Fortunately, it all got done—at least, most of it did. Prior to assuming my role as president of Division 45 (2000–2001), I was invited by Derald Wing Sue to bring the AMCD multicultural competencies to APA. From 1999 to 2002, I worked vigorously along with Nadya Fouad, in particular, as well as Michael D'Andrea, Allen Ivey, and many other supporters to develop a document that was unanimously approved and has become policy for APA: *Guidelines on Multicultural Education, Training, Research, Practice, and Organizational Change for Psychologists* (APA, 2003). There was much celebration, but for me the journey brought important new learning points: (a) Organizational change built on inclusive objectives is possible; (b) organizational change is a collective process that takes time (there are no overnight successes); (c) through diversity comes change; and (d) involvement and persistence require clarity about personal values, the ability to be tenacious and open-minded, and a willingness to persevere.

Entre Fronteras: The Borderlands

The themes of double and triple tracking continue to be a strong mantra, reinforcing the *entre fronteras* theme as well. According to Chicana feminist writer Gloria Anzaldúa (1987), Chicanas and Latinas continuously find ourselves crossing from one zone to another, adapting as we go and negotiating unfamiliar and sometimes unfriendly terrain. One of the skills I learned as a child was to observe the "Other" and determine her or his intentions. Vigilance coupled with excellent listening skills has helped guide me in lonely situations, such as being the only woman in a group of White males in the corporate world or being the only Latina in ACA meetings with no other people of color. In the early 1980s, I felt intimidated by this numerical imbalance. When I was asked what Latinos thought about a particular issue, I experienced the burden of my role. When I heard others question the credentials of other colleagues of color, I also felt obligated to give voice to their credibility. I hope that White professionals will recognize that walking and working entre fronteras is very tiring. People of color simply want to be respected for who they are and what they have to offer professionally. We all get tired of proving that we can do as well as our White counterparts, justifying why ethnic minorities merit special consideration in various academic issues, and sitting on many committees and boards because we have to be the ethnic minority representative. This often becomes exhausting for me, because if I don't serve, it may mean there is no other ethnic minority voice. I hope that my White colleagues will appreciate this point.

Gathering and Maintaining Strength With Colleagues and Mentors

Familismo, personalismo, and *hermandad* describe the values of interpersonal and interdependent relationships from Latino cultural perspectives. Family or *familia* is core to individual Latinas and Latinos. By extension, *familismo* describes the sense of family or familia experienced by and among Latinos. Familismo can also be felt with nonbiological family members. I have participated in Latino professional groups that also embody this sense of familismo or *hermandad* (brotherhood or kinship) because of our shared cultural identity. *Personalismo* also conveys an emotional connection and valuing of a relationship. For me, personalismo is evident in close friendships and even professional relationships in which I have come to know and work closely with peers.

As my career has matured, I have become more intentional about drawing upon these Latino cultural values and applying them in my professional life. I never feel totally alone when it comes to accomplishments or stumbling blocks because there are innumerable individuals and groups in my life. I have met all of these individuals, with few exceptions, through ACA, APA, NLPA, UNH, and other civic organizations in Boston and Phoenix that are a part of my personal and professional support system. For example, coauthorship or copresentation at conferences is never for show. My collaborators and I are either friends or become friends as a result of these engagements.

In my ambition to promote a focus on women and ethnic minority professional leadership, the value of multicultural competency development, Latino issues in counseling and psychology, and multicultural organizational development, I have become part of numerous networks that require mention. For the establishment of the ACES Women's Interest Network, six women who are today still active in ACA were part of that pioneering endeavor. They are Holly Stadler, Bea Pressley, Rie Rogers Mitchell, Margaret Bloom (Fong), Jo Hayslip, and Sunny Hansen. In particular, Sunny and Jo served as important role models for me because they were long-term advocates for women's career development.

As many individuals who have dedicated themselves to promoting multiculturalism as the "fourth force" in counseling (Pedersen, 1991) are well aware, the journey has had many ambushes, pitfalls, critics, and organizational challenges. However, in 1994, Michael D'Andrea and Don C. Locke hosted a very important gathering for those who made it to the ACA conference in snowbound Atlanta (remember?!). This meeting kicked off the establishment of the National Institute of Multicultural Competency (NIMC), a movement that has led to institutional changes within ACA and APA, as well as at schools and universities across the country. I am proud to be part of this special group of individuals who are undeterred in the promotion of multicultural counseling competencies and social justice. This special group includes Judy Daniels, Michael D'Andrea, Mary and Allen Ivey, Don C. Locke, Beverly O'Bryant, Thomas Parham, and Derald Wing Sue. Outcomes of our various initiatives have been documented in a case study (D'Andrea et al., 2001).

The Latino Interest Network of AMCD has truly brought me the feeling of familia. There is great emotion when others in this group who share your heritage and often are bilingual get together. Regardless of age, professional status, or ethnic-specific heritage (e.g., Puerto Rican, Colombian), we experience the feeling of being *raza* or part of the cosmic race (Ramirez, 1998). Bernal Baca, Azara Santiago-Rivera, Robert Davison-Aviles, and Miguel Arciniega have succeeded me as vice-presidents of the network since its inception in 1992.

I know there are many omissions in this brief accounting, because I have limited myself to a few groups and individuals within ACA. However, there are others like Janet Jones, Judy Lewis, Mark Pope, Renee Middleton, and

Maritza Gallardo-Cooper who have brought special gifts to me when I needed to ease my mind and feel motivated to keep moving ahead with ideas and goals despite frustrations.

In some respects, I believe that peer mentoring is more descriptive of my professional journey. Yes, my academic advisors, Ralph Mosher and Maria Allende Brisk, guided and supported my interests in working with immigrants and bilingual counseling, but there were many other professionals that emerged after graduate school. John Whiteley demonstrated the possibility of using video for education and training purposes, an avenue I have pursued with Mary and Allen Ivey. Beverly O'Bryant showed me how a woman of color leads an organization in the midst of crisis, and Judy Lewis demonstrated the benefits of bringing people with shared interests together to establish Counselors for Social Justice. I have learned and matured because my life has been blessed by so many gifted and honorable persons.

Connecting Theory to Practice and Beyond

I have strong beliefs in different models that I have helped develop. However, these beliefs are the result of a different equation: practice, evaluation, theory, practice. I believe it is important to acknowledge that theories do not come from the air or from a good night's sleep. Beliefs, values, biases, assumptions, and experiences, in my estimation, inform theory and practice, which is why multiculturalism is an essential theme in all of our professional lives. Everything we do is culture bound because we are all cultural beings influenced by familial, national (heritage and place of birth), religious, political, socioeconomic, and educational forces. These forces are alive within all of us and infuse our teaching, practice, and everyday interactions. My mission as a counseling professional is to continue to promote the valuable role of culture in counseling, psychology, and organizational development.

For up-and-coming professionals, I encourage focused attention on the important literature regarding the role of ethnic and racial identity development, multicultural competencies to guide all forms of counseling practice, and the development of bilingual skills, particularly in Spanish. The Latino immigrant population continues to increase in all parts of the United States. Opportunities are emerging for collaboration with institutions in Spanish-speaking countries that want to focus on counseling. With careful and systematic career planning, all professionals can improve their multicultural proficiency and perhaps even become bilingual. My other piece of advice to students and young professionals is to be active in your profession, whether it is on the university, local, state, regional, or national level. From these engagements you will grow in your professional identity.

Future Directions

When I met with my financial planner, Al, recently and after reviewing my latest work and travels plans, he stated flatly, "It doesn't sound like you are going to retire any time soon." From my vantage point, all I see are wonderful possibilities ahead of me—some that I cannot even imagine. The future involves completing two books accepted for publication, more active mentoring of students here at Arizona State University as well as across the country regarding their professional career development, and attention to the National Latina/o Psychological Association. I served as president from 2002 to 2004 and intend on nurturing the organization's growth and development. I want all students to succeed, and I especially want to be available to students of color in graduate training. Having said all of this, I also want to restate or reemphasize my passion for my career. I enjoy supporting students' research in the area of ethnic minority concerns such as academic persistence and mentoring. I also believe the future will allow me to work in the capacity of ambassador to Spanish-speaking countries where there is a growing desire for community mental health counseling models. To not scatter my energies, I have learned to involve others in my plans. I believe the boundaries for exchanging counseling practices from different cultural backgrounds will become more fluid. There are many good reasons to learn about the benefits of culture-specific practices such as *cuento* (storytelling) therapy, the use of testimonials in counseling, and the Hawaiian tradition of *Ho'oponopono* (harmony and positive family relationships). Personally, I want to continue to expand my multicultural proficiency and encourage others to do the same.

In my experience, horoscopes are never quite accurate and neither are tarot cards. Who can really predict the future? My preference is not to know the future. I would rather live my life with a five-year time line and let the rest take shape based on the events of the next five years. I am confident that anticipated and unanticipated experiences will continue to open doors to greater career possibilities. I will keep an open mind and be willing to be surprised because *sí se puede* (yes, we can). Meanwhile, I will continue to make time to enjoy nieces and nephews in Boston and Ohio, and my extended family of stepchildren and their children. We care a great deal about each other. I also have wonderful friends who are around to see a movie, take a walk, or play golf. These outlets are just as important as my academic endeavors. I strive for balance, and yoga and golf can get me there 50% of the time. My professional journey is in high gear, but I know there is nothing to prove. I am simply enjoying each day and hoping that what I do and who I am will provide inspiration for another's journey.

References

American Psychological Association. (2003). Guidelines on multicultural education, training, research, practice, and organizational change for psychologists. *American Psychologist, 58,* 377–402.

Anzaldúa, G. (1987). *Borderlands/la frontera.* San Francisco: Spinsters/Aunt Lute Book Co.

Arredondo, P. (1996). *Successful diversity management initiatives.* Thousand Oaks, CA: Sage.

Arredondo, P., Toporek, R., Pack-Brown, S., Jones, J., Locke, D., Sanchez, J., et al. (1996). Operationalization of multicultural counseling competencies. *Journal of Multicultural Counseling and Development, 24,* 42–78.

D'Andrea, M., Daniels, J., Arredondo, P., Ivey, A. E., Ivey, M. B., Locke, D. C., et al. (2001). Fostering organizational changes to realize the revolutionary potential of the multicultural movement: An updated case study. In J. G. Ponterotto, J. M. Casas, L. A. Suzuki, & C. M. Alexander (Eds.), *Handbook of multicultural counseling* (pp. 222–254). Thousand Oaks, CA: Sage.

Johnson, W. B., & Packer, A. H. (1987). *Workforce 2000: Work and workers for the twenty-first century.* Indianapolis, IN: Hudson Institute.

Pedersen, P. (Ed.). (1991). Multiculturalism as a fourth force in counseling [Special issue]. *Journal of Counseling & Development, 70*(1).

Ramirez, M. (1998). *Multicultural/multiracial psychology.* Northvale, NJ: Jason Aronson.

Sue, D. W., Arredondo, P., & McDavis, R. J. (1992). Multicultural counseling competencies and standards: A call to the profession. *Journal of Counseling & Development, 70*(4), 477–486.

Chapter 5

With a Little Help From My Friends: The Tapestry of My Career

Jane Goodman

I can tell the story of how I became a counselor and then a counselor educator as if it were a series of logical, sequential, planned events or as if it were random, chance, happenstance, to use the term created by Mitchell in her theory of planned happenstance (Mitchell, Levin, & Krumboltz, 1999). They are both true. In hindsight, the process looks logical. While living it, however, it felt accidental—and lucky!

Influence of the Past

When I finished college in 1963 with a degree in sociology but with the "insurance" of many women of my generation, an elementary education teaching certificate, I needed to find a job. I had just gotten married (my husband was still in school), and I wanted to work at the university that I had attended and where we were living. I made the rounds of the deans and professors with whom I had a good relationship and ended up being hired to work in the career planning and placement office doing teacher placement. Luck? Yes, but the fact that I knew deans and professors and that they wanted to help me find a position was a result of being involved in student activities, making connections with faculty and administrators, and I hope, being seen as capable. I also took the initiative to talk to these university folks. So what felt like luck had elements of planned happenstance (Mitchell et al., 1999).

When I then moved to Michigan, I worked for two years as a fourth-grade teacher as planned until I had my first child. I was certainly following a typical female script at that time in my life, but I was uneasy enough in the role to begin work on a master's degree. But in what? Chance intervened again. I had taken a course called "The Role of the Teacher in Guidance" as part of the continuing education requirement to keep my teaching certification. I was not happy as a teacher of young children because I found the discipline and rigid requirements counter to my personality. I suspect my immaturity also played a part in my dissatisfaction with my abilities and my performance. So I went to the local university and wandered the halls trying to find out how I could do again what I had done after college: work in student affairs. But since I didn't have any idea that that was its designation, or that there was even training in such a field, it was a frustrating day. I had used one of my two business days—the only two days I could take off all year. I was standing in the halls of the university, close to tears, when the professor from my one guidance class came by. Being a good counselor, and a caring man, Ed Adamek asked me what the matter was. As I tearfully explained, he told me his department had just hired someone who was starting a program in college student personnel work—the exact field I was looking for. He then walked me upstairs and introduced me to Nancy Schlossberg. Chance? Of course. But mediated by the fact that I was searching for a program, had taken a class, had done well enough to be remembered by the professor, and had followed up on his invitation to come upstairs and meet his new colleague.

Let's fast-forward six years, to 1972. Two babies, a master's degree in college student personnel, and several part-time temporary jobs have intervened. I am at a party and another guest says to me, "What do you know about this test that has a pink form for women and a blue form for men?" I promised to look into it, and the next chapter of my professional career was born. My first step was to talk to Nancy Schlossberg, who had become a mentor and friend. We began a research study into what was then called the Strong Vocational Interest Blank. We gave both the men's and women's forms to groups of both men and women, did an item analysis, and determined that the test had a clear gender bias. Although the test authors claimed that the colors were a chance decision, we found clear status differences in the way the instrument interpreted identical sets of responses from men and women. Armed with this information, we brought a resolution to the senate of what was then called the American Personnel and Guidance Association (APGA). It was referred to what was then called the Association for Measurement and Evaluation in Guidance (AMEG). We worked with AMEG and the test publishers to change the inventory.

Needless to say, this is an oversimplification of an arduous and sometimes controversial process. I felt great satisfaction in this result. It was perhaps the first time as a counseling professional that I had been able to see the connection between my political activism and my chosen profession. In addition, not only did I get to know a number of professionals in the counseling world but also I acquired some post-master's credits. (Because there were no funds to support the research, I registered for some independent study hours.) Nancy Schlossberg then suggested that I apply for the doctoral program to take advantage of some of those credits. Although I was somewhat distracted with my family, which now numbered three children, I applied, was admitted, and began doctoral study.

Was Pascal right that chance favors the prepared mind? Had I not heard about the pink and blue Strong Vocational Interest Blank, I might be in an entirely different field. But had I not pursued it, and had the good fortune of finding Nancy Schlossberg to pursue it with me, that chance would have made no difference. Schlossberg (personal communication, July 2, 1994) refers to this type of experience as being cobiographers.

Savickas (2003) discusses the importance of childhood experiences, especially our earliest memories, in determining what line of work we choose and how we implement that career option. Although I considered myself a shy child, my earliest memories are of adventure and rebelliousness. I read and reread Lewis Carroll's *Alice in Wonderland* and *Through the Looking Glass*, reveling in Alice's experiences. I would have to say today that helping others is my chief value. But after that, variety and novelty stand out in importance. They make me good at idea generation and much poorer at follow-through. I have to work hard at being organized. I enjoy buying a new calendar each year and choosing pretty file folders and labels; it is using them in which I often fall short. Perhaps that is a reason I enjoy collaboration so much. There is someone else to keep me on target.

In tracing my political beliefs, I think they are also the result of the fact that I was an unpopular child, especially at school, where being bright but without artistic or athletic talent made me unattractive to my peers. Perhaps my concern for the underdog stems from those experiences—or perhaps because in my neighborhood we rooted for the perpetual underdogs, the Dodgers, against what we saw as the domination of the rich Yankees! I grew up in Yonkers, New York, famous in those days for being next to the biggest city in the world—New York City. This pun on Yonkers proximity to New York also expresses our feelings of being second-class citizens. So my enthusiasm for the underdog has varied roots.

I received very mixed messages from my parents regarding achievement. They were pleased that I got good grades but also told me that girls shouldn't be seen to be too smart. One of my mother's favorite adages was "Be good, sweet maid, and let who will be clever." This from one of the cleverest women I have ever known! I was fortunate to be able to attend a high school and college where I was no longer one of the cleverest. This gave me the freedom to really stretch and to enjoy my academic abilities. It also led me to believe that the academic environment was one in which I could be comfortable. I suspect that is also why I have continued to seek out smart women as role models and to try to be a role model for other women, younger or newer in the field.

I don't think any of us traverse a life without challenges. I experienced several unlooked-for transitions during my 30s and 40s: the deaths of both of my parents within eight months of each other, a divorce, the struggles of my youngest child to find his place in the world, a new marriage, and new work, to name a few! Perhaps that is why I am so fascinated professionally by transition theory and why I feel so privileged to have had the opportunity to work with Nancy Schlossberg and Elly Waters on that topic on the second edition of *Counseling Adults in Transition* (Schlossberg, Waters, & Goodman, 1995). I am pleased that I will have the opportunity of passing on that privilege as I work with my doctoral student Mary Anderson on the third edition—with Nancy Schlossberg.

I have always been an optimist. I take great pleasure in being alive, enjoying my five senses, and looking for the best in situations. I decided many years ago that being down in the dumps wouldn't change the political situation, lead to world peace, or solve the problems of hunger and homelessness. I know this sounds positively Pollyannaish, but it is true. I am not a woman of religious faith. I was raised in a Jewish home by parents who were staunch atheists. I have come to the understanding that not being religiously observant does not mean that I do not have a spiritual side, however. I feel deeply connected with the natural world—maybe I am a true pagan—and often feel a sense of oneness with the universe when I experience great art, music, or architecture. I suspect it is hard to be an optimist without some sense of greater purpose. There is so much sadness and tragedy in the world; I have to believe that we were meant to appreciate all of the joy that comes our way, both the little moments and the big.

Perhaps a story will best illustrate what I mean about connectedness with nature. I was walking my dog on a railroad right-of-way near a golf course one very foggy, bleak winter day. The sky and the ground were the same color: gray. It was a lowering sky; you could hardly see where the earth ended and the sky began. There was snow on the ground, but it, too, was gray. The trees were bare, and I was feeling about as drab as the scenery. I encountered another dog walker who turned to me and said, pointing to the landscape, "Isn't it beautiful? Just like a Dürer engraving," referring to the 16th-century German artist. As I looked again at the scenery, it suddenly leaped into focus, as if I had just put on 3-D glasses. The tree branches created beautiful traceries against the gray sky, and the gray acquired gradations of hue and intensity. I was transported. And grateful to this stranger who had changed my day and my perspective.

Political Influences on My Career

I mentioned my political beliefs briefly above. They are an important part of who I am as a person and as a professional. I was raised in a middle-of-the-road liberal family, pro-union and democratic, but very frightened by the red-baiting of Joe McCarthy and the House Un-American Activities Committee (HUAC). My parents knew people who had lost their jobs, and having grown up poor and survived the Great Depression, they were very worried that any political activity could be dangerous. I discovered folk music in my mid-teens and was radicalized by singers such as Pete Seeger and the Weavers. I worked summers at a camp for poor children, where the burgeoning Civil Rights Movement and the possibility we felt of "changing the world" excited my fellow counselors and me. This camp was an opportunity for me not only to meet children from a variety of backgrounds but also to spend time with other young adults who shared my worldview.

Moving away (literally 500 miles) from the fears of my parents, I began college in 1959, at a school, the University of Chicago, noted for its student activism. I became involved in student politics, marched against HUAC and sat-in in front of the university administration building when we found out that the university owned segregated housing. The 1964 murders of three civil rights workers in Mississippi, one of whom was the brother of a friend as well as the son of friends of my parents, added to their fears but spurred me to greater involvement. I helped raise funds for the "freedom schools" in the South, was a part of forming the union in the elementary school in which I taught, and became involved in the movements protesting the war in Vietnam and seeking equal rights for women.

My political views continued to shape my sense of self and led me toward wanting work where I could continue making a difference. An opportunity arose to do an internship at one of the first women's centers in the country, the Continuum Center at Oakland University. Founded in 1964 with a Kellogg demonstration grant, the Continuum Center in 1972 (when I began working there) was a full-service counseling center dedicated to helping women achieve their potential. I did my internship there, was lucky enough to be hired, and stayed for 17 years, working part time at first and then taking on more hours as my children grew older. The center, in the words of its long-time director Elly Waters, "desexegrated" in 1978, although we continued to serve a largely female clientele. As I honed my counseling skills in an organization that made ongoing training and feedback a high priority, I also began to increase my interest in career development. Most of the women who came to the center in the 1970s and early 1980s had been full-time homemakers since the birth of their first child, and now, through desire or necessity, wanted to work. I became fascinated by the decision-making process, the integration of career and personal issues, and the relationship issues that caused or were caused by these transitions. We also soon learned that men had similar needs to rethink their self-definition, their relationships, and their careers. Elly Waters coined the phrase "affective men and effective women" to describe the phenomenon of women finding a greater sense of autonomy while men were rediscovering their feeling side (Goodman & Waters, 1985).

Because we were dependent on grants and contracts, and because funders usually wanted products that were easy to disseminate, I had the opportunity to develop materials, train professionals and paraprofessionals in their use, and work with a wide variety of clienteles. With colleagues at the center, notably Judy Hoppin and Sarah Uhle, I worked with students in the public schools, particularly high school and what was then called vocational education. I worked with active and laid-off automobile and telecommunications workers. I worked with displaced homemakers and community college and university students and the counselors who served them. One of my fondest memories is having two laid-off tool and die makers serve on a grant advisory board. They kept us grounded in reality and helped us to understand the depth of feelings of men and women who had lost their jobs.

Again, because granting agencies often requested dissemination as part of the grant, I began to write articles for professional journals. I discovered that although I did not always enjoy the process of writing (and still don't), I do enjoy having written! All of my early writing was done with coauthors, and I still prefer to collaborate whenever possible. I was fortunate to have the opportunity to work with another woman who became a mentor and good friend, Elly Waters, with whom I cowrote many articles and ultimately two books. Indeed, I only wrote alone after attending a National Career Development Association (NCDA) Women's Gathering, where I set a goal of writing something by myself, just to prove I could!

I also enjoyed the fact that some of our earlier writing was iconoclastic. The work on the Strong Vocational Interest Blank described earlier was followed by an article titled "Down With the Maintenance Stage" (Goodman, Walworth, & Waters, 1975) that questioned Super's (1957, 1980) model, which we viewed as deterministic. I had the good fortune of coediting a monograph for the NCDA's Women's Commission entitled *Resocialization of Sex Roles* (Waters & Goodman, 1980). Based on a conference that I helped plan, the monograph and conference brought me in contact with leaders in the field, such as Sunny Hansen and Juliet Miller, women I still consider my friends. So my good fortune extended to meeting and being supported by several extremely able and generous women. I hope I have been able to pass that support on to newer members of the counseling field.

From Practice to Professing

My counseling career began when I accepted a job at the Continuum Center, the women's center referenced earlier. I had done an internship there, and being hired for a half-time position was a dream come true. I was in charge of the evaluation component of a grant and conducted and supervised group personal growth and career development programs, primarily for women. These groups were time limited, structured, and led by volunteer paraprofessionals whom we had trained intensively and supervised closely (cf. Waters, Fink, Goodman, & Parker, 1976). This was a time of enormous learning for me. Coleading with experienced helpers gave me the opportunity to see master therapists in action. Sitting in on the groups led by our volunteers was also an opportunity to learn from their skills as well as their errors. My induction into group work began a love affair with the group process—one I have continued to carry into my teaching and professional organizational work.

Development as a Multicultural Counselor

I grew up in a virtually all-White, working-class factory town, a suburb of New York City, in the years immediately following Word War II. Although we were Jewish, I didn't know anyone else Jewish, except my relatives, until I was about 12 years old. Our predominantly Irish Catholic neighborhood accepted me fully; I went to church almost every Sunday with one friend or another. My Jewish identity remained, and remains, strong, although I am not religiously observant. The first African American person I knew socially was a fellow member of an organization in which I became active in high school, the National Conference of Christians and Jews. In college, I met a few other people of African American descent, but I still lived in an almost all-White world. (My mother's best friend when I was in high school was Puerto Rican, but I knew no other Hispanic people until much later in my life, except the children I worked with at the aforementioned summer camp.)

Then I moved to Detroit. My husband at the time joined his father's law firm, which was perhaps the first integrated law firm in the country. (In the 1960s my husband had been written up in *Jet* magazine when, as a law student, he joined with a Black attorney to integrate a Southern law office.) For the first time, I got to know middle-class African Americans whose education and lifestyle were similar to mine. When our oldest two children were one and two years old, we moved to a neighborhood that was rapidly losing its White population, and I began, at least residentially, to inhabit a Black world. My children were among the very few White kids in their schools, leading to some interesting family discussions about what majority and minority meant in this context. When, after a divorce and remarriage, I moved to the suburbs to be closer to my and my new husband's work, it looked so White! I had a difficult adjustment to the more aloof attitudes of my new neighbors; I was used to the warmth and outgoing friendship of the Black community.

Professionally, I became concerned that African Americans and Hispanics were poorly represented in counseling in general and in counseling leadership in particular. With the aid of a small grant from the Michigan Department of Education arranged by a wonderful professional, Gertrude Bonaparte, I joined with a group of Black counseling professionals (chiefly Janice Green from Wayne State University and Yvonne Calloway from Eastern Michigan University) to put on a workshop that invited minority counselors to become involved in organizational leadership. In the process of planning and delivering the daylong conference, I learned much more than I imparted. This lack of minority representation in counseling leadership continues to trouble me, and I continue to look for ways to encourage minority coprofessionals to get involved.

As I became more knowledgeable about multiculturalism, I began to realize that my understanding needed to move beyond issues of race and ethnicity. I have detailed elsewhere (Goodman, 2005) my growing knowledge of the issues faced by gay, lesbian, bisexual, and transgendered people. This knowledge grew out of individual friendships, mostly with men and women whom I met through my counseling work and professional organizational activities. I also had the privilege of attending an all-day workshop at the American Counseling Association (ACA) conducted by leaders from the Association for Gay, Lesbian, and Bisexual Issues in Counseling (AGLBIC). Although, unfortunately, there were only about a dozen attendees, the day was powerful and I had the opportunity of getting to know some of these fantastic people, several of whom are still my friends.

More recently, I have become concerned with the paucity of research into issues of counseling and social class. I am encouraged by a small but growing body of scholarship in the career development arena, but I wish there were more in the general counseling literature. I attempted to address this deficit, at least a little, in my first professional article, "A Woman's Place: Children's Sex Stereotyping of Occupations" (Schlossberg & Goodman, 1972). In that study we not only examined children's views of who could do what, in both the first and sixth grade, but also compared the children in a middle-class school with those in a school in a very poor neighborhood—which happened to be literally on the other side of the tracks. Interestingly, the only major difference was that the poorer children were more open to women being doctors than the middle-class children, probably because at that time, many female physicians worked in the kind of salaried positions accessed by the poor, as opposed to being in private practice.

If the reader is looking for a fruitful field for research, I recommend looking at issues of social class as it relates to any of a number of areas of counseling theory and practice. In investigating the intersection of career development, family, and multiculturalism for a book chapter (Hawley, Goodman, & Shaieb, 2002), we found very little written that included all three elements. Apparently, many of the people working in each of these areas were focusing on two elements (e.g., issues of ethnicity and family systems) but were not looking into more complex interactions. I hope that future researchers will undertake this important, although perhaps difficult, work.

My Style of Working and Accomplishments

I have been accused of being somewhat hyperactive. I also, paradoxically, need to sleep eight and a half or nine hours per night. I have a high energy level, with a great capacity for loafing! I write by setting mini-goals—500 words a day, for example—and reward myself with computer games, a walk, or sometimes a few minutes with my current novel (often a mystery). My work style is one of persistence and occasional flashes of inspiration. I work best with others, as described earlier in regard to writing. I think aloud and think best when I am involved with others' thinking, for example, in a brainstorming session. I have strong values around keeping promises and see my work commitments as promises to my students, my colleagues, or organizational associates. I have been told that the hallmark of maturity is the ability to delay gratification. I think, therefore, that I am semimature, because I can delay it for only a brief time. My biggest professional challenge is saying no. I hate to leave a party early because I might miss something. I think this "greediness" has actually stood me in good stead professionally, as it has led me to seek out and accept challenges. It has also gotten me very tired!

While writing this chapter, I had the unpleasant experience of having heart problems. Some very minor pain led me to a cardiologist, an angioplasty, and a stent to repair an over 95% blockage of an artery. Although I am told that this repair will lead to even more energy, it has also, as seems typical of life-threatening experiences, led me to reexamine how I spend my time. At the risk of sounding smug, what I have realized is that I am spending my time exactly the way I wish. I see my children and grandchildren as much as possible and spend most of my free time with my husband doing things we both enjoy. I travel, and I play a lot: tennis, bridge, walks with my dog or with friends. I read light fiction as well as professional literature and more edifying material. And I work at something I love: teaching and mentoring the next generation of counselors. I also realized during this experience how fortunate I am to have so many people who care about me—and for whom I care. A fringe benefit of this scare has been discussions with friends about how important we are to each other—something we perhaps take for granted too often. As Noel Coward said, "Life is for living. What else could one do with it?" I try to live by that philosophy.

One of the elements of Nancy Schlossberg's four-S transition theory is "support" (Schlossberg et al., 1995). When I teach this part of the theory, I have each of my students construct a support wheel, listing all of the people and nonpeople supports in their lives. I encourage them to include family, friends, and other people in their lives, but I also encourage them to look at nonpeople supports such as faith, pets, memories, outdoor activities, music, and books. Were I to draw mine today, it would be very full.

I can also be extremely compliant—a paradox for a rebel. I finished my dissertation when I had no real plans to do so, because my advisor, George Leonard, told me I had to. I am eternally grateful, because my internal motivation to do so was nonexistent and my work did not require the degree. When people I respect, mentors perhaps, tell me they think I can do something, I usually believe them and give it a try. I am often reminded of the words to the song in Oklahoma: "I'm just a girl who can't say no. I'm in a terrible fix. I always say, 'come on, let's go,' just when I oughter say, 'nix.'" I am lucky that so many wonderful people have said, "Come on, let's go!"

I am a wife, mother to three, stepmother to four, mother-in-law to five, and grandmother to seven. I am fortunate to have many dear friends. I have a wonderful yellow Labrador retriever who takes me for walks every day. I lead a full and busy life. When my children were young I worked part time. I am not a night person, so I often arose at 5 in the morning when I had writing to do rather than try to work in the evenings. I worked on and typed my dissertation, before computers, mostly from 5 to 7:30 a.m. When asked how I did it, the answer was, "I get tired." I was impressed with the words of Bernie Siegel when he said in a speech to the Michigan Counseling Association something like, "You don't get burnt out doing what you love. You get tired. When you are tired, you can rest." And for the most part, as I said before, I love what I do. I began my career as a counselor educator when I was 49. My children were grown and I was able to work the evening hours required by this kind of position. And I was able to concentrate on the writing and leadership activities necessary for tenure and promotion. I would have found it hard to do earlier. I have sympathy for young women and men trying to find balance in such a demanding career.

We have been asked by the editors of this volume to discuss the "secret" of our success. That is an interesting question because it presumes that one calls oneself a success. I have been fortunate to have had wonderful opportunities in my career. I believe that I have worked hard to capitalize on these opportunities. So the secret is work hard and be lucky! One of the other things that I did was to believe my mentors when they said I could do something, even if I didn't truly believe it myself. Why would they, people I respected, lie to me? So I often tried new activities, shaking in my boots, and discovered that I was, if not good at least okay. For example, I had never given a speech before working at the Continuum Center. I was the only member of the staff attending an ACA (then APGA) conference in San Diego in 1973. Elly Waters had been accepted as a presenter and could not attend, so I agreed to read her speech. It was thereafter filed in our office under *M* for "My name is Jane Goodman, and I am here . . ." This particular experience was a disaster! I felt compelled by loyalty to read as much of the speech as possible, yet we were in a section of the exhibit hall only closed in by a curtain. No one could hear anything. Today I would scrap the speech and speak briefly with the audience. But what I learned is that even a disaster did not cause the sky to fall or cause me to be drummed out of the association. So I tried again, and again, and eventually acquired decent speaking skills.

My early training and experience was as a group counselor. I use my group skills in every class I teach and in every meeting I lead or in which I participate. I believe that my teaching is enhanced when I use group skills in the classroom. Group workers develop the skill of being aware of the nonverbal behaviors of all group members. I wish I had had that skill when I taught fourth grade. I attempt to draw people out when they are quiet, sometimes using structured activities to do so. I also use my group counseling skills to help some people speak less. I have found that often people need to perseverate when they do not feel heard, so a simple restatement or summary of their points can help them to allow the class or meeting to move on. Summarizing the feeling of a meeting can also allow the group to move on toward appropriate action, even when divided. I am amazed again every day of my life how powerful reflection of thoughts and feelings can be! I have also found it useful to remember a maxim I learned early in my training, "State the obvious." Acknowledging what has been called the elephant on the table has frequently broken impasses and allowed the group to discuss the real issue, not a stand-in or tangential matter.

The Shape of My Future Journey

As I have said earlier, one of my paramount career values is variety. I have enjoyed being open to opportunity and following interesting paths as they beckon. I expect that I will continue to do that, so predicting the future seems unrealistic. But . . .

I will certainly continue in my position as a professor of counseling for a few more years. I plan on continuing my involvement in professional association work if the opportunities are there. As I write this I have a year as treasurer of ACA ahead of me and three more years on the ACA Foundation Board. State and local associations are always appreciative of volunteer hours, so I am sure I can stay involved. I plan to continue to write and am hoping that my sabbatical study of career development in the formerly Communist countries of Eastern Europe will be the impetus for an area of inquiry that I can continue. I am currently working with my first doctoral students (we are a new program), and I anticipate extending and expanding my mentor role through this avenue.

Ideas percolate for me from some sort of unconscious well—from meditating while I walk, from free association, and from wide and varied reading. I read newspapers, but I watch very little television, so I am often out of touch with the modern world, but I get great stimulation from talking to—or rather listening to—other people, whom I find endlessly fascinating. I have always thought it is an asset as a counselor to be nosy. I anticipate that this nosiness, more politely called curiosity, will remain with me into retirement and will help me find new projects and activities.

Advice for Younger Professionals

Graduate students can best prepare for becoming a faculty member, advanced-level practitioner, and future professional by working hard, being open to feedback and learning, and becoming closely networked with other counseling professionals (I did say, didn't I, that I was good at stating the obvious?). My best advice is to find experienced members of our field who believe in you and trust them when they offer opportunities. Saying yes, even when you don't really have the time or the confidence, will lead to more opportunities and more confidence. (There is never enough time, so you might as well do exciting things.) If your goal is to be on a counselor education faculty, begin writing as soon as you can. Offer to collaborate on articles with faculty, push yourself to identify areas of your dissertation to turn into articles, and identify an area of scholarly inquiry that interests you enough to stay with for a while. Journal editors are usually very helpful with feedback and suggestions, so try to see rejections as learning experiences. (I find that the first couple of days after I get negative feedback, I am hurt, then irritated, and by the fourth day, I am ready to read the feedback and try again.)

Attend the meetings of as many professional associations as you can possibly afford, at the local, state, and national level. Meet people. Even if you are shy, this is a time to push yourself. Find a way to meet people that works for you. Some folks can walk up to strangers and begin a conversation; others need to join an interest group or volunteer to work on a committee. When I am at a conference where I don't know people, I find that getting to sessions a few minutes early allows me to engage in conversation with a person seated next to me. When I see those people later in the conference, I feel as if I know somebody and I feel a little less alone. It often happens that the same people will attend a similar series of workshops because we are interested in the same things. I still count people I have met that way among my professional friends.

Final Thoughts and Reflections

Perhaps a tapestry is a clichéd image, but it is one that fits my story. There are threads to be woven together, although some have premature endings and some start in the middle. The warp of my personal tapestry is my personal life: family and friends. The weft includes my political, academic, professional, and organizational lives. I have been so fortunate to be in the counseling profession at a time of unparalleled growth and acceptance. I have been fortunate because I have had a wonderful career, wonderful professional opportunities, and the wonderful experience of spending most of my working time with people who when they ask, "How are you?" really want to hear the answer!

References

Goodman, J. (2005). From naïf to activist: Personal reflections of an ally. In J. M. Croteau, J. S. Lark, M. A. Lidderdale, & Y. B. Chung (Eds.), *Deconstructing heterosexism in the counseling professions: A narrative approach* (pp. 77–82). Thousand Oaks, CA: Sage.

Goodman, J., Walworth, S., & Waters, E. B. (1975). Down with the maintenance stage: Career development for adults. *Impact, 3*(6), 44–51.

Goodman, J., & Waters, E. B. (1985). Conflict or support: Work and family in middle and old age. *Journal of Career Development, 12,* 92–98.

Hawley, L. D., Goodman, J., & Shaieb, M. (2002). Research in context. In K. M. Evans, J. C. Rotter, & J. Gold (Eds.), *Synthesizing family, career, and culture: A model for counseling in the twenty-first century* (pp. 123–138). Alexandria, VA: American Counseling Association.

Mitchell, K. E., Levin, A. L., & Krumboltz, J. D. (1999). Planned happenstance: Constructing unexpected career opportunities. *Journal of Counseling & Development, 2,* 115–124.

Savickas, M. L. (2003, September 4). *The career theme interview.* Paper presented at the meeting of the International Association of Educational and Vocational Guidance, Bern, Switzerland.

Schlossberg, N. K., & Goodman, J. (1972). A woman's place: Children's sex stereotyping of occupations. *Vocational Guidance Quarterly, 20,* 266–270.

Schlossberg, N. K., Waters, E. B., & Goodman, J. (1995). *Counseling adults in transition* (2nd ed.). New York: Springer Publishing Company.

Super, D. E. (1957). *The psychology of careers.* New York: Harper & Brothers.

Super, D. E. (1980). A life-span, life space approach to career development. *Journal of Vocational Behavior, 16*(30), 282–298.

Waters, E. B., Fink, S., Goodman, J., & Parker, G. (1976). Strategies for training adult counselors. *The Counseling Psychologist, 6*(1), 61–66.

Waters, E. B., & Goodman, J. (Eds.). (1980). *Resocialization of sex roles: A guide for educators.* Falls Church, VA: National Vocational Guidance Association.

Chapter 6

A Meaningful Life—Personal and Professional—Has Many Twists and Turns
●●●●●●●●●●●●●●●●●●●●●●●●●●●●●●●●●●●●●●

Gerald Corey

In this chapter, I begin with a brief sketch of some key events and memories in my life and share some lessons that evolved from my personal pathway. My aim is to show the connection of past events to my current personal and professional life, including my development as a multicultural counselor and my working style. I end this chapter by speculating about the future of the profession in general and my work in particular, and offering some advice to younger members of our profession.

Turning Points and Reflections on My Journey

School Daze

At age five, I was a kindergarten dropout. On the first day of school I ran down the street after my mother, which was symbolic of my dependency and my fear of being thrust into the world. At this period in my life, I was lonely, scared, and insecure, and I did not want to face the demands of the world. My confidence level was zero!

My entire elementary school experience was one long painful road of frustration and rebellion. I went to Catholic grammar school, and I did not do well at all. To be blunt, I hated school. We were expected to memorize the catechism, the times tables, and the imports and exports of major countries. I was utterly bored and could not see how any of what was being taught would be of any use. My resistance in the fifth grade was met with the punishment of being held back in the same grade for another year. I felt humiliated that I could not measure up and that I had let down my parents. I believed I was very different from all the other kids who went on to sixth grade. For the rest of my grammar school years, I was a class clown, a trait that is still part of my personality.

With nine years of grammar school under my belt, you might think I had finally found the road to school success. But my transition to a Catholic boys school at age 15 did not go much better than my earlier schooling. Although

I really wanted to succeed, I felt totally overwhelmed and had not a shred of confidence that I could pass my courses. The road of my life had turned rough and unfriendly, and I wondered if I would ever steer my way out. I flunked algebra, geometry, chemistry, and typing. I endured four years of Latin, and all I can now remember is, *Mea culpa, mea culpa, mea maxima culpa.* These adolescent years were particularly painful, and my strategies for staying sane were denial and withdrawal. I felt rather insignificant, and I lacked any sense of direction or purpose.

I began learning to play the alto saxophone my first year in high school and joined the band. This made going to school more enjoyable and brought me my first taste of success. With new-found confidence, I began to apply myself academically. I did fairly well in many of my classes and even decided I wanted to become a high school teacher. The band teacher (Jim Del Mano) and one other teacher (Father Mann) provided me with support and encouragement. These teachers modeled a caring way of being for young people, and they were instrumental in my decision to work with adolescents. If I could help other adolescents find their way, I thought maybe then I could understand myself.

Connecting With People

During my early 20s, I attended Loyola University, a Catholic institution taught by Jesuits. My confidence that I could succeed in my goal of becoming a high school teacher expanded, and being a part of the university band added to my self-esteem. I even got a partial scholarship for playing the saxophone and becoming the "property manager" of the band equipment. Although I did not have extraordinary musical talent, I enjoyed being part of a community endeavor. In the academic realm, I was finally finding some direction, primarily because of my excitement over the psychology courses I was taking.

My best efforts finally started yielding dividends, and eventually, I graduated with a master's degree in counseling. My decision to major in psychology was greatly influenced by Father Peter Ciklic, founder and one-man faculty of the psychology department at Loyola. I took all of his courses and felt encouraged by him to pursue doctoral studies. I learned an important lesson about the power of a mentor to keep me focused and motivated, even when I had self-doubts. Soon after I graduated, Father Ciklic hired me to teach a few psychology courses, which solidified my career decision as a teacher and as a counselor.

In the early 1960s, I began teaching English, social studies, and psychology at Whittier High School in Whittier, California. Teaching was a most rewarding endeavor, and my own elementary and high school experiences gave me a clear picture of what I did not want to be as a teacher. I did everything possible to personalize student learning and to make learning relevant, meaningful, and interesting. I was willing to take risks, and I experimented with novel ways of teaching in all of my classes. I asked students to write essays on topics such as "The meaning of my life," "What I would do if I had 24 hours to live," and "My values and life choices." My aim was to help students get a clearer sense of who they were and what they most wanted from life.

Four years of teaching high school students was followed by two years of teaching psychology in a community college. I found it relatively easy to structure introductory psychology in a way that challenged students to engage in self-exploration and to talk about personal concerns. My courses emphasized discussion and small-group work, which tweaked my growing interest in group counseling.

Mentors Found in Unusual Places

During the six years that I was teaching in high school and community college, I was also attending the University of Southern California's doctoral program in counseling. Although I enjoyed my counseling courses, I detested statistics and feared that I would not be able to pass these courses. Dr. Jane Warters was instrumental in putting my fears in perspective. She did not believe my extremely low Graduate Record Examination (GRE) scores were accurate, and she encouraged me to take the exam again. I took the GRE twice more, but neither trial elevated my anemic scores.

The semester I struggled with statistics, I came home with a splitting headache after each class. Jim Johnson was the custodian for my high school classroom. He was studying to become a math teacher, and he took a special interest in my progress. Jim put math problems on the board, and I worked on solving these problems. Whenever I felt like dropping out of the program because of my math anxiety, both Dr. Warters and Jim Johnson calmly assured me that my goals were attainable if I was willing to work hard and to persist. A lesson this experience taught me was that by challenging my fears, they became manageable, and that self-discipline pays off. It is easy to feel engulfed by fear and to stop too soon, yet fears can be put into perspective by viewing obstacles as challenges that can be overcome. Eventually, with the help of a tutor, I passed statistics.

Having people who believed in me gave me a sense of hope when discouragement set in. An important lesson for me at this time was recognizing the power a mentor can have in inspiring others to strive for their dreams. Mentoring is an important part of my professional life today, and I derive a deep sense of satisfaction from the encouragement I continue to provide to students.

By the way, Jim and I developed a long-term friendship, which continues to this day. In 1984 he convinced me to purchase my first Macintosh word processor, and he patiently taught me how to use it. Today, Jim is still the person I turn to when I encounter problems with my computer.

Personal and Professional Challenges

My early 30s presented me with many turning points. I received my doctorate and landed a new job at California State Polytechnic University. My professional tasks included doing both individual and group counseling in the university counseling center and teaching courses in abnormal psychology, adolescent psychology, and educational psychology. During my five-year tenure at this university, I taught psychology courses for students preparing for a teaching career. As before, I tried to personalize the learning by encouraging students to review their personal experiences as learners and to decide how they might want to teach differently than they were taught. Along with teaching, supervising student teachers, doing individual counseling, and conducting personal growth groups, I was also working toward becoming a licensed psychologist. The supervised experience required included seeing clients in private practice for individual counseling and cofacilitating marathon encounter groups.

This was an extremely challenging time for me, both personally and professionally. I had been married for only a few years, and we had two young daughters. I was not prepared for all that this entailed, and I struggled through the process of learning how to be a husband and a father. These were difficult roles for me to learn, partly because I threw myself into my work.

I received wonderful feedback as a teacher, and I could see the results of my work in my students. But I was impatient and anxious with the pace of my counseling clients. It was difficult for me to allow them to struggle and to find their own way, and I also struggled with feeling ineffective as a counselor. When clients made little progress, I interpreted this as being due to my inadequacy as a practitioner. Many of my unresolved issues stemming from childhood and adolescence reappeared at this time. I often told myself that I was in the wrong profession and was not cut out to be a therapist. To make matters worse, I did not get much recognition or support from my supervisors during my training. One of them suggested that I might be better off as a teacher and that I should give up on becoming a counseling psychologist.

A lesson that this taught me was the importance of persisting, even with the absence of external validation. Although it is difficult to persist when reinforcement from others is not forthcoming, I began to learn to look to myself for the kind of approval I had sought from others. I also learned that I could not inspire clients to pursue their in-depth personal work if I was avoiding my own problems. I returned for additional personal therapy and attended many different intensive groups, and both were very useful to me in exploring my personal issues and honing my therapist skills. I learned that I could not take my counseling clients any further than I had gone on my own personal journey.

Taking Risks and Facing Self-Doubt

One of my former supervisors was beginning an innovative undergraduate human services program at California State University at Fullerton. I visited his classes and was impressed with his students, and he encouraged me to apply to teach in the program at this university. At age 35, I gave up a tenured position and accepted this new role with some anxiety yet with a belief that this was a good move. Our program involved an integration of both the cognitive and affective domains. Students majoring in human services found their classes both academically demanding and personally meaningful. A lesson I learned was to think through a rationale for a program and to have the courage to stick with a vision, even when this vision is threatened.

The human services program that I helped to develop was the target of considerable controversy on campus. The more traditional departments viewed us as the "touchy-feely" major and did not see a justification for giving students credit for self-exploration. What did that have to do with cultivating the intellect and transmitting knowledge? My task was to educate administrators about the value and relevance of courses in the major.

In my role as a new professor in an innovative program, I had an opportunity to design and teach a variety of group courses and a course on the theories of counseling. I also wrote my first book, *Teachers Can Make a Difference* (G. Corey, 1973), and shortly after, a second book, *The Struggle Toward Realness* (G. Corey, 1974). Although the books were not widely read, having them published was a turning point for me. I learned that writing textbooks could be a reality if I wrote about the subjects I was teaching and if I followed my interests. Focusing on my goal of completing a book also supplied the motivation to continue when I felt discouraged. Indeed, when I first began my writing career, I often struggled with getting words on paper and doubted that I had anything worthwhile to say. Here is an excerpt from my journal (in the early 1970s) that illustrates this self-doubt:

> Today I really wanted to write a chapter in my book. I sat down and just nothing would come. I write and it seems trite and stilted. I just can't organize or develop my thoughts—nothing comes. I feel like junking the whole damn thing. I wasted a whole day—and what do I have to show for it? A few disjointed paragraphs—nothing hangs together, and it seems that I just can't write. I hate that frozen feeling—immobility.

The Fruits of Perseverance

Early in my 40s, I began writing textbooks for just about every course I taught, including my first successful book, *Theory and Practice of Counseling and Psychotherapy* (G. Corey, 2005). The impetus for this book came from teaching the course and wanting to pull my ideas together on the subject. Close to this time, Marianne (my wife and colleague) and I began writing together, which resulted in several books: *Groups: Process and Practice* (M. Corey & Corey, 2006), *I Never Knew I Had a Choice* (G. Corey & Corey, 2006), *Issues and Ethics in the Helping Professions* (G. Corey, Corey, & Callanan, 2003), *Theory and Practice of Group Counseling* (G. Corey, 2004), and *Group Techniques* (G. Corey, Corey, Callanan, & Russell, 2004). Some of these books we did with our friends and valued colleagues. (For all of the books listed above, the initial publication dates ranged from 1977 to 1981.) Although *Theory and Practice of Counseling and Psychotherapy* (currently in its seventh edition) is widely used, my road to completing the first edition was rocky and full of potholes. A few reviewers gave some very harsh, critical, and discouraging feedback, and others thought my style of writing was too informal and not empirically sound. One lesson that grew out of my early experiences as an author was that writers should be open to feedback from reviewers but question their input as well. It would have been easy to throw in the towel and let discouragement get the best of me, but I continued to see the value of persistence, hard work, and self-discipline as a route to reaching my goals. I also learned to persist in the face of self-doubts.

In my mid-40s, I began conducting workshops in various parts of the United States and also in Europe, often with Marianne and other colleagues. This was challenging, exciting, demanding, and fun. These opportunities were sparked by our books, and they represented yet another way to teach both students and mental health professionals. I continued to have the inspiration for topics for new books. Certainly this was a period in my life that was in stark contrast to my early years in school when I felt I had no voice. I had finally come to believe that I had a voice and that I could use it to make a difference.

This was a demanding time. Not only was I teaching full time in human services, but I also assumed the responsibility of program coordinator (the equivalent of a department chair) for about nine years. During summers and semester breaks, I was busy writing and revising books, conducting workshops, and training students and professionals in the area of group counseling. I was challenged with learning how to balance a multiplicity of professional roles, learning how to formulate long-range and short-term goals, acquiring time management skills, and learning how to create some personal life amid all the fury of my professional life.

Early in my years at California State University at Fullerton, I developed a weeklong residential group course that was held in a mountain setting. My colleagues and I offered this course for 25 years (both here and abroad), and those of us who cofacilitated these groups found them to be of immense value both personally and professionally. Most of what we learned about the power of groups came from being a part of these personal exploration groups. Our underlying philosophy was the belief that we have choices and can take steps to redesign our lives. Once group members identified early decisions and their faulty beliefs surrounding these decisions, they were in a position to replace self-limiting core beliefs with functional beliefs. In essence, the intensive group evolved into a dynamic community that encouraged interpersonal honesty and gave the participants permission to be themselves.

My colleagues and I learned a great deal about how healthy relationships can be established when people feel safe enough to explore their lives in a therapeutic community. We did our best to provide boundaries and to create a climate of safety that permitted the group participants to take risks that they would normally not take. Sometimes the participants shared with us that they experienced the group as an ideal family. In this new family, they felt safe, trusted one another, expressed themselves without fear of being judged, felt accepted and protected, and were encouraged to be themselves instead of trying to be what others expected of them.

On several occasions I had to convince university administrators to allow me to continue offering this unusual course, and in 1998 the university canceled the course because of liability concerns. This is but one example of how anxiety surrounding legal action can interfere with a creative program in a university setting. I felt a keen sense of defeat at the loss of this project that was so dear to my heart. Despite my willingness to fight for what I believed to be educationally sound, I lost this battle.

Choosing a Road Less Traveled

By my mid-50s, I was doing everything I wanted to professionally. However, I continued to feel challenged in learning limits and finding a balance in nonwork areas of my life. I was still attempting to do too many things at once. Many of my personal needs were met from my involvement with so many projects, yet I came to realize that I couldn't do everything that I loved doing. I decided it was time for someone else to accept the administrative role of directing our undergraduate program, and I also began taking a leave without pay every fall semester to devote more time to the ever-demanding task of writing. Teaching full time each spring semester kept me active in the classroom and made life less crowded with activity.

A hard lesson for me to learn was to pause before too readily accepting yet another invitation for doing another workshop, another keynote speaker engagement, or another book project. Because I lived with an overcrowded schedule and accepted too many invitations, I was challenged to learn the value of carefully reflecting on the pros and cons of accepting any invitation, no matter how tempting it appeared. Although I enjoyed most of what I was doing, I eventually recognized that it took time and energy. I had the difficult task of learning to say no to some delightful offers.

I formally retired from the university system as a full-time professor at age 63, but I continue to teach courses in group counseling and ethics in counseling as an adjunct faculty member. In addition, each year I teach at least four courses at several different universities. My writing schedule now is almost full time, and I revise at least two textbooks each year. Over the past few years, Marianne and I have become involved in making educational videos, which is another way to reach students beyond the realms of textbooks or the confines of a classroom. Making and editing video programs has proven to be as much work as writing textbooks. I continue to be challenged to take a side road, to slow down, to pause along the way. But the unwinding road has provided me with a wonderful ride!

Connection Between Theory and Practice

The main way I practice counseling is through facilitating groups of various sorts. Here is a brief summary of what I attempt to convey to those who participate in our groups about how change occurs.

The more we attempt to deny some aspect of our being, the more we remain the same. If we desire change in some area of our personal life, we must first accept who and what we are rather than striving to become what we should be. Recognizing who we are at the present time is the starting point for the path toward change. Change is not facilitated by guilting ourselves over all that we are not. Rather, change occurs when we are able to view ourselves as we are and to treat ourselves kindly. We must be willing to take small steps in the direction we want to move. Perfection is best viewed as a direction, not a goal that we reach once and for all. Wanting to be different is the beginning of a new direction. Taking charge of our lives exacts a price, and each of us needs to decide if we are willing to endure a degree of discomfort that is often associated with making changes.

What are the implications of my perspective on change for the practice of counseling? How does change occur in the therapeutic endeavor? What is my role in facilitating change? I do not view my role as a problem solver or a giver of advice. Instead, I create a climate where clients can evaluate what they are doing and how well it is working for them. It is their job to determine what changes they want to make. From my perspective, counseling is a process of engagement between two persons, both of whom are bound to change through the therapeutic venture. At its best, this is a collaborative process that involves both the counselor and the client in co-constructing solutions to concerns.

Much of psychotherapy research demonstrates that it is the quality of the therapeutic relationship that makes the difference. It is precisely within the context of a person-to-person relationship that the client experiences growth and the power to change. What facilitates healing is a process of genuine dialogue with our clients. If we hide behind the safety of our professional role, I believe our clients will keep themselves hidden from us. If we become merely technical experts and leave our self out of our work, the result will be sterile counseling. It is through our own genuineness and our aliveness that we can significantly touch our clients. If we possess wide knowledge, both theoretical and practical, yet lack human qualities of compassion, caring, good faith, honesty, realness, and sensitivity, we are merely technicians. I think our clients need more than our technical expertise if we hope to make a significant difference in their lives.

Much of my writing has been devoted to helping students understand the basic concepts of the contemporary theories of counseling so that they might be able to apply these concepts to actual practice. I view theory as a road map that helps us keep our focus, know where we are going, and make sense of what we are doing in our counseling practice. My emphasis in both writing and teaching is on the practical applications of the various theories. Ultimately, I hope counseling students will learn the fundamentals of the various counseling models and begin to develop their own integrative approach. I encourage students not to become devotees of one theoretical model but to be open to multiple counseling models and to base their practice on elements from diverse theoretical perspectives.

Development as a Multicultural Counselor

I am a first-generation Italian American, and I learned about cultural diversity first from my family of origin. Both of my parents were from Italy, yet neither of them seemed to think it was important that I learn how to speak Italian. When I was a child, we spent almost every Sunday at a family gathering at my grandparents. I felt lost because most of the conversation was in Italian, and I didn't feel that I fit in.

My father was a brilliant and sensitive man, but a depressed person. Sent from Italy to New York when he was seven years old, he was raised in an orphanage. Eventually he became a dentist, and he practiced dentistry during the Great Depression. Because he was convinced that many people would not want to come to an Italian dentist, he changed his name from Cordileone (meaning heart of the lion) to Corey.

My mother, who lived until she was 94, was a great teacher by her modeling. From her early childhood years, she worked hard on her father's peach orchard and learned the values of a simple life. Despite having a hard life, she retained her wit and sense of humor until the end. She taught me the value of hard work and showed me that one can change even in old age.

Being around a nuclear and extended immigrant Italian family, I learned at an early age that people see the world through different eyes and express themselves in different ways. I came to appreciate differences rather than judge them. Because of my father's experiences, I became aware that people were discriminated against because of their heritage. My extended Italian family encountered some discrimination, yet some of these family members harbored their own prejudices as well.

I learned more about cultural diversity from Marianne than I did from my family of origin or extended family. Marianne immigrated to the United States from Germany at the age of 19. We were married in Germany about three years later, when I was 27. Each summer we spent time in Marianne's village in the Rheinpfalz, which gave me an opportunity to experience the values associated with living in a small, rural town in another country. Living in two cultures has helped me to appreciate the complexities of culture and various ways of perceiving the world. Without a doubt, Marianne has been my primary mentor in teaching me about culture—and she has been one of the major forces in challenging me to think about what I do and say.

Our daughters, Heidi and Cindy, were greatly influenced by their experiences both in Germany and in the United States. Both of our daughters are bilingual and bicultural. Cindy earned a PsyD in clinical psychology, with a specialization in multicultural and community counseling. We share common interests and concerns about multicultural issues, and she has challenged me to reexamine some of the assumptions underlying my clinical practice. Cindy has copresented with Marianne and me at several conferences and cofacilitated several weeklong residential groups with us. Cindy has taught me valuable lessons about how culture influences the therapeutic process. Heidi took another route in the healing arts, that of teaching yoga. Heidi's influence is a reminder of the importance of paying attention to the body and not getting lost in words, which certainly has relevance in multicultural counseling.

In my student years, there were no discussions of how culture influences the assessment and treatment process, and no multicultural courses were offered. When I began my university teaching, my emphasis was largely on counseling from an individualistic perspective and studying internal psychodynamics, with little discussion of the cultural context of the therapeutic process. In the early 1980s, our human services faculty grew to include two persons of color with multicultural perspectives and backgrounds in social work. Both of them were very instrumental in enabling me to see the limitations of functioning strictly with the spectacles of a counseling psychologist. They broadened my scope to consider the person-in-the-environment. In fact, these two professors did a great deal to broaden the scope of our human services program to encompass the clients' culture and the impact of the community on the individual.

Marianne and I both expanded our horizons considerably through our travels to other countries where we conduct workshops. In Mexico, Hong Kong, China, Korea, Scotland, Germany, Belgium, Canada, and Ireland, as well as in many regions of the United States, our group counseling workshops have shown us how cultural variables influence an individual's functioning within a group. Each of these experiences provides Marianne and me with a different way of looking at what counseling is about and offers powerful avenues for learning about the interface between counseling and culture. In addition, I have found it extremely useful to read and to participate in workshops on multiculturalism.

My Work Style and Accomplishments

My Work Style

In all honesty, I must admit that a central facet of my life is work, yet I have come to realize that balance is essential. Although it may sound as if I work constantly and get little sleep, such is not the case. Over the past four years, I have kept my work down to about 42 hours a week (when I am at home working and not on vacation), which represents only a few hours less than when I worked "full time." I also make the time to exercise at least an hour every day. Yes, I do monitor activities involving work and exercise. Maintaining fitness in all areas is a priority for me. Walking and bike riding are patterns that I established about 40 years ago and are two ways I keep fit and maintain my stamina. I never miss a meal and have healthy nutritional habits. Taking time to enjoy the serenity of the mountain setting where we live is a priority in my life. My weekly schedule also includes getting deep body-work sessions, listening to meditation tapes, doing stretching exercises, and making the time for church several times a week. When I am at home, I frequently do not begin my workday until after lunch, and I rarely work beyond 10 in the evening.

Throughout my career I have been able set long-range goals, establish a schedule for getting things done, and take the steps needed to satisfactorily complete projects. I am typically working on several book projects at the same time, each in different phases of development. This demands careful planning and making the time to keep up to date with the various cycles associated with publication.

In addition to our writing, Marianne and I take time to enjoy a circle of friends and our family. We have been married for 40 years, which is an accomplishment in itself. Marianne is an exceptional person, as all of our friends would agree, and she is the one person most responsible for contributing to my productivity. We collaborate on group work, writing, making videos, and conducting workshops. Marianne provides input to books and chapters for which I am the sole author, and she continues to be my most demanding, honest, and useful critic. Over the years, the nurturing home that Marianne has created for our two daughters, herself, and me has given me the opportunity to be very productive.

Over the years I have learned how essential clarity of purpose, motivation, and self-discipline are for engaging in productive work. Realizing that I am the one who decided to commit to these projects keeps me focused and energetic. If I were doing what someone else expected of me and was externally motivated, I would long ago have lost my enthusiasm for these projects. This ties into my existential orientation, which emphasizes the role of personal responsibility in shaping our existence. A valuable lesson I try to share with students is for them to strive to discover and pursue their own passions and dreams.

Combining Work and Personal Life

During much of our married life, Marianne and I have made time for vacations, even short times away, but too often we link our professional travels with vacations. For example, recently we did a couple of five-day training workshops in group counseling with people in the helping professions in Ireland. We arranged our schedule so that we had time both before and after the workshops to visit the sites and to enjoy the country. We also took the opportunity to spend some vacation time in other countries such as Germany and Norway. Even when we travel to another state to present at a professional conference, we allow several days before we work to enjoy the natural beauty of that state.

In the past few years we have become better at blocking out time exclusively for personal travel rather than sandwiching a vacation into a work situation. For many years we have enjoyed taking cruises to Alaska and the Caribbean, sometimes with our family, other times with friends, and sometimes just the two of us. We have also found renewal on our scenic hikes in Hawaii. We rarely travel with a computer on our vacations.

Professional Accomplishments

I have greatly enjoyed the various facets of my work and have a sense of pride in all aspects of my work. I have never had any regrets about focusing my energy in areas of keen interest and following my passions in doing what I really valued. When I advise college students about pursuing graduate study and a career path, I typically encourage them to discover what excites them and to make a decision based on this rather than focusing on where they will make lots of money or what is currently in fashion.

In addition to the courses I have taught, the books I have authored or coauthored have been a way to extend my role as an educator beyond my university campus. Almost all of my books grew out of my need to have materials for my own classes, and my writing has given me an opportunity to apply the ideas in our books in the classroom. A facet of textbook writing that has definitely exceeded any dreams or expectations I may have had is the popularity of our books in many places in the world. Some of our books have been translated into Arabic, Chinese, Japanese, Korean, Portuguese, Polish, Russian, and Spanish. It is good to hear that much of what we've published appears to be useful in various cultures, with adaptations.

What matters to me most are the rewards of working with students in my teaching career of over 44 years, but I consider myself fortunate to have attained a fair number of external signs of professional accomplishment as well, including the university's Outstanding Professor Award in 1991. Helping students move ahead in their personal and professional journey has given me a great deal of satisfaction. Getting my students to challenge themselves by questioning life and stretching their personal and professional boundaries has always been more significant than merely presenting academic knowledge. What counts for me is knowing that I am continuing to make a difference in the lives of many students.

Alfred Adler's idea that feelings of inferiority are the wellsprings of creativity has real meaning to me. Along with the Adlerians, I believe that our striving for superiority (a sense of personal competence) grows out of our feelings of inferiority. My own fear of failing, feelings of inadequacy, and struggles to define who I am have been my best teachers. The lessons I have learned from these experiences are the essence of what I hope to communicate to my students. I encourage students to dare to dream what may seem like impossible dreams, to believe in themselves, and then to work hard to make their dreams reality.

Future Directions

What's Next Personally?

Basically, I do not see retirement in my picture until they put me six feet under—and then I may continue writing from my new location! I have too much fun in my work, and it provides me with purpose and meaning. I greatly enjoy teaching and doing what it takes to keep our books current, so at age 67, I am hardly thinking of retirement in the sense of not being engaged in professional work. Interacting with colleagues on exciting projects is meaningful and enjoyable, and I continue to find joy in working with appreciative and eager students who have kept me young in my "advancing" age.

Although I have enjoyed more than my share of professional accomplishments, I realize that any talents I have in teaching and writing are ones that God gave to me. Without these gifts, I do not fool myself into believing that I could be of significance to others. I feel blessed with excellent health and a good life, which has allowed me to strive toward meaningful goals. Much of what I have achieved professionally is the result of interaction with colleagues and friends in the profession. Our work together and our discussions are the impetus for new ideas and new projects, and I expect that these collaborations will continue in the years ahead.

Future Directions of the Profession: Some Speculation

Although I don't have confidence in my ability to predict the future of the profession, I have some general sense of the direction the profession is taking. Four trends that strike me are (a) an increased use of brief therapy, (b) use of technology in counseling, (c) integrative approaches to counseling, and (d) the role of spiritual and religious values in counseling.

Brief therapy appears to be "in," and long-term therapy seems to be a thing of the past in most settings. Certainly, solution-focused brief therapy has made a number of significant contributions, including focusing on the strengths of clients. Instead of viewing the therapy experience as a one-time endeavor, recurring shorter commitments to therapy at various cycles in life may be more beneficial. As individuals face new challenges in life, they can seek additional therapy when needed.

Technology is another emerging direction in the counseling profession, and it has some unfortunate aspects as far as I am concerned. It is now possible to get advice on personal problems and to work with a therapist online. Counseling students can take many of their counseling courses online—including a course in group counseling and ethics! Frankly, this disturbs me. I do see some benefits to using technology as a supplement to the interpersonal relationship, but I do not see online counseling as the main diet. Technology cannot replace human contact in the therapeutic relationship.

Some research indicates that therapy outcomes are roughly equal regardless of the theoretical orientation of the practitioner. I basically agree with this, yet I don't think this means that we are moving toward one unified theory. This is too ambitious a task! Instead, the trend over the past couple of decades or so has been away from single-theory practice and toward an integration of therapeutic approaches. Psychotherapy integration is best characterized by attempts to look beyond and across the confines of single-school approaches to see what can be learned from—and how clients can benefit from—other perspectives. The integrative approach is characterized by openness to various ways of integrating diverse theories and techniques.

Because of the complexities of human behavior, especially when the range of client types and their specific problems are taken into consideration, no single set of counseling techniques is always effective in working with diverse client populations. In order to develop an integrative perspective, practitioners need to be thoroughly conversant with a number of theories, open to the idea that these theories can be unified in some ways, and willing to continually test their hypotheses to determine how well they are working. An integrative perspective is the product of a great deal of study, clinical practice, research, and theorizing—and this is indeed a lifelong endeavor that is refined with experience.

Traditionally, religion and counseling have been viewed as antagonistic forces, but there is now widespread interest in the topic of spiritual and religious beliefs—both the counselor's and the client's—and how such beliefs might be incorporated in therapeutic relationships. From my perspective, spirituality is a factor that needs to be addressed if it is a concern of the client. There are many paths toward fulfilling spiritual needs, and it is not the counselor's task to prescribe any particular pathway. The key here is that the counselor remains finely tuned to what the client wants to explore and the purpose for which he or she sought therapy. It is essential to understand and respect the client's religious and spiritual beliefs and to include such beliefs in assessment and treatment practice, for the client's spiritual beliefs can be a major source of strength as he or she makes crucial life decisions.

Suggestions to Other Professionals

I have been asked to share some advice I would offer to graduate students preparing for a career in the counseling profession. Here are a few tips to add to those highlighted in this chapter.

- Find a group of supportive people to offer you encouragement when you may be tempted to give up, and never let discouragement get the best of you.
- Seek out at least one mentor. Talk with your favorite professors and ask how you can get involved in projects with them. You might be able to facilitate small groups in their classes, assist in research projects, or participate in writing a journal article. Ask them for tips in succeeding in school and in your career.
- Don't interpret making mistakes as failure. Understand that your learning will be limited if you are not open to making mistakes. Do your best to learn from mistakes.
- Seek out a variety of self-exploration experiences, especially individual and group therapy. Your own therapy can be your best teacher in learning how to effectively counsel clients.
- Make the time to read books that will broaden your academic understanding and that will enrich you personally. Along with your read-

ing, keep a personal journal. This is a good way to keep track of what you are doing and where you are going.

- If you think you would like to write a book, begin now. There may be a book within you that is waiting to be written. You do not need to look for a publisher yet, but you could begin by writing your thoughts and reflections in your journal.
- Now is the time to join professional organizations on the state, regional, and national levels. Read the journals of these organizations, attend the conferences they offer, and submit a proposal to present at conferences. Go to the presentations that interest you and look for ways to network with presenters with whom you share similar interests.
- Establish long-term goals and short-term goals, and make a concrete timeline for accomplishing specific tasks. Learn time management and apply these skills to your projects.
- Reflect on ways that you can make a difference in the lives of others and what special talents you have that you can put to the service of others.
- Take care of yourself in all ways. If you do not learn and practice self-care, you will not last long in the counseling profession. If you find yourself saying you don't have time to take care of yourself, then re-evaluate your priorities and determine the direction your behavior is taking you.
- Dare to dream and have the courage to pursue your passions. Let your interests be your guide. Envision what you would love to do and then figure out how to move in that direction.

I hope you take time to reflect on what you are doing that has worked for you in the past and is currently working for you, and then continue these patterns. Trust yourself to come up with your own plan for creating the kind of professional life you want—and then take steps to put your action plan in place. A well-known Chinese saying states, "A journey of a thousand miles begins with a single step." What steps are you willing to begin taking today on your journey?

References

Corey, G. (1973). *Teachers can make a difference.* Columbus, OH: Charles E. Merrill.

Corey, G. (1974). *The struggle toward realness.* Dubuque, IA: Kendall/Hunt.

Corey, G. (2004). *Theory and practice of group counseling* (6th ed.). Belmont, CA: Brooks/Cole.

Corey, G. (2005). *Theory and practice of counseling and psychotherapy* (7th ed.). Belmont, CA: Brooks/Cole.

Corey, G., & Corey, M. S. (2006). *I never knew I had a choice* (8th ed.). Belmont, CA: Brooks/Cole.

Corey, G., Corey, M. S., & Callanan, P. (2003). *Issues and ethics in the helping professions* (6th ed.). Belmont, CA: Brooks/Cole.

Corey, G., Corey, M. S., Callanan, P., & Russell, J. M. (2004). *Group techniques* (3rd ed.). Belmont, CA: Brooks/Cole.

Corey, M. S., & Corey, G. (2006). *Groups: Process and practice* (7th ed.). Belmont, CA: Brooks/Cole.

Chapter 7

The Continuing Journey to Multicultural Competence
• •

Derald Wing Sue

I was born and raised in Portland, Oregon, during World War II, the second oldest of six siblings. My father emigrated from China; indeed, he stowed away on a ship to the United States at the age of 14. Not knowing how to speak English and unfamiliar with this country, my father survived. And that has been the story of our family—surviving. My brothers and sister have learned that lesson well, and watching my mother and father deal with our early experiences of poverty and discrimination has taught us to struggle and fight against social injustice. I attribute my work on social justice, multiculturalism, and diversity to these early experiences.

As a family, we have always been in awe at the courage it must have taken for our father to journey to a strange country without family, friends, formal education, and employable skills. Yet, my father married, raised five sons and one daughter, and was able to provide for the family. He met my mother and married her when she was 16, both never attaining an education beyond the third grade. My mother taught herself how to read and write English, but my father refused to part with the "old ways." His pride in being Chinese was immense, and he eventually made his mark in Portland's Chinatown, where he became a respected elder in the community. Prior to that, he found work in the shipyards and as a gambler, and provided as best he could for the family. Despite the limited schooling of my parents, they always stressed the importance of an education. They instilled within us the value and importance it had for our future. It always amazes my colleagues when I tell them that I have three brothers with doctorates, all in the field of psychology. My sister, unlike her brothers, became a computer programmer.

Early Childhood Memories

The earliest memories of my childhood are filled primarily with images of a close-knit family that struggled economically to make ends meet. For the brief period we were on welfare, I could sense the shame and humiliation my parents felt. Everyone in the family worked to contribute until we could again stand with our heads held high. People who have never seriously lacked for the necessities of life will never truly understand the experience of being poor: constantly worrying about how to pay even the most inexpensive bills, not being able to pay for school field trips, walking miles every day to save bus fare, working after school until midnight to help the family financially, purchasing soda or candy as holiday gifts for one another, having to completely support ourselves through college and graduate school, and knowing that others seemed to shun us because we were poor. To deal with our isolation, we kept to ourselves as a family and learned to depend only on ourselves and one another.

In graduate school I recall how my classmates in counseling psychology often expressed the desire to help those less fortunate than they, actively spoke out against inequality in our society, and declared their desire to work on behalf of social justice. I often doubted, never their sincerity, but their ability to understand what they spoke about so passionately. To them, the many social injustices they talked about were purely an intellectual exercise. Although well-intentioned, they seemed much more interested in private practice, opening an office, and hanging out their shingles. Perhaps I am being harsh on them, but that was how it struck me then.

When I was in fourth grade, my father wanted better housing for his family and moved us outside of Chinatown. Our new neighborhood, which was primarily White, was not receptive to a family of color, and we were not only objects of curiosity but also subjects of ridicule and scorn. As I reflect on it now, this was the beginning of my racial/cultural awakening and my experience with racial prejudice and discrimination. And although I did not know it then, it was the beginning of my journey to understanding the meaning of racism and the many social injustices that infect our society. But in those early days, I allowed the reactions of my classmates to make me feel ashamed of being Chinese.

My older brother David and my younger brother Stan entered Abernathy Grade School with me, where we became immediate objects of hostility and constant teasing. We were called "ching-chong Chinaman" and made fun of because of our "slanty eyes" and strange language. In Chinatown we lived among other Chinese Americans and were accepted by the community and protected and buffered from the larger society. In the southeast district of Portland, we were no longer in the majority and were considered undesirable by many. As I recall, this was the most unpleasant and painful part of my early childhood. We were the victims of stereotyping, considered "nerds," passive, weak, inhibited, and subhuman aliens. Because my brother Dave was the oldest, he was often forced to fight White classmates on behalf of his younger brothers.

I vividly recall one incident that forever changed my perception of being a Chinese American. A large group of White students who had been antagonistic to us for the better part of our early school years chased the three of us to our front yard and surrounded us. There they circled us, chanting unmentionable names and told us to leave the neighborhood. I was truly frightened but stood shoulder to shoulder with Dave and Stan to confront the large group. All three of us were much smaller than our White peers, and I kept glancing to our house porch, trying to get my brothers to break for it. Dave, however, kept inching toward the group, and I could see he had somehow turned his fear to anger. I realized later that for us to start running would reinforce the stereotype that Asians were weaklings and afraid to fight.

Just as it appeared a fight was imminent, my mother opened the door of the house, strode to the edge of the porch, and in a voice filled with anger asked what was going on. When no one responded, she said if a fight was to happen, it should be fair. She identified one of the ringleaders, probably the biggest of the boys in the group. Then she asked my brother Dave to fight him. This shocked not only us, but the entire group of boys. To make a long story short, Dave gave the other boy a bloody nose from a series of lucky blows. The fight ended as fast as it had begun. At times, I have often wondered what would have happened if he had lost. It was a gamble that my mother was willing to take, because she believed that despite the outcome, pride and integrity could not be lost.

I will never forget that incident. It taught me several important lessons in life that have remained with me to this day and form the basis of much of my professional work. First, we live in a society that has a low tolerance for racial/cultural differences. Our unconscious social conditioning makes it easy for us to associate differences with deviance, pathology, and lesser value in society. Second, stereotypes held by society can also do great harm to racial/ethnic minorities. Not only are they held by the majority culture but they can become deeply ingrained in minorities as well. When facing the wrath of the band of boys, I never imagined Dave would stand his ground and fight as he did. More astonishing, however, was to witness a tiny Asian woman, my mother, take charge of the situation and encourage a fight. Any thought on my part that Asians were weak and unable to fight back disappeared that day. Third, I felt a sense of pride in being a member of the Sue family and in being Chinese, something my dad had always stressed. No group, I realized, should be made to feel ashamed.

The College and Graduate School Years

In my college and graduate school years, I continued to feel like an outsider. Perhaps that was the reason I chose to go into the field of psychology. Not only was I always trying to understand people as an observer but also I became aware of myself as a racial/cultural being. Although my classmates were friendly and accepting, I felt that the curriculum was often invalidating and did not seem to match my experiential reality. I found psychology fascinating, but the theories of human behavior seemed culture bound and limited in their ability to explain my own personal journey as an Asian American. This was especially true when I entered the counseling psychology program at the University of Oregon.

I had purposely chosen counseling rather than clinical psychology because the field seemed more open and receptive to new ideas and was less rigid with respect to racial and cultural issues. At Oregon, I was exposed to the teaching of Leona Tyler, a counseling psychologist who I quickly learned was a well-respected figure in the field. Her teachings and the humanness of her approach resonated with what I believed psychology should be. She talked about the need to stress the positive aspects of the human condition, the importance of vocational and career development for mental health, the need to balance an understanding of individual and systemic interactions, and the importance of understanding familial, social, and cultural influences in human development.

Despite being enthused and motivated by her vision, my education continued to be monocultural. Indeed, although the terms *multicultural, diversity, cultural competence,* and *racial identity* are common in psychology curricula today, they were nonexistent during my graduate school years. Although issues of minority groups were occasionally raised in my courses, the focus was always on the uniqueness of the individual or the universal aspects of the human condition. My professors operated with the certainty that similarities could bridge all differences, that the stressing of differences was potentially divisive, and that we were all the same under the skin. It was only later that I realized why I was so alienated from these concepts, although they had a degree of legitimacy. First, as an Asian American, the avoidance of discussing racial differences negated an important aspect of my racial identity. Second, I realized that my professors knew little about racial groups and felt uncomfortable talking about group differences.

During my undergraduate and graduate years, I became very involved with the Vietnam antiwar movement and participated in teach-ins, demonstrations, and other educational forums trying to get others to see the moral injustice of the United States' actions. For the first time in my life, I no longer felt like an outsider. I felt a powerful kinship and camaraderie that made me realize the power of the collective and group action. At times it was almost spiritual. I also became involved intellectually with the free speech movement and the Third World strike. I longed to be at Berkeley or San Francisco State University, where all the demonstrations and outpouring of intellectual thought emerged. I could relate well to the denunciations of oppression and injustice, and it stirred up feelings from my childhood. The Black Power movement; rise of the Black Panthers; and the words of Malcolm X, Huey Newton, H. Rap Brown, and other activists seemed to resonate with my experiential reality. They spoke about oppression, injustice, prejudice, and discrimination in a way that made more sense to me than much of my graduate school education.

First Job as a Counseling Psychologist

I guess you would say that it was no coincidence that my first job was as a counseling psychologist at the University of California Counseling Center in

Berkeley. Throughout my doctoral studies, I always believed that I wanted to practice and work with clients. Although I interviewed at places that offered me a larger salary, the allure of Berkeley and its social activism was too much to resist. Although it was at the end of the Third World strike, my Berkeley years represented a racial and cultural awakening for me unsurpassed in any other period of my life. In Oregon, there were few Asian Americans, but at Berkeley, the student body was greatly represented by Asian Pacific Islanders.

While I was working at Berkeley, I had the good fortune to meet my future wife, Paulina. She was in her last year of obtaining a teaching credential and was a resident assistant at one of the dormitories on campus. I must confess that I was originally attracted to her because of her startling beauty. But it did not take me long to realize that she was exceptionally intelligent and firm in her beliefs and values. I marveled at her racial/ethnic pride (like me, she was an Asian American). Contrary to my early feelings of inferiority associated with being Asian, she had never experienced such feelings. This was another important seed that was planted in my journey to cultural awareness and pride. We eventually married and raised two children, a son and a daughter, who I hope will always feel pride in their ethnic heritage.

At the counseling center, I saw many Asian American clients, many of them expressing personal and social problems that were similar to mine. It was not the cultural differences and the invalidation of being a racial minority in this country that seemed to affect their lives but the sociopolitical pressures placed upon them. Like me, they were made to believe that being different was the problem. It was at that period in my life that I came to the realization that being different was not the problem. It was society's perception of being different that lay at the basis of the problems encountered by many racial/ethnic minorities. Although I like to think that I helped them in their adjustment to societal intolerance, I confess that they helped me more. They validated my thinking and made me see how counseling and therapy attempted to adjust them to an intolerant system, how the practices of clinical work were antagonistic to their cultural and life experiences, and how important it was to realize that much of the problems encountered by minorities lay in the social system.

Going Into Academia

Although I enjoyed working with clients, I was not satisfied with the slow pace of therapy and the knowledge that the problems encountered by many clients were due to external circumstances. I discovered that many of the problems encountered, for example, by Asian Americans and other people of color were due to systemic forces such as discrimination, prejudice, and injustice. Having access to data at the Berkeley Counseling Center on Asian American students led me to conduct a series of studies on Chinese and Japanese students. The results reaffirmed my belief that sociopolitical forces were important considerations in the lives of people of color. The results of my early research instilled a "hunger" in me to contribute to the knowledge base of psychology. At that time, getting multicultural research published in top-notch psychology journals was difficult. Editors and editorial boards did not consider ethnic research important or relevant to the profession.

My early work on Asian American psychology and eventual movement into academia, however, eventually brought me to the attention of the American Personnel and Guidance Association (now the American Counseling Association [ACA]), and I was appointed editor of their flagship journal. The youngest editor ever appointed, at the age of 31 I was still quite naive about the internal organizational politics of the association. I radically altered the appearance of the journal, appointed many racial/ethnic minority members to the editorial board, and changed the philosophy of the journal to be more inclusive. The journal published major articles on racial/ethnic minority mental health, work with minorities, systems intervention, and psychoeducational approaches. Many of our special issues pushed the envelope on social justice, and a special issue on human sexuality caused quite a stir in the profession. There was a move to remove me as editor because of the controversial nature of the topics and my stand on social justice issues. Although it was one of the most painful periods of my professional life, many colleagues rallied to my defense. Nevertheless, the toll from those who called for my resignation or removal made me decide not to continue in my second term. The lesson, however, that I learned from this experience was that "swimming upstream," or going against the prevailing beliefs and practices of the times, can lead to great stress and pain.

Work on Multicultural Counseling and Therapy

Throughout the 1970s, my clinical experience and research on minority mental health led me to conclude that traditional counseling and psychotherapy were Western European constructions and often inappropriate in application to racial/ethnic minorities. Indeed, I began to realize that although mental health providers could be well-intentioned in their desire to help clients of color, the goals and process of counseling and psychotherapy were often antagonistic to the life experiences and cultural values of their clients. Without awareness and knowledge of race, culture, and ethnicity, counselors and other helping professionals could unwittingly engage in cultural oppression. Studying the culture-bound nature of counseling led me to study other racial groups as well. What I found were similar concerns among African American, Latino/Hispanic American, and Native American colleagues. All felt that traditional mental health concepts and practices were inappropriate and sometimes detrimental to the life experiences of the very clients they hoped to help.

My work led to several publications (D. W. Sue, 1977, 1978; D. W. Sue & Sue, 1977; S. Sue & Sue, 1977) that attacked the culture-bound nature of mental health practice and suggested radical changes in the delivery of services to a diverse population. Because I took great pains to document my work, it was well received on an academic level but failed to have a major influence on mental health delivery systems. Psychologists continued to believe that traditional forms of counseling and psychotherapy could be universally applied to all populations and situations.

In the early 1980s, things began to change. Increasingly, ethnic minority psychologists voiced concerns about the need for counselors to "own up" to their biases, stereotypes, and inaccurate assumptions of people of color. I credit two major events with radically altering my work and influence in the field. First, Leo Goldman, a valued colleague and elder in the field of counseling psychology, asked me to write a book for his series on counseling and human services. He was one of the few White psychologists who seemed genuinely to understand my research and ideas. More importantly, being a critic himself of traditional counseling, he encouraged me to put what I had to say in a book that would be unconstrained by reviewers. Concurrently, Allen Ivey, then president of the American Psychological Association's (APA) Division of Counseling Psychology, asked me to chair the Education and Training Committee and to develop standards or competencies for multicultural counseling. These publications became two of the most frequently cited in the field (Ponterotto & Sabnani, 1989).

Counseling the Culturally Different: Theory and Practice (D. W. Sue, 1981) can only be described as a labor of love. As suggested by Leo Goldman, I wrote from the heart and let loose with all the passion, frustration, and anger I felt about the harm our society and counseling psychology have done to people of color. I knew it would be provocative and accusatory and make many in the field defensive and angry. And that was what happened. I received calls from colleagues who criticized the book and claimed it was a prime example of "White bashing." Strangely enough, although many colleagues and students found the book distressful and disturbing, it became a success that surprised even my publisher. I had been told by the publisher that although few minority mental health or cross-cultural counseling courses existed in academic programs, the book stimulated creation of such courses. In general, faculty of color and adjuncts were the first to adopt and use the book in seminars or courses that they proposed. Since its publication, *Counseling the Culturally Diverse* has gone through four revisions (D. W. Sue & Sue, 2003), and I am proud to say it is the most frequently used text on multicultural counseling. Furthermore, it forms the knowledge base of many items on the Examination for Professional Practice in Psychology.

Likewise, the work of the Division 17 committee on cross-cultural counseling resulted in "Cross-Cultural Counseling Competencies: A Call to the Profession," which was published in *The Counseling Psychologist* (D. W. Sue et al., 1982). Many have identified that piece of work as the forerunner of the cultural competence movement. In actuality, the product was the result of the work of many pioneers of color whose important contributions were either overlooked, ignored, or neglected.

The Cultural Competency Movement

Although the Division 17 "Cross-Cultural Counseling Competencies" report was accepted by the Executive Board, according to Allen Ivey, it was not endorsed. To many of my colleagues, it was "too political" a stance and statement. I have since discovered that my writings are often seen by people in the profession as too filled with emotions, too provocative, and not consistent with the objective style so prevalent in academia. That has been one of my major criticisms of so-called scholarly writing in the field. It appears that many of my colleagues operate from the mistaken notion that rational thought can only come from being objective and devoid of emotions. To me, speaking from the heart and with passion is not antagonistic to reason. Furthermore, speaking the truth, especially about how counseling and therapy have oppressed and damaged people of color (although unintentionally), is difficult for many of my White colleagues to hear. They are likely to react with anger and defensiveness, making it difficult for them to accept challenges to their concept of mental health practice, and perhaps their own complicity in perpetuating unjust treatment of clients of color. I suppose they see my writings as accusatory and off-putting. Yet, how does one nicely and objectively speak about stereotyping, prejudice, and discrimination in the helping professions and the helping professional? Should I soften the message and not speak about the "unspeakable"?

As the document languished in the literature without action by the profession, Thomas Parham, then president of the Association of Multicultural Counseling and Development (AMCD), asked me to chair the Education and Training Committee to again work on the multicultural competencies. This time, we became very specific in identifying 31 multicultural counseling competencies. The document produced by AMCD was considered sufficiently important to be published jointly in both the AMCD and ACA journals to maximize distribution (D. W. Sue, Arredondo, & McDavis, 1992a, 1992b). Again, I emphasize that this historic document was the product of many, not just the three authors who are often credited with its production. Since that time, cultural competence has become almost a rallying cry in the counseling psychology field. Models of cultural competence have infiltrated research, practice, and education and training. In 2002, through the work of many, APA finally passed "Guidelines on Multicultural Education, Training, Research, Practice, and Organizational Change for Psychologists" in *American Psychologist* (APA, 2003). As such, the multicultural guidelines have become official APA policy, and I am hopeful that they will become a guiding force in the profession's movement toward multiculturalism. Needless to say, the actions by APA in passing the guidelines represented a high point in my personal and professional life.

Expanding Social Justice Horizons

In 1997 I was invited to address President Clinton's Race Advisory Board on what the average American could do to help eradicate racism. As some may recall, the National Dialogue on Race was one of former President Clinton's attempts to address what many of us consider to be one of the great social ills of our society, that of racism. The preparation that went into the national address (which was shown on C-SPAN, CNN, and many major outlets), my increasing awareness of racism, and the hate mail that I received as a result of the testimony made me realize several things. First, honest discussions of racism are difficult for our society, and strong buttons are pushed in people when racism is brought to their attention. Second, the negative reactions are often the result of defensiveness brought forth by individuals' denial of personal responsibility for racial inequities in our society. Third, it made me realize the reason that many have difficulty in the battle to eliminate racism: It is because they are unaware of their own personal and professional complicity in perpetuating racism.

That experience has had a major effect on my current work and my burgeoning belief that "social therapy" or work toward social justice is also a part of what helping professionals should be doing. I do not mean to minimize the importance of counseling and therapy (it will always be needed), but such an approach tends toward remediation rather than prevention. If injustice in the guise of racism, sexism, homophobia, and other types of social oppression form the basis of the many individual and social ills of society, do we not as helping professionals also have a moral and ethical responsibility to address those systemic forces responsible for psychological problems? R. D. Laing, an existential psychotherapist, once made a statement that went something like this: "Is schizophrenia always a sick response to a healthy society? Or, can schizophrenia be seen as a healthy response to a sick society?" Changing the individual to adjust or conform to a sick system or unhealthy situation may be unwittingly the goal of unenlightened therapy. If depression, anxiety, and feelings of low self-esteem are the result of unhealthy societal forces (stereotyping, limited opportunities, prejudice, and discrimination), shouldn't our efforts be directed at eradicating societal policies, practices, and structures that oppress, rather than simply changing the individual?

Although all of us must make choices about where to place our efforts, it is now clear to me that multiculturalism and the eradication of racism are about social justice. Social justice is about equal access and opportunity and about building a healthy, validating society for all groups. That is why it is so important that psychology and especially counseling move toward cultural competence and multiculturalism. Since my testimony before the Race Advisory Board, I have turned most of my attention to the eradication of racism and the development of antiracism strategies and tactics. This focus led to publication of my most recent book, *Overcoming Our Racism: The Journey to Liberation* (D. W. Sue, 2003). Like *Counseling the Culturally Diverse: Theory and Practice* (D. W. Sue & Sue, 2003), it represented a labor of love. Written originally for a lay audience, *Overcoming Our Racism* has been described by *Publishers Weekly* (2004) as an "anti-racist manifesto" that is unsparing in its analysis of everyday racism. It stated that although readers may find the book "accusatory" and "off-putting," it will disturb readers by jarring them from their complacency when they recognize themselves in many of the scenarios and descriptions. What has surprised me, however, has been the fact that the book has increasingly found its way into the academic market as well.

In the book, I make several important points that have since guided my understanding of prejudice and racism. First, the goal of our society and, by association the helping professions, should be to "make the invisible, visible." What I call ethnocentric monoculturalism and "Whiteness" represent invisible veils that define the reality of most White Americans. Second, power resides in the group that is able to define reality. Last, the group that "owns" history possesses the power to impose its worldview or reality on less powerful groups. As such, if one's reality or truth does not correspond with that of those in power, unintentional oppression may be the result. From viewing the importance of changing individuals so they can function better in our society to work with organizations and systems, I have become increasingly involved in social policy issues. I now see that my role in life is much broader than when I first received my doctorate in counseling psychology and desired to work primarily with individual clients. As I have gotten older (and hopefully wiser), working toward social justice from a broader sociopolitical perspective has become my personal and professional life.

Personal Reflections on My Career Journey and Advice to Younger Colleagues

It may seem strange to say so, but I find it difficult to characterize my profession or career as work. To me it represents my goal in life, something that gives me meaning and is intimately linked to my personal integrity as well. So, when asked how I balance my personal and professional life, it is very difficult for me to answer. I believe I am blessed with discovering my lot in life or why the creator has placed me on this planet. I absolutely love what I do, because to advocate on behalf of multiculturalism, diversity, and social justice is not just an intellectual and professional undertaking but one that is deeply personal and allows me to express my racial/cultural identity and humanity. There is nothing more rewarding than to realize that my contributions to counseling and the mental health professions have resulted in significant changes in the field—and that my contributions stem primarily from just being who I am, Derald Wing Sue.

So, when younger colleagues and students ask me how I achieved what I have accomplished, telling them to be true to themselves is the answer. At the same time, I realize that students and younger colleagues are just beginning their own journeys. So, here is some advice I would give them.

1. Strive to integrate both your professional and personal journeys. If you are able to do that, the dichotomous distinction we often make between work and personal life becomes less an either/or choice and more a manifestation of your total being.

2. Remember that you are where you are because of the sacrifice of family, friends, and significant others. You are not an island onto yourself. Spending time with others and giving back the love, support, and nurturance they provided you throughout your life and career are important.

3. Counseling is about understanding the human condition and helping others. If you are dedicated to this, then getting a good education is important. Studying theories of counseling and psychotherapy, keeping up with the research literature, and getting hands-on experience in working with others are important aspects of your education.

4. Formal education, however, is not enough to make you a good counselor. If you rely just on book learning, taking classes, and attending workshops to become culturally competent, then you have obtained only a partial education. Becoming a culturally competent counselor means lived experience. You must have experiences and relationships with people you hope to serve.

5. Know that as an aspiring helping professional or academician, you will encounter obstacles and disappointments along the way. You are also likely to experience failures and negative events in your professional journey. Use these experiences as teachable moments in your life. Learn from them. I have learned that one of the most precious attributes of my journey to cultural competence is my own experiential reality. The struggles you go through, the disappointments in your life, your hopes, aspirations, and fears tell you much about yourself. Don't be afraid to listen to your intuitive voice and to extract lessons from them that will add meaning to your life.

6. Become culturally competent. Know that your formal and informal education is likely to be monocultural in nature. Know that theories of counseling and psychotherapy, research findings, fieldwork experiences, and other aspects of your social conditioning are likely to be culture bound. Thus, getting multicultural experiences, working to understand yourself as a racial/cultural being, and being open to differences are important.

In closing, I would stress the four major ongoing goals that hopefully will guide your own journey to cultural competence.

1. You must become aware of yourself as a racial/cultural being. You must own up to your biases, beliefs, stereotypes, and assumptions about human behavior. Without this awareness, you may unwittingly impose them on clients whose worldviews differ from your own.

2. It's important to understand the worldview of people who differ from you in race, culture, ethnicity, gender, and other sociodemographic variables. As I have stressed earlier, this does not come about through formal education only but must be tempered by lived experience. You must make an effort to place yourself in the communities and lives of the people you hope to understand.

3. Work on developing culturally appropriate intervention strategies to fit the cultural values and life experiences of those you hope to serve. There is no single universal strategy or technique of helping that is equally applicable across all populations, problems, and situations.
4. Always be cognizant of sociopolitical forces that affect the life experiences of your clients and your role as a helping professional. This knowledge and awareness should help you see the helping professions as wider than simply a one-to-one relationship (counselor–client), involving you in systems analysis and interventions, as well.

References

American Psychological Association. (2003). Guidelines on multicultural education, training, research, practice, and organizational change for psychologists. *American Psychologist, 58,* 377–402.

Ponterotto, J. G., & Sabnani, H. B. (1989). "Classics" in multicultural counseling: A systematic five-year content analysis. *Journal of Multicultural Counseling and Development, 17,* 23–37.

Publishers Weekly. (2004). [Review of the book *Overcoming our racism: The journey to liberation*]. Retrieved August 3, 2004, from http://www.amazon.com/exec/obidos/tg/detail/-/B00018BMOY/103-3456033-1222249?v=glance.

Sue, D. W. (1977). Counseling the culturally different: A conceptual analysis. *Personnel and Guidance Journal, 55,* 422–425.

Sue, D. W. (1978). Eliminating cultural oppression in counseling: Toward a general theory. *Journal of Counseling Psychology, 25,* 419–428.

Sue, D. W. (1981). *Counseling the culturally different: Theory and practice.* New York: Wiley.

Sue, D. W. (2003). *Overcoming our racism: The journey to liberation.* San Francisco: Jossey-Bass.

Sue, D. W., Arredondo, P., & McDavis, R. (1992a). Multicultural counseling competencies/standards: A call to the profession. *Journal of Counseling & Development, 70,* 477–486.

Sue, D. W., Arredondo, P., & McDavis, R. (1992b). Multicultural counseling competencies/standards: A call to the profession. *Journal of Multicultural Counseling and Development, 20,* 64–88.

Sue, D. W., Bernier, J. B., Durran, M., Feinberg, L., Pedersen, P., Smith, E., et al. (1982). Position paper: Cross-cultural counseling competencies. *The Counseling Psychologist, 10*(2), 45–52.

Sue, D. W., & Sue, D. (1977). Ethnic minorities: Failures and responsibilities of the social sciences. *Journal of Non-White Concerns in Personnel and Guidance, 55,* 99–106.

Sue, D. W., & Sue, D. (2003). *Counseling the culturally diverse: Theory and practice* (4th ed.). New York: Wiley.

Sue, S., & Sue, D. W. (1977). Barriers to effective cross-cultural counseling: *Journal of Counseling Psychology, 24,* 420–429.

Chapter 8

Personal and Professional Journey
•••

George M. Gazda

In this chapter I trace my personal and professional development from childhood to my current state of retirement. I describe the importance of developing early on a strong work ethic, first because of the need to carry my load in supporting my family of origin and later as a means of making my contribution to my profession and to society.

Throughout my development I have been influenced by numerous individuals, especially parents, siblings, spouse, my son, pastors, teachers, coworkers, students, and grandchildren. The unique contributions toward my development of each of the individuals and groups are acknowledged and described. There were also a number of defining moments that significantly influenced the course and direction of my personal and professional life. Each of these defining moments and their subsequent effects is described, as well as some of what I consider to be my most significant professional contributions.

I close the chapter with suggestions for newcomers and mid-career professionals on how they might first select a graduate program for their training and later how they might manage their professional development. Also, I describe three areas of personal and professional development that I am pursuing and share some predictions of what the future holds for the counseling professions.

Past Influences of My Journey

Coal Miner's Son

I was born on March 6, 1931, the second child of Thomas Gazda and Mary Wargo Gazda. Their first child, Thomas Jr., was two years older than I. Three more boys were to be born to my parents: Andrew in 1933, Lawrence in 1937, and Charles in 1941. Being the second child, I responded much like Adlerians would predict: I was competitive, and as a result, an overachiever in most activities that I undertook. Being born into a family of all male siblings meant that my activities were masculine-dominated, especially play, work, and sports. Of all my siblings, I was least interested in what then was considered to be more feminine activities, such as cleaning the house, cooking, and the like.

Ironically, my career choice was at the time considered to be more feminine than the choices of my other siblings, all of whom became engineers.

I was born during the Great Depression, and my family and I experienced economic hardships. These hardships were alleviated somewhat by developing a strong work ethic from a very early age. My father was a coal miner with a limited education. When the mine closed, he, like many in our small town in central Illinois, worked in government jobs such as the Work Projects Administration (WPA) and the Civilian Conservation Corps (CCC).

Work was a necessity for everyone in our family. When we were old enough to work outside the home, we had paper routes, mowed lawns, did farmwork, and had various summer jobs in nearby factories and farms. I believe that developing a strong work ethic as a youth became one of the most important assets in my career development. What success I may have achieved in my professional life is closely related to my early work habits.

Three areas dominated my early childhood and youth. Work has already been addressed. In addition, schooling/education and church were the other areas around which our family life was centered. Neither of my parents graduated from high school, but both realized the important role that education played in improving one's economic status and cultural condition. Schooling was valued very much, and my parents supported us through many personal sacrifices so that we could maximize our educational opportunities.

My parents had strong religious beliefs and stressed the importance of religion in our lives. My brothers and I all attended public schools because there was no parochial school in our community, but we attended religious education classes on Saturday and religious education vacation school in the summer. We attended mass on Sundays and all holy days of the Roman Catholic Church. Our household strictly observed fast days and abstinence, and only essential work was allowed on Sundays. Religion in my childhood and youth, and still today, has been a source of refuge and strength for me and my family.

Although my family of origin set the basic parameters and standards for my life, I would be remiss if I did not credit my wife, Barbara, for her constant support, encouragement, and assistance. She was responsible for deciphering most of my handwritten manuscripts and typing them for submission for publication. She also assumed many of my parenting duties with our only child, David, when I was traveling or closeted with writing and editing tasks. Our marriage was a defining moment in my life.

Life's Motivation Discovered

David, our only child, was born on June 3, 1960, during the end of my first academic year of teaching at the University of Illinois. My purpose and motivation was forever changed with David's birth, another defining moment. I recall what one of my former employers (when I was working construction) said to me one Saturday morning as we sat around his kitchen table and watched his children eating breakfast: "George, this is really what

I work for; this is what it is all about." This profound statement still motivates me even as it is now directed more to my grandchildren.

While in senior high school, I was asked by the principal to fill in for teachers in an elementary school adjacent to the high school. I do not know how the principal was able to arrange this, but it gave me a very early experience teaching young children in a classroom setting, and this experience played some part in my interest in becoming a teacher.

During the summer between my junior and senior years in high school, I was a page in the Illinois House of Representatives, and this experience led me to consider law and politics as possible careers. (My father had been a precinct committeeman in our small community, and his experiences also helped me to understand politics.) Following completion of my education to prepare me for teaching and school administration, I entertained the idea of going to law school at night but later gave up that plan to enter graduate education at the University of Illinois. More will be said about this later.

In 1949, my senior year in high school, I was still undecided on a college major. I was considering engineering because by now my older brother had returned from the military and was using the GI Bill to attend Purdue University as a civil engineering major. When I discussed this with our high school librarian, who also doubled as guidance director, she discouraged me because she said there were too many ex-GIs enrolled in engineering schools and there would not be jobs for all of them. This was my first experience with someone who acted in the capacity of a school counselor. What neither she nor I knew was that most of these GIs would not complete an engineering degree, and in fact, there would even be a shortage of engineers.

In order to attend college, I had to pay for most of the expenses. Fortunately, I received a state teacher's scholarship that paid for tuition. I decided to attend Western Illinois State College (now Western Illinois University) because a close friend of mine had completed his freshman year there and suggested that we room together. We found a room in a private home about a mile from campus. We were able to pay for our room by working for the landlady and doing odd jobs in the neighborhood. I also got a job working at the college and doing construction work on weekends with a contractor for whom I worked during the summers. I always had three jobs during my undergraduate schooling. I learned that I could use my tuition scholarship for four years and that if I took an overload each quarter and attended summer school one year, I could complete my degree in three years and use the scholarship for a fourth year to complete my master's in school administration. This is the course I took. At some point in my first four years of college, I began to consider the possibility of someday teaching in a college or university.

During my senior year in college, I had to make plans to complete two years of military service. I passed all the exams to enter pilot training in the U.S. Army Air Force and expected to be called up after completion of my bachelor's degree. However, at this point in time, the Korean War was ending and the need for pilots was significantly reduced. I therefore decided to begin work on my master's degree until I was called up. As fate would have it, I injured my right eye while diving off the high board in the college swimming pool. Surgery corrected the detached retina but also ended my chances of becoming a pilot.

Because I was unsure of my future military status, I took a teaching position in a small rural community in north central Illinois. A friend of mine was going there to be the high school principal, and he encouraged me to go with him because they needed someone to coach middle school and teach high school science. During that year I did a wide variety of teaching in Grades 5–9. The superintendent of schools turned out to be incompetent, and I made up my mind not to return for another year. During the course of the year, I was also called up by the draft board for a physical. With my recent eye surgery, the army did not want to chance adding another disability pensioner to its list, so I was sent home. This was a defining moment in determining my future career.

Now, with the uncertainty of military duty removed, I could do some long-range planning. First, I obtained a position in Auburn, Illinois, near my home, teaching and coaching in a junior high school. I also was in a position to get married to my fiancée, who I had dated throughout high school and college. We were married on July 3, 1954. Barbara continued to work for an insurance company, and I taught school for the next four years. During this time I started taking evening extension courses from the University of Illinois and attending summer school in Champaign-Urbana. My original intention was to major in educational measurement and statistics, but after taking a first course in counseling, I discovered that this field had many of the answers to classroom management that I never received from all the teaching methods courses in my previous course work, and it offered many other possibilities for a career.

I Discovered My Life's Work

During my fourth year in Auburn, Illinois, I applied for a scholarship in order to work full time on my doctorate at the University of Illinois. What I thought was an application for a tuition scholarship turned out to be a fellowship that covered tuition and a stipend for living expenses. This award permitted us to move to Champaign-Urbana and allowed me to work full time on a doctorate, which was another defining moment in my career. After having taken counseling courses with Drs. Merle Ohlsen, Walter Lifton, C. H. Patterson, and Fred Proff, I realized that I wanted to major in counseling. My major professor in measurement and statistics was Dr. Thomas Hastings, and he agreed to continue in that role until I passed qualifying exams, after which Dr. Merle Ohlsen would be my major professor for my dissertation research.

With my fellowship and my wife's job as secretary to the director of the University of Illinois scholarship program, I was able to complete two full years of course work and dissertation research. Dr. Ohlsen had a large grant to study gifted underachievers, and he was doing group counseling with them. I was caught up in his excitement of this relatively new counseling intervention, and under his guidance I did a dissertation on the effects of group counseling on prospective counselors. The choice of my dissertation topic became a defining point in my future professional emphasis.

It was in the academic atmosphere in the counselor training program at the University of Illinois, observing the faculty of Drs. Ohlsen, Lifton, Proff, and Patterson going about their professional duties, that I was inspired to emulate them in my own professional life. These men all had distinguished professional careers and made significant contributions to the counseling profession, but they also were dedicated to mentoring their students. They instilled in their students an excitement about learning and the need to use their expertise and leadership to advance the profession and, through it, humankind in general.

Another defining moment in my life and career occurred as I was finishing my dissertation and preparing for my defense in August of 1959. I had already been accepted for a postdoctoral internship with the Veteran's Administration (VA) in Danville, Illinois. We were planning to remain in Champaign, from which I would commute to Danville daily. Unexpectedly, Dr. Lifton resigned his position in the counseling program to assume a position with Science Research Associates in Chicago. The faculty asked me if I would fill his position for the new academic year. I went from student to faculty member immediately after my dissertation defense. This one-year temporary appointment was changed a year later to a research assistant professor. A major portion of my time for the next two years was spent working on Dr. Ohlsen's research grant, leading counseling groups of underachieving middle school children (all of which were recorded on kinescopes), and leading counseling groups with the parents of these underachievers. I also continued to teach basic courses in the department. These three years following graduation further enhanced my professional development because of the continued association with my former teachers and mentors.

It was during this three-year period in the department that I was learning risk-taking behavior by being given speaking and training consultations with a variety of professional groups. Although many of these assignments offered to me seemed to be beyond my level of expertise, my mentors convinced me otherwise. Some of the assignments went well for me, but not all; nevertheless, the willingness to submit myself to this kind of challenge served me well in future years.

Having spent three years in postdoctoral work at my alma mater, I began looking at position openings at other universities. I had this belief that I needed to get out of the nest and fly on my own if I were to fulfill my potential. As usual, my mentors assisted me by alerting me to openings at major universities. I interviewed at four of them and accepted an offer at the University of Missouri in Columbia. I was well received by the faculty, and I expected to spend the rest of my career there. There were a couple of factors that led me to change this plan. None of them, however, was of a serious nature, and I believe that I could have had a successful career had I stayed at the University of Missouri. Basically, I left because I learned that our dean was going to retire, and I felt that I would need to prove myself to a new dean over a couple of more years before possible promotion to associate professor. (I had already been assistant professor at the University of Illinois for three years.) Also, a good friend of mine had just taken a position as department head at the University of Georgia, and he invited me to join him in building the department. I was offered a good raise and promotion to associate professor, and now being more of a risk-taker, I accepted the new challenge. I felt, too, that I could grow more completely in a new program than in one that was well established and only required maintenance. Moving to the University of Georgia was another defining moment in my life and career.

In my new position at the University of Georgia, I was given the opportunity to serve as major professor for two doctoral students and to direct their dissertation research. I had the good fortune to have two excellent students as my first doctoral advisees. I discovered that mentoring doctoral students was to be my greatest joy and reward in my career. I also discovered that they were a great source of assistance in research and writing. My first book was coauthored with one of these two students (Jonell Folds) and published by R. W. Parkinson and Associates of Urbana, Illinois. It was also Parkinson's first attempt at publishing. The book, *Handbook of Guidance Services,* was published in 1966 (Gazda & Folds, 1966). Parkinson and Associates became Research Press, now a very successful publishing company. My other student, Jack Duncan, was cofounder with me of the Association for Specialists in Group Work (ASGW) and also coauthor of several publications. Both of these students became university professors, leaders in the counselor education field, and lifelong friends. I learned that involving my doctoral students in research and writing was mutually beneficial. We stimulated each other and learned from each other. I continue to coauthor articles and books with my doctoral students to the present day.

My mentors at the University of Illinois had encouraged me to become active in professional associations, so very early on I became a life member of the American Personnel and Guidance Association (APGA), which is now the American Counseling Association (ACA), and several of its divisions. I attended national, regional, and local conventions and served on various committees in the divisions. I was fortunate to be elected president of five national professional associations and be cofounder of one. I was first elected as president of the Association for Counselor Education and Supervision (ACES) followed by cofounder and first president of ASGW, then president in 1976–1977 of APGA, and 10 years later, president of the Division of Counseling Psychology of the American Psychological Association (APA). Most recently, I was elected president of the Division of Group Psychology and Group Psychotherapy of APA.

In these leadership positions I learned the important political roles that were necessary to gain support and recognition for the counseling profession. I also learned of the need to monitor our professional conduct through the development and constant revision of training standards and codes of ethics, especially since counseling was such a young profession.

In 1967 I was contacted by a faculty member in the Department of Psychiatry of the Medical College of Georgia (MCG) to consult with a group of department heads and help them improve their management and human relations skills. I worked with this group for a year and was then invited to become a part-time faculty member of MCG, another defining moment in my career. I was appointed as a professor in the Department of Psychiatry, and my first obligation was to lead a personal therapy group for psychiatry residents once a week. In addition, I did human relations training with administrators, department heads, and medical departments and taught group dynamics for nurses. I also began to consult with the adjacent VA Department of Psychiatry. After some 13 years with the MCG Department of Psychiatry, I became a consulting member of the faculty and spent some 20 years in a similar capacity with the VA Department of Psychiatry. At the VA I set up a patient program in Life-Skills Training, which I supervised on a weekly, then monthly, basis until my retirement in 1994. A clinical nurse specialist, Mildred Powell, was the on-site manager and was instrumental in the success of the program.

In 1980 I initiated a counseling psychology program in the Department of Counseling and Human Development Services, which became APA-accredited in 1984. I was director of the program for 10 years while also assuming the position of associate dean for research (I was made a research professor in the 1970s) in 1984, which I held until my retirement in 1994.

Experiencing My Professional Journey

Having briefly described my personal and professional journey, I shall respond to what the experience was like. My professional journey was almost always fulfilling, enjoyable, and exciting. Except for a few years when our department leadership was absent and I became discouraged about our future, I rarely had a day when I did not look forward to going to work. Teaching, supervising, advising, collaborating with, and developing close friendships with doctoral students provided me with my most fulfilling moments.

Some of my scariest moments came when I was taking high risks in attempting to practice my professional skills with groups with whom I had not previously worked. For example, when I agreed to work with administrative officers and department heads at MCG, some asked me what expertise I had that led me to believe I could help them. Interestingly, it was the two department heads who raised this question that later were the first to ask me to work with their entire department. Other scary moments were when I first worked with groups of inmates in a prison setting, alcoholics in a rehabilitation setting, psychiatric patients in a medical setting, psychiatry residents in a therapy group, medical students in a therapy group, peer groups in my college and university, psychodrama demonstration groups in national convention settings, and my professional peers in training workshops, to cite but a few. Each time that I was willing to risk my expertise with a new challenge, it became easier to risk in the next challenge. Growth and self-confidence for me came through risk-taking and exposing vulnerabilities to a test.

Most burdensome for me was balancing duties to family with duties to job and profession. I often missed events in which my wife or son were involved. I discovered that once you get into the "professional circuit," commitments and demands on your time are greater than you can accommodate. The more you're involved, the more that is expected. However, one can learn to juggle writing commitments, for example, by spacing contract dates between book publications and having some flexibility in the contract. Invited articles can sometimes be accepted if those who are requesting them are willing to allow you to include a junior author.

Keeping one's focus is related to one's self-discipline and time management. In my case, most of my writing had to be done in the evening (after school hours), on weekends, and on vacation. There was virtually no time to do serious writing other than correspondence during 8–5 office hours. I managed to stay focused on my writing commitments by scheduling short-term, intermediate, and long-term due dates. Long term could mean up to a year and a half in the future for a book due date. Six months would be intermediate, and anything less would be short term.

Because I began most of my writing prior to word processors and computers, I did it by hand, and my wife Barbara, who was a much better typist than I, would type from handwritten copy. We did not have enough secretarial help to type manuscripts at this time. When I did get a full-time secretary, I had lost most of my typing skills, and so I continued to write by hand and still do. (I do not recommend this for current authors.)

In addition to the time crunch challenge and mechanics of manuscript preparation, the most discouraging impediment to productivity, in the early years, was lack of colleague support. Most moral support came from family, doctoral students, and fellow professionals from other institutions.

Major Influences and Sources of Strengths

I have previously indicated that my family of origin, my wife Barbara, and my son David were my major influences. Teachers at all levels of the education ladder were also sources of motivation and influence. I had one or more teachers in elementary, high school, college, and university who took special interest in me or were models for me to imitate. My major professor, Dr. Merle Ohlsen, at the University of Illinois was, and still is, a major part of my life. There were a number of professors at Illinois, Missouri, and Georgia who were excellent models. Dr. E. Paul Torrance at Georgia exemplified most of the best in these models.

Dr. Robert Carkhuff's work on human resource development and his models for therapeutic intervention gave me a whole new strategy for counseling and skills training. Dr. Dean Elefthery trained me to be a psychodramatist and provided me a rationale and skills in action therapy. Dr. Ray Corsini introduced me to a radically new, futuristic model for education that can be a remedy for current failures in our system. My spiritual life has been strengthened by many friends and pastors, especially by a former pastor, Father Joy Nellissery, PhD, who is living an exemplary life. Mother Theresa also exemplified for me unselfish giving to suffering humanity.

Connection Between Theory and Practice

My broad goal for clients is to help make them responsibly independent. This implies a number of things, including an understanding of self and one's purpose in life, an understanding of environment, the ability to communicate, the ability to make decisions and be responsible for one's actions, and the ability to solve problems. I believe that people are impaired or even dysfunctional either because they are not educated or trained sufficiently to cope with life's problems and need to be taught effective coping skills or, through experiencing trauma and resultant debilitating anxiety, they are unable to apply the knowledge and skills in their repertoire that are appropriate to solve the problem at hand.

I further believe that the counselor's role is to assist the client in understanding his or her condition of impairment, its likely causes, and steps to be taken to alleviate the problem. If clients are permitted to explore their strengths and deficits in a safe, nonthreatening environment, they can recognize what they are thinking or doing that is ineffective and learn preferred strategies and responses that may require guided practice.

My practice as a counselor began in practicum where I worked under supervision from theorists who followed Rogerian theory, psychodynamic theory, and eclectic theory. I used a psychodynamic theory when working with children in a playroom and with families. I used Rogerian theory with young adults in a military base, and I used an eclectic theory working with preadolescents and adolescents. The fact that I worked with different age spans of young children through preadolescents, adolescents, and adults gave me a developmental perspective, which led me to develop a developmental group counseling theory. I recognized that a different theoretical rationale was necessary to accommodate the different strategies to fit the various age levels. Talk therapy appropriate for adolescents and adults was not appropriate for young children who expressed themselves best through play and motor activity. Likewise, preadolescents were better able to express themselves through games and activities. The developmental level of the client determined which theoretical model was emphasized—a developmental eclecticism. This model was first described in *Group Counseling: A Developmental Approach* (Gazda, 1973). The latest version was published in *Group*

Counseling and Group Psychotherapy (Gazda, Ginter, & Horne, 2001). In my theory development, I began with my practicum supervisors' theories and modified and developed them based on my practice experience. In teaching I covered the basic theoretical models but let the clientele dictate for the student the most appropriate theoretical model to implement. Basic to all theoretical models is the climate the counselor establishes for helping. It is essential that the counselor can operationalize the core conditions of a helping relationship.

Suggestions for Newcomers and Mid-Career Professionals

Whether you are a newcomer or mid-career professional, carefully assess your assets and liabilities. Seek training and exposure to situations in which you can sharpen your strengths and reduce your deficits. Take calculated risks and pursue those activities in which you can sustain interest and excitement. Assume the role of lifelong learner, including learning from your students and colleagues as well as from so-called experts. Get involved with your professional associations and be willing to start with minor assignments. To paraphrase an astute observation made by Frankl that I have found to be valid: If you seek directly success and happiness, it will evade you. The alternative is to apply yourself diligently each day to each task and enjoy the rewards of the success that will come.

If you are in the university setting, look for a successful senior colleague to be your mentor. This person can help you avoid potential pitfalls and keep you advised on your progress toward promotion. If you find yourself in an unhealthy work environment, be willing to seek employment elsewhere.

Development as a Multicultural Counselor

I became aware of cultural diversity as a child growing up in a small rural community in central Illinois. No one called it cultural diversity in those days, but in my community there were a number of first- and second-generation families of diverse ethnic backgrounds. There were families from Eastern European (Czech and Slovak) backgrounds such as my own; there were a number of Italian, Irish, Scotch, and English families also. Slovaks were referred to as "Hunkies," Italians as "Wops," English as "Johnny Bulls." There were no people of color in my community. My first contact with an African American was as a 17-year-old page in the Illinois House of Representatives when I worked with a 30-year-old African American page. He took me under his wing, and I had a very positive experience in our brief time together.

Most pronounced in my community were religious prejudices. Even these prejudices were subtle in their expression. Protestants perceived Catholics as second-class citizens because they were viewed as late arrivals on the scene.

My first regular contact with racial minorities occurred when I went to college, and then it wasn't until I was in graduate school that I was in classes with an African American who had been a football star as an undergraduate in the college. He was singled out by our graduate advisor because of his race. Although our advisor was obviously supportive of this young man, he went overboard in his encouragement and unwittingly called attention to this young man's minority status.

My next encounter with diversity was in my doctoral courses, where I was in classes with a male African American once again. We became friends during our doctoral work and kept in contact for several years. Following graduation, I became friends with an African American visiting professor in our department at the University of Illinois, and we continued our friendship for several years until his untimely death. He helped me to understand the racial divide in the South. I encouraged him to visit our home in Georgia when he was coming through Athens from North Carolina on his way to visit his mother in Alabama. He would call me from a phone booth to say hello but wouldn't visit our home. One day when I pressed him very hard to visit us, he said diplomatically, "I don't think your neighbors would appreciate that."

When I had African American doctoral student advisees in Georgia, they helped me to better understand the race issue of cultural diversity. The same was true for my Jewish students. When I became an associate dean in the College of Education, I was in a position in which I could facilitate the hiring of minority faculty. We hired two African American women in our counseling department and several others in other departments, as well as an associate dean. These faculty members were a continuous source for increasing my understanding of cultural diversity. After the death of my wife Barbara in 1995, I met and married a widow who was born in Spain and later lived in England and Venezuela. She has helped me to better understand especially the Spanish and Hispanic cultures, and our circle of friends has expanded to include many from these two cultures.

Multiculturalism as an area for research and practice is an area of great need and one of great promise for the counseling profession. The diversity of our population continues to increase and problems created will continue to require research and resolution. Counselors who are bilingual will be in great demand, especially if they are proficient in Spanish.

Work Style and Accomplishments

My work style is related to and controlled by my priorities. My goal was to make a contribution to my profession and help to build a national reputation for my department. In order to accomplish my goal, I had to limit leisure activities and unrelated work activities. I chose to give up playing golf entirely and limit the time that I went fishing. I also limited the time that I went to sporting activities, watched TV, or went to movies. I also limited vacation time. However, I realized that I needed to keep active physically, so I began jogging regularly in 1973 and I have been in an exercise program ever since. Since I enjoy outdoor work, I always did my own yard work and had a vegetable garden. In 1978 I bought a small farm and expanded my outdoor work to include raising a small herd of Angus cattle. The physical labor required for farmwork provided a release from the mental and emotional strain of academic duties. Development of the farm operation also allowed my wife and son to become more involved with me as we collaborated in various farm projects.

Major Accomplishments

Although I do not claim credit for their accomplishments, I especially value the support I was able to give to my wife Barbara during the time that she began and completed her bachelor's degree in elementary education and then her master's degree in library education at the University of Georgia and later rose to librarian for the U.S. Department of Agriculture Richard Russell Research Laboratory in Athens, Georgia. I was able to support our son David while he completed his degree in agricultural economics at the University of Georgia and later help him and his family develop a registered Angus farming operation.

Professionally, I would like to think that I was able to add to the theory and practice of group counseling and therapy through the development of my own developmental models of counseling and life skills training and editing and publishing works of others. I believe that I was able to add to the expansion and professionalization of the field of group work by cofounding ASGW, by hosting the Georgia Symposium of Group Counseling and Psychotherapy from 1970 to 1980, by serving on the first Board of Directors of the Division of Group Psychology and Group Psychotherapy (Division 49 of APA), by chairing the selection committee for the first editor of its journal *Group Dynamics*, and by serving as president-elect of Division 49 of APA.

I would like to think that I made some professional contribution to the overall field of counseling while serving as president of ACES, ASGW, APGA (ACA), and Division 17 (Counseling Psychology) of APA. I think that my presidential project for Division 17, the Third National Conference for Counseling Psychology, held in Atlanta, Georgia, advanced the profession of counseling psychology.

I am pleased to have had a major role in the development of an APA-accredited counseling psychology program at the University of Georgia and to have served as the director of the program for its first 10 years. Perhaps my greatest contribution to the profession was serving as major professor for more than 80 doctoral students and teaching hundreds more who have in turn taught and trained thousands for the profession.

No one can accomplish anything entirely on his or her own. I have already indicated that I owe so much to my family, my major professor and mentors, my graduate students, my colleagues, and administrators who allowed me to "do my thing." I learned early of the power released through group involvement and shared leadership. Therefore I usually involved many people in my projects, which meant I could have many more projects than if I acted alone. I owe much of my success to being able to obtain collaborators or partners to invest in my projects.

Ideas for my projects come from needs uncovered in teaching, such as textbooks appropriate for the course and training materials needed when attempting to illustrate interventions, leading to the making of training tapes. Teaching current models for training and therapeutic intervention led to developing new therapeutic models. Ideas also came from the writings and research of other professionals and from attending training workshops and convention programs. However, most of my ideas came from the practice of group and individual counseling in a wide variety of settings.

Future Journey

I have three major professional areas of interests I wish to pursue. First, I want to finish a project begun several years ago. I want to develop a Developmental Life Skills curriculum from preschool through high school, at least. A first draft was put aside many years ago and is waiting for revision.

Second, I want to increase efforts to promote a new system of education formulated several years ago by Ray Corsini, now known as Individual Education. I have been involved in some pilot schools using this system, and I believe it could revolutionize how we educate and, if adopted, would alleviate most of the problems created in the current system.

A third area that I plan to continue is to lead bereavement support groups for my community. I began after my wife Barbara's death in January 1995. My avocation continues to be the development with my son and his family of our Angus cattle farm, especially assisting my granddaughters, Katie and Taylor, in breeding and showing registered Angus cattle.

I have no crystal balls for predicting the future. One thing seems certain is that technology will continue to influence the profession both in training and treatment online. I can understand and accept teaching theory courses online, but I cannot understand how it can work with practicum courses. Neither can I understand how counseling can be done ethically and effectively online. Television programs such as *Dr. Phil* may also affect counseling for better or for worse. The economics of health care is already driving practice and is likely to become an even greater factor. It has already pushed brief therapy to the forefront of treatment. The question remains, How brief can it get before it is no longer therapy? To maintain a medical dominance and maximize brief interventions we may see even greater use of psychopharmacology.

Another trend might be greater use of group counseling and therapy for its economic value, especially with Medicaid clients. Group examinations of pregnant women are already being tried by medical doctors to reduce overall time and costs.

With increased federal government intervention in the schools, we might also see ancillary school services such as counseling contracted out to private clinics, thus reducing the need for the traditional type of school counselor. At least one state is experimenting with this approach.

Suggestions for Prospective and Young Professionals

As a prospective professional, you must decide whether you want to prepare for a career as a practitioner or as a faculty member. If you plan to go into private practice or work full time in a college or university counseling center, you may wish to go to a professional school and earn a PsyD. If, however, you plan to teach and do research, a PhD or EdD from an accredited program is preferred and almost essential because of the research requirements of a university faculty member.

If you plan to become a practitioner, be prepared to pass a state licensure exam in order to practice as a psychologist or counselor. Licensure workshops and study guides will need to be used in many cases to prepare for the examination. Also, licensed supervisors may need to be located for meeting postdoctoral supervision requirements of some states. Searching for a practice position may require a placement agency or considerable independent searching. Joining a group practice may be more economical than solo practice with the greater overhead.

The first choice to be made by a person who plans to train for a faculty position in a college or university is the selection of a major university with a nationally recognized faculty and a program that is APA accredited. This is a must for someone seeking a counseling psychology position. For someone seeking a counselor education position, the same basic tenets hold, but the program would need to be accredited by the Council for the Accreditation of Counseling and Related Professional Programs. Selecting a major professor and future mentor also is very important. Choose one whose research interests and theoretical orientation most closely resemble your own. Compatibility along as many dimensions as possible between student and major professor will be the best assurance of success in the graduate program.

If you choose to become a faculty member in a college or university, you should have, while still a graduate student, selected a line of research and at least have submitted dissertation research for publication. Preferably, you should have already published a couple of papers in refereed journals.

When seeking a faculty position, consult your mentor regarding the suitability of an advertised position with your qualifications. Role-play interviews and be critiqued.

Finally, research the promotion and tenure policies of the institution where you plan to apply. Some schools have developed a history of using new assistant professors for cheap labor and releasing them before they can be promoted and tenured. Once employed, seek a successful senior faculty member as a mentor and develop a long-range plan for publication, quality instruction (ask for colleagues to visit your classes and critique your instruction), and appropriate service work.

References

Gazda, G. M. (1973). *Group counseling: A developmental approach.* Boston: Allyn & Bacon.

Gazda, G. M., & Folds, J. (1966). *Handbook of guidance services.* Urbana, IL: R. W. Parkinson and Associates.

Gazda, G. M., Ginter, E. J., & Horne, A. M. (2001). *Group counseling and group psychotherapy.* Needham Heights, MA: Allyn & Bacon.

Chapter 9

There Is an Eagle in Me: Touching the Spirit
• •

A. Michael Hutchins

Past Influences on My Journey

I was born in Clinton, Massachusetts, in 1943. My mother's family migrated to Boston from Ireland during the potato famines and worked in the factories in central Massachusetts. My father was from a Maine Yankee family with ties to the fishing and shipbuilding industries. My paternal grandfather lost contact with his Maine forebearers when he married an Irish Catholic from Boston. Both parents, who grew up in large, single-parent families during the Great Depression, were committed to providing their children with a secure home. As a child, I remember stories of Ireland and our connections to it and large lively family gatherings. Despite stories of family connectedness, I was aware of being different and separate from a very early age.

Family and School Influences

As a child, I did not seem to fit into the large extended family and the close-knit neighborhood. When my peers were playing, I was reading. At the local Catholic elementary school, I did well academically. I did not seem to share common interests with my peers and often felt lonely. I began to realize that I was attracted to boys in ways that were not to be acknowledged. Some sexual "experimentation" with peers occurred, leaving me feeling ashamed, guilty, and frightened. I wanted to escape.

My escape came through academics when I was accepted at St. John's Prep in Worcester, Massachusetts. My parents did not have the financial means for me to attend St. John's, but the local parish provided a scholarship that allowed me to further my education and make my escape. The seeds of being grateful and experiencing joy were planted in the discussions I had with my pastor as I began high school.

At St. John's, I encountered my first mentor. Brother Neil was the first man who seemed to understand my social awkwardness and support my intellectual curiosity. There were times when I wanted to seek his counsel, to ask him about sexuality and my experiences of feeling different, although

I didn't have the courage. Upon reflection, I realize it was my early discussions with this man that led to my interest in becoming a teacher and counselor. I continued to feel guilty about exploring my growing attraction to other boys but believed that, eventually, I would grow through this attraction and meet a woman with whom I would fall in love, get married, and live with forever. I dated girls I met through friends and strove to fit into the Catholic high school social scene. There were times of joy and times of discontent. Some of my teachers encouraged me to continue in my intellectual and spiritual pursuits by inviting me to involve myself more completely in my community. Other experiences, such as hearing Senator John F. Kennedy challenge the students to put our beliefs into action, caused me to want to make a difference.

College Influences

I was accepted at the College of the Holy Cross and entered in a daze. Most of the students at Holy Cross were from a completely different socioeconomic world from the one in which I was raised. I changed majors almost every semester and was frightened and losing direction. Joseph H. Maguire, then a new faculty member and later to become dean of students, became my mentor. Struggling to find my place in a culture that was foreign to me, I tried to interpret, and then defy, the rules in this society. Joe helped me through this transition from adolescence to young adulthood.

On November 22, 1963, I was in a social psychology class when I learned that President Kennedy had been shot. I was devastated. In trying to understand what had happened, I started to tap into my anger and sense of injustice. Joe Maguire and I spoke of paths to creating different ways of being-in-the-world. These discussions led to my joining the Jesuit Lay Volunteer Corps after graduation, serving for two years as a teacher in a Jesuit-operated high school for Iraqi boys in Baghdad.

Throughout my college years, I dated several different women. Although my friends were entering into relationships that would lead to marriage, my relationships were briefer and coincided with secret "experimentation" with other men. I became quite adept at rationalizing these experiments, denying that they were meaningful, and believing that sooner or later, my attraction to women would overcome any attraction to men. At this point in my life, I believed that sexuality was about behavior but remained unaware of the spiritual, social, emotional, and cultural components of healthy sexuality.

Journey to Baghdad

I left the States for Iraq shortly after college graduation. My parents never really understood my need to take on this experience. I was terrified, excited, and ready to explore. This world was completely different from the world in which I was raised. I was welcomed into the homes of Bedouin sheiks; explored biblical sites with a brilliant archaeologist; traveled throughout the Middle East, including places Westerners rarely went; and sat at dinner with Chaldean seminarians and their families in Mosul. On one occasion I found myself climbing up a date palm along the Tigris River, tearfully holding on. For the first time in my life, I felt connected to life, learning about simplicity and authenticity. My core values were challenged. I learned that the way I had been taught to view the world was profoundly different from the way my students viewed the world.

Father Joseph Carty, the rector of the mission, became my spiritual advisor. He helped me to understand that the success of the mission was not in conversions to Christianity but in educating Muslims and Christians alike in order to learn about each other and work together. It was through my teaching and my discussions with the men of this community that I began to experience a more integrated worldview. They taught me that the world can be seen most effectively in terms of unity and collaboration. It was in this community that I began to learn ways to live in love and respect. Here, life was simple yet profound.

While I was in Iraq, I felt centered. I was doing the kind of work that made a difference in people's lives. My sense of being excluded was minimal—a new experience for me. In my work with the students at Baghdad College, I became aware of wanting to explore in greater depth the different cultural factors involved in the way people learn. Teaching was rewarding, yet I wanted to make different kinds of connections. It was during my second year at Baghdad College that I decided to return to the States and get a master's degree in counseling.

My Professional Journey

I left Iraq the day before the Arab–Israeli War broke out in 1967 and spent the war in Libya, Tunisia, and Algeria. I was never certain what was happening, but I had learned that American news sources were seldom reliable when reporting events in the Middle East and Arabic sources were even less so. I was treated with honor and respect as I traveled through North Africa and found my Islamic hosts to be gracious and welcoming, just as had the families of my students in Iraq.

I returned to the States to enter a master's of arts program in counseling at Assumption College in Worcester, Massachusetts and had the opportunity to work with Dr. Frank Buckley. Frank became a mentor, encouraging me to do my own work in counseling as a way of becoming a more effective counselor. It was from him that I learned that when we believe in our field, we will become willing participants in the counseling process as clients.

Becoming a Counselor

When I returned to the country in 1967, America was a different place. We were becoming more involved in the Vietnam War. Disturbed by our position and believing that we were involved in an unjust war, I was becoming more socially active, while also traveling from Massachusetts to the Washington, DC, area to spend time with the woman I had met upon my return to the States. In 1968, I received my master's degree and took a school counseling position at an exciting place called Cardinal Gibbons High School in Baltimore.

In 1968, the Catonsville 9 in Maryland objected to the Vietnam War by destroying draft files. I was angry and sad about the American position and our approach to foreign policy and wanted to support the antiwar work of Daniel and Patrick Berrigan. I joined the Central Committee for Conscientious Objectors and became politically and socially active while working as a counselor. When Martin Luther King Jr. and Bobby Kennedy were assassinated, it moved me deeply, causing me to be personally devastated and furious.

While I was establishing myself professionally, I was dating the woman I would eventually marry. On several occasions, I secretly attempted to go to one of Baltimore's gay bars, although I was afraid and never got the courage to go inside. Getting married was a relief, and I believed that my attraction to men would end. My son, Adam, was born in June 1970. His early life was spent in a backpack at antiwar rallies and listening to the cries of my students who were hurt and saddened by the killings at Kent State. At times, our sense of helplessness was excruciating.

A Next Step

I went to the American Personnel and Guidance Association (APGA) convention in Atlantic City in March 1971. I decided to stop for lunch at a café between my hotel and the convention center and sat next to Dr. Tom Hipple, who was a counselor educator at the University of Idaho. We spent the afternoon talking. Six months later, I was a doctoral student at the University of Idaho. Moscow, Idaho, was a very new culture for this New Englander. I had never come into contact with the Mormon Church, which had a significant impact on most of my colleagues and on the students with whom we worked. I soon recognized that their worldviews challenged mine in new ways.

At the insistence of Tom Hipple, I took a group dynamics course and became excited. A cadre of faculty members and students from a variety of disciplines formed the Center for Human and Organizational Research and Development (CHORD). This group engaged in task, psychoeducational, counseling, and psychotherapeutic group work in a variety of settings throughout the university. Through my work with CHORD, I was afforded the opportunity to do much of the personal growth work that Frank Buckley had encouraged when I was a master's student. Although much of what CHORD did was insight-oriented verbal group work, the experiential and adventure-based work ignited my passion. One particular workshop stands out clearly. It was a 10-day workshop focused on anger. I knew that I had anger building that was related to social injustice. Through this workshop, I began to explore some of the fear and hurt beneath my anger. However, I still was not prepared to explore issues directly related to sexual orientation.

Coming Out, and Then Some

Upon graduation, I accepted a position as a visiting assistant professor on the counselor education faculty at Oakland University in Rochester, Michigan. I chose to take this position because it afforded me the opportunity to learn more about group work and because the university had a racially diverse faculty and student body. As I drove from Idaho to Michigan with my wife and my son, all seemed well in my world. I remember driving east, thinking that my attraction to men was the only remaining piece of the puzzle that was not in place. I was determined to find a counselor in Michigan and resolve the dissonance.

My year at Oakland was another transition. I was introduced to friends who are still an important part of my life, and I was becoming an effective teacher. I was presenting at conferences and becoming more skilled, and my wife became pregnant with my daughter. During this time, I met a man. This man was becoming more intriguing. I received a call with a job possibility at New Mexico State University, Las Cruces. The "intriguing man" told me that he was in love with me. I went for a job interview in New Mexico. On my way back to Michigan, I realized that I loved him, too.

As my family and I moved to Las Cruces, I told my wife that I had met a man with whom I was in love. She was seven months pregnant with my daughter, Aidan. Over the next three years, my family and I went through anger, fear, hurt, shame, love, and, for me, excruciating loneliness. My wife and I made the decision to work through our experiences together, even as we prepared to separate. We cared about each other but knew that we could not continue as husband and wife. We also knew that we loved our children and wanted to go through the separation in a respectful and loving way. When we finally separated, I left the university. Las Cruces was a very small town, and in 1976, we were not prepared to publicly confront discrimination on the basis of sexual orientation. My own homophobia complicated the decision-making process. I believed that although my counselor was supportive, there was no one who really understood the turmoil that I and those I loved were going through. I was alone.

Moving Toward Integration

Leaving New Mexico State University opened new doors for me. Having made the decision to leave academia and to step back from direct work with clients, I needed to explore what it meant to be an openly gay man. I experienced a wide range of emotional responses in the beginning of my "coming out" process. My first male relationship was a tumultuous exploration—at times joyful, at other times excruciating. I was not in a position to provide direct services to clients until I had become clear about who I was myself. As a result, I left direct client service from 1978 until 1986. During these years, I worked in clinical administrative positions in a community mental health organization and in a juvenile corrections facility.

I was increasingly aware that sexuality was about more than behavior. I had such information intellectually earlier in my life, but now this information had deeper, more integrated meaning for me. As an emerging gay man in my 30s, I began to learn about the social, emotional, psychological, spiritual, and cultural aspects of being sexual. I began to write, explore, and put together workshops for men who were clarifying their own sexuality. It was the late 1970s and early 1980s, a time when being a gay man in America was about to change. At this time in my life, I would have welcomed an openly gay male role model in my profession and was aware of gay men in counseling and in counselor education who were not open about their sexual orientation. I read Vivien Cass's (1979) model for gay identity development and was able to recognize aspects of my own journey, with relief, sadness, and hope.

Throughout these years, I had separated myself from the religious structure in which I was raised and which was the source of much of my strength as an adolescent and young adult. Where others might have had painful experiences with Roman Catholicism, I had not. It was through the Catholic educational system that I had learned to think critically, to value integrity, and to learn respect for diversity. It was through my association with the Church that I had become involved in social activism. As an emerging gay man, I came to believe that, for me, the Roman Church was no longer a safe and supportive community. John Fortunato (1982) writes about the grieving process for gay Christians. I experienced the loss of a supportive religious structure and the challenge of creating a new spiritual community.

A series of synchronistic events brought me to Tucson and provided the opportunity to work in juvenile corrections. Again, I found myself face-to-face with young men and families whose worldviews challenged mine. More than anything else, these young men taught me about respect. There were times when I was embarrassed about being "over-educated" for the position in which I found myself. As I was exploring new relationships and learning how to become a member of the local gay community, the dissonance built. A crisis in my son's life led to clarity for me, and I left my position in juvenile corrections to become a full-time father.

Several months after leaving juvenile corrections, I opened a private counseling practice. My first contracts were with the juvenile court, working with young men and their families. Struggling with coming out as a gay counselor, I decided to do so and got more referrals from the juvenile court system. In the years since that decision, I have come to work extensively with adolescent and adult males who are exploring ways to become healthy, integrated men, and I continue to learn from each of my clients.

Professional Involvement

Upon starting my counseling practice in 1987, I rejoined the American Association for Counseling and Development, which later became the American Counseling Association (ACA), after a 12-year absence. As a practitioner, I became a member of the Association for Specialists in Group Work (ASGW). Soon after, Diana Hulse-Killacky invited me to chair the new Gay and Lesbian Task Force. Through this initial contact, I became active in ASGW and moved into positions of leadership, eventually serving as president. In a series of synchronistic events, I discovered a meeting of the Association for Gay and Lesbian Issues in Counseling, later to become the Association for Gay, Lesbian, and Bisexual Issues in Counseling (AGLBIC), and signed up to go to dinner. This was my first experience with openly gay, lesbian, and bisexual counselors. I cried in my room that night.

I was appointed to represent ASGW on the first ACA Human Rights Committee and selected to chair the committee. This gave me the opportunity to collaborate with bright and committed professionals, many of whom, including Judy Lewis, have moved into leadership positions within ACA. It was from this committee that many of the human rights and social justice issues that are now a part of the profession emerged. For me, much of this work helped forge my identity as an emerging gay professional.

As a counseling practitioner, I continue to seek the balance between staying involved in my profession, providing the best possible service to my clients, and maintaining a fulfilling personal life. At times, this means taking a step back financially so that I can step forward in advocacy for my clients. In 1994, when I was looking for ways to invigorate my counseling practice, I contacted a friend from Cottonwood de Tucson, a dual-diagnosis in-patient treatment program. As a result of this contact, I began an association with Cottonwood that continues to this day. Currently, I facilitate groups for men who have histories of sexual abuse and trauma and who engage in sexually compulsive behavior. Through my work with these men, I am coming to a much clearer understanding of the underlying dynamics of male sexual trauma and compulsive behavior.

Social Justice Advocacy

Throughout my development as a man and a counselor, I have experienced an ongoing desire to address issues of advocacy and social justice, paralleling ACA's commitment. In the 1990s, it became apparent to many within the association that we could do more. As the forces gathered, Counselors for Social Justice (CSJ) emerged. Some of my CSJ colleagues are brilliant at articulating the issues and creating strategies for social action. Hopefully, I bring a set of supportive group work skills to the association. I like to believe that these skills were part of what made the early ACA Human Rights Committee so creative and proactive. As CSJ emerged, I was fortunate enough to serve as the first president, and I now serve as the CSJ representative to the ACA Governing Council. In this capacity, I hope to be able to continue to bring a focus on social justice concerns to the ACA decision-making process, the field, and the community we serve.

Staying Balanced

Throughout my personal and professional development, I have reflected upon those early years as "the outsider" in my family and neighborhood. I no longer wish to spend my life as an outsider, although it would be easy for me to do so. I wish to be a part of a community that operates from love and respect for different worldviews. When confronted by dissonance in a group, I am likely to ask the question "Are we spending our time the way we want to spend it?" I want to be respectful, collaborative, and harmonious in all arenas in my life.

When my son was 16, he confronted me with the importance of being a father. I recognized that I often did not balance my personal and professional life. As a result, I experienced loneliness and pain. I am now better at learning to balance. My greatest teachers have been my children. When I believe, as I often do, that I am going along just fine, my son or my daughter is likely to remind me that sharing our simple daily events with each other is what is really important. They remind me that when we lose contact, we lose meaning. As a gay man, I have developed an "intentional family." These are those special people with whom I spend special time. They are all over the world. In this age of the Internet and cell phones, keeping in regular contact can be excitingly creative. I have built up lots of frequent-flyer miles, too. In order to stay physically healthy, I take the time to work out with a trainer three days a week and supplement lifting weights with cardio exercises three days a week. I read voraciously and have promised myself to read fewer political books. Being in touch with spirituality is central, so that I receive energy from the desert in the morning, from the scent of orange blossoms in the spring, from the shadow of a red-tailed hawk in the desert sky, from the taste of cranberries, from diving into the cold surf on an August day in Maine, from remembering that life can and should be simple and judicious.

Connection Between Theory and Practice

I believe that we change when we experience dissonance in our lives. Dissonance can be described as the awareness that our lives are not what we want them to be and that change must occur on some level. I want what I say I believe to be consistent with how I feel, and I want my behavior to reflect this congruence. It is where my behavior, thoughts, and feelings intersect that my spirit is nurtured. We all deserve to be loved and respected. Life experiences may diminish or enhance the experiences of love and respect. As a result, we begin to experience core feelings that can be either life enhancing or life inhibiting. Along with these feelings, we create beliefs about who we are, who we are with others, and what our world is like. Beliefs that serve us well at some points in our lives may inhibit us at other times. Much of who we are is framed by the community in which we grow and how we relate to that community.

I see the struggling within the communities in which we live as comparable to the experiences faced by individuals. We are all part of a greater community-at-large, which takes many forms. This community-at-large continues to explore ways to integrate all members. When a community or an individual engages in an either/or approach to being-in-the-world, we are likely to experience increasing dissonance, making one of our tasks as members of a community to work for harmony and collaboration. Those of us who have had greater privilege and access to power are morally and ethically bound to work more diligently for greater respect and social change so that all people are included and respected. It is incumbent upon each of us to acknowledge that there are multitudinous ways of viewing the world and that we can all grow from working to understand and integrate all worldviews.

Counseling Practice

In my counseling practice, I work with individuals, couples, and groups. Although my beliefs provide the foundation for my work, I am also aware that working with individuals is significantly different from working with couples, which, in turn, is different from working with groups. Hopefully, I have developed the insight and skills to work differently while maintaining respect for my clients and for the methodology.

As a counseling practitioner, I learn from each of my clients. I have come to believe that each of us is here to learn about love and respect. Each person who enters our lives teaches us a lesson about loving and being respectful. Sometimes those lessons are difficult ones to learn. Each of my clients deserves respect for who he or she is. My role as a counselor is to walk with my clients along their paths and explore the world that they know. My frequent questions include, What is your life about? What do you want your life to be about? What are you willing to do to change? How are you going to manifest the changes you wish to make? These are starting places for the journey.

In exploring such questions with my clients, I continually have the opportunity to examine those questions myself. Additionally, my work with clients allows me to explore ways of integrating my feelings, thoughts, and behaviors and, hopefully, nurturing my spirit. I believe that as part of being effective counselors, we must be advocates for social change. When the community in which we live is disconnected from respect and collaborative, creative problem resolution, we have a responsibility to address injustice as it plays itself out. As a result, we must participate in creating change by taking the next step, whatever that may be for each of us.

Balancing Practice and Theory

A critical aspect of being a counseling practitioner is having the opportunity to participate in ongoing peer supervision. My peer supervision group is essential to my growth as a counselor. As part of our relationship, my colleagues and I consistently explore and clarify our beliefs about the counseling process and our roles in it. We question the interventions we make; our beliefs about change; the dangers of pathologizing behaviors, thoughts, or feelings; the role of community and individual development; differing cultural norms; the need for advocacy in the community; our own blind spots and biases; and our willingness to take community action to address issues of injustice. In addition to peer supervision, I participate in my professional association on several levels, at times taking on tasks that open new worlds to me. I am not an academic and am inclined to participate in experiential training to increase my professional skills and expand my worldview. At this point in my career, I am invited to conduct workshops or teach classes.

Advice to New Professionals

Before anything else, remember to BREATHE. Trust in yourselves and your observations. Learn from others—your clients, your supervisors, the community in which you live—and integrate that learning into who you are. Be a member of some community (however you define community) where you can speak up for issues of human rights and social justice. Continue to be a participant in life. Most of what you bring into the counseling session is the integration of cognitive information that has been learned in the classroom with the experience of being alive in the world. Constantly check your assumptions. Actively participate in some form of supervision in which you can safely explore your fears, frustrations, pain, joy, and passion, and continue to work in a respectful manner. Put yourself in uncomfortable situations and grow from the experience. Reach beyond your culture of comfort. Be a client. Do your own personal spiritual, emotional, cognitive, and cultural work. Recognize that there are many ways of being-in-the-world. What may entice one person or group may stifle another. Remain curious and humble. And finally, don't give advice.

And for Those of Us Beyond "New"

My message is quite similar. I want simplicity and authenticity in my life and invite others to explore ways to maintain their simplicity and authenticity. There are many questions that those of us at mid-career may ask: What is your life about? What do you want your life to be about? Are you living your life in a loving and respectful way? Are you doing what you want with your life? If not, what changes are you willing to make? How are you contributing to your community? What kind of difference are you making in the world? How are you speaking up for those who cannot speak for themselves? How do you get in your own way? How do you keep your spirit alive? Where do you go for support? Who knows who you are? How do you move toward or maintain congruence? Are you willing to take creative and healthy risks? What are you doing to increase harmony in our world?

Development as a Multicultural Counselor

As a child, I was aware that my perceptions of the world were different from the perceptions of others. Though I was unable to articulate it, I experienced dissonance in attempting to fully accept an Irish American, Catholic, heterosexual model of the world. I believe that I first became aware of socioeconomic differences as a high school student and then again as an undergraduate. This information was not clearly defined for me but was experienced as a dissonance between my perception of myself and my fellow students. I knew that many of my classmates, all of whom were male, took for granted much of what I had to work hard to attain. I had not framed these experiences as social class difference or "privilege" at that point in my life.

The most significant experiences of diversity came when I lived and worked with the Jesuit Lay Volunteer Corps in Baghdad, Iraq, from 1965 to 1967. When I began my teaching, I had some cognitive information about Islamic and Arabic cultures, but I was unfamiliar with the customs of daily living. I had grown up in an Irish American version of Roman Catholicism. When I went to Iraq, almost half of my students were Christians; however, none were from Western Christian traditions. There was much for me to learn about Christianity. Additionally, my Muslim students came from a variety of Islamic sects, each with different customs, beliefs, and practices. My students and their families in Iraq processed the world in ways that were very different from the way I had learned to process the world, and the differences were profound and, at times, difficult to understand. In many ways, I believe that this lack of understanding of the cultures of the Middle East has contributed significantly to problems in that area of the world.

Certainly, living in Iraq was a significant experience in my life. Additionally, living in Moscow, Idaho, was a similar opportunity for exploration, as I was fortunate enough to have contact with communities throughout the state of Idaho. I learned about rural America and about the influence of the Mormon Church. Again, I needed to explore my own assumptions of how the world is and how each of us fits into the greater community of being. Later, I continued to learn about the diversity of Tucson and its many cultures. Perhaps one of the most significant concepts I have learned came from my work in juvenile corrections in Arizona. In working with Spanish-speaking street gang members from South Phoenix and South Tucson, I learned the importance of respect. Although I had a cognitive understanding of respect, these young men challenged me to examine how and when I was being disrespectful. I also came to a fuller awareness of ways to be respectful when working with them and their families.

In my own search as an emerging gay man, I have learned much about the gay community. In the early stages of my sexual identity development, I believed that sexuality was about behavior. As my sexual identity emerged, I have become more closely connected to the spiritual, social, cultural, emotional, and psychological dynamics of sexuality and community. Participation in an "intentional family" is particularly important for me. In addition to an individual's sexual identity development, I believe that communities, and the community-at-large, develop in terms of their understanding and integration of sexual diversity.

My Style

I am active. At 61, I continue to love experiential group work and do not see myself retiring any time soon. I continue to seek ways of being involved in a variety of professional and personal activities. I am not as quick as I used to be, so I spend more hours each week doing work that I enjoy. I do my best to find joy in my work. I am learning to fly with less baggage. I also need alone time. In the morning I walk in the desert near my home, breathing in the life of the desert, hoping to keep my life simple. I work out physically, and whenever possible, I head for a beach and play in the surf. It is important for me to have some involvement with the gay community. I have wonderful friends with whom I spend time or keep in touch through the Internet. As I shift priorities, I am reconnecting with gay, lesbian, bisexual, and transgendered social advocacy agencies in Tucson and Arizona and now serve on Tucson's Commission on Gay, Lesbian, Bisexual, and Transgender Issues.

My greatest accomplishment has been being a father to my son, Adam, and my daughter, Aidan. Adam is currently doing environmental research for Hawkwatch International. He is passionate about environmental concerns and is doing his part to protect the world in which we live. My daughter, Aidan, is currently working as a wilderness instructor with at-risk students from the New York City public school system. She is exploring ways to go to graduate school to combine her passion for biology, theater, and environmental activism. I believe my children have emerged as they are, in part, because their mother and I worked together when they were growing up. As they grew into adulthood, we were fairly effective at stepping forward when needed and stepping back as they created their own worlds.

Professionally, I hope that I have contributed to opening doors and providing opportunities for emerging gay, lesbian, bisexual, and transgendered counselors and the clients we serve. From the time I began my personal and professional explorations, I ached to have openly gay male mentors. Despite frequently questioning whether it was possible to be a successful gay man, my experiences with ASGW, AGLBIC, CSJ, and ACA have been crucial in my development, leading me to work to assist others.

Perhaps my greatest professional accomplishment is an ongoing one. I would like to believe that the clients with whom I work move forward creatively in their lives and their communities. I continue to commit myself to working with men in their emerging sense of who they are and who they can be. My work providing individual counseling and leading groups for men who have been sexually abused as boys has helped me develop a greater understanding of the effects of early trauma and the shame, hurt, fear, loneliness, and anger associated with these early life experiences. It is exciting to observe men awakening to their life experiences and healing.

As I reflect on my career to date, I believe that the most challenging events in my life were those related to sexual identity development. Much of my personal work has focused on moving through the shame initially associated with my sexual orientation. Although my early life experiences in my family of origin were founded in Roman Catholicism, as an openly gay man, I no longer find a place in the Roman Church. I have sadness about this. My passion is for group work, specifically for adventure-based, experiential group work. I have been able to find parts of myself that I had not known and to help others discover who they are, who they are with each other, and who we are as a community.

I am learning humility. Just when I believe I have reached a way of being-in-the-world, someone will come along to let me know that I know significantly less than I thought I knew. I am a student of life, believing that each person who comes into my life has a lesson to teach me about what it means to be loving and respectful. I am learning to not take myself too seriously, and to trust that others are more skilled than I am in many areas. Slowly, I am becoming more effective at collaborative decision-making and problem-solving. I am learning to "keep it simple." I get new ideas from watching the red-tailed hawk that flies in the skies above my home, from watching desert sunsets, from paying attention to my body, from listening, from reading and the Internet, from early morning discussions with colleagues and friends, from my children, from the explorations of my clients, from slowing down to pay attention to the light on the mountains north of my home, and most recently, from listening to the stories of my mother.

What Does the Future Look Like

My attempts to look into and predict the future have always been less than stellar. But I will look into the stars and speculate!

My Personal Direction

I wish to continue exploration in my personal and professional life, continuing to involve myself in my profession and my professional association. I currently serve on the ACA Governing Council, representing CSJ, and I hope to be able to continue to address social justice issues in my life, my profession, and the community at large. I wish, also, to continue to work as an advocate for social change. My particular area of interest is working for equal rights for gay, lesbian, bisexual, transgendered, queer, and intersexed people and confronting homophobia (my own and others). I continue to enjoy providing individual, group, and couple counseling. Although I have not published much about what I do in my work, I would like to write about my work with men in a way that would be helpful to others. I have been blessed with excellent health. Hopefully, this will continue. As mentioned earlier, I continue to explore the balance of mind, body, and spirit and try to live in a loving and respectful manner.

Future Directions of the Profession

I am deeply concerned about the immediate future of the world in which we live. I perceive a growing need for counseling and other mental health services and a shrinking pool of resources. Executive, legislative, and judicial decisions in the past few years have challenged the balance between societal security and individual civil rights. As counselors, we need to become advocates for social change, adopting and integrating the ACA Advocacy Competencies. The economic situation in our world is remarkably inequitable. As a profession, we will need to explore the methods used to provide services and ways of consolidating and integrating those services. Additionally, we must work diligently to ensure that counselors are acknowledged and rewarded for the services we provide while building collaborative relationships with other helping professions.

On a more long-term basis, as national borders become less important in understanding the world, as cultures weave new threads into the fabric of our community-at-large, and as we become more aware and skilled in multicultural work, we will see new theories, approaches, and techniques becoming essential in counseling. I believe the models of mental, social, and spiritual health will need to expand and evolve so that our profession can draw on new resources and integrate ideas, beliefs, traditions, activities, and approaches from different groups within our community at large. We will begin to honor and acknowledge some of the cultural healing systems that are already in place in the many cultures that exist in our world. Hopefully, we will honor the diversity within our community, regardless of the basis for the differences.

I see group work continuing to grow as an approach to working with individuals and communities. This will require an increase in the number of opportunities for and quality of group work training. Additionally, we will need to draw on group work modalities and approaches from cultures in which group work is indigenous. Technology will also continue to build as a force and a resource in the profession, providing new methods of teaching and training. The Internet will become a more and more effective counseling tool. This is evident in the current online meetings of our association on a regular basis. There will be a need to explore the evolution of our ethical standards in order to accommodate our rapidly changing technology. Finally, there will be an increasing integration of spirituality into the work being done by counselors, in order to provide healing that was previously done by shamans and other healers.

Advice to the Next Generations

Some thoughts: Don't give advice. Learn from the mistakes that my colleagues and I have made. Don't interpret mistakes as failures, but rather as opportunities to grow and change. Be gentle with and trust yourself. Don't take yourself too seriously. Explore new ideas and new ways of being-in-the-world. Explore ways of being-in-the-world that have been around for generations and are new to you. Do not be discouraged easily. Create a support system built on trust in which you can explore who you are and where you are going. Participate in supervision. Be active in your professional association.

We can create greater change when many of us speak with one voice. Make a difference. Create your own path and share the process of path-creating with others. Keep life simple and be passionate.

Concluding Thoughts

As we develop as people and as professional counselors, we must take the steps to move outside of the world in which we are comfortable. We must continue to challenge our assumptions about who we are in the world, how the world is, and how our views differ from those of others. Before pathologizing another person's or group's experiences, we must examine the cultural context, recognizing that although our view of the world may work well for us based on our cultural assumptions, it may not work for others. See the world in terms of inclusiveness, exploring ways to include others and be included, as we change our language to be more inclusive. Be a learner, going into new situations as someone who has something to learn from others. We must take the lead in becoming advocates for social justice in our community-at-large. For each of us, this means taking the next step forward—whether it is writing to a newspaper, becoming active in a local or national organization, running for public office, serving on a community advisory board, voting in local and national elections, or becoming mentors and models for our peers and the client populations we serve. We must never lose our commitment to respect for differences.

References

Cass, V. C. (1979). Homosexual identity formation: A theoretical model. *Journal of Homosexuality*, 4, 219–234.

Fortunato, J. (1982). *Embracing the exile: Healing journeys of gay Christians.* San Francisco: Harper & Row.

Chapter 10

A Work in Progress: On Becoming a Culturally Competent Counseling Psychologist

Madonna G. Constantine

Early Background

I grew up in a small, somewhat segregated, predominantly White southern city in Louisiana during the 1960s. I came from a working-class family of seven individuals and am the third of five children. My siblings (three sisters and one brother) and I were relatively close in age, and as a result, we spent a lot of time playing with each other. My parents, who did not complete college, put every spare dime they had into our education by sending us to private, Catholic, predominantly Black elementary and high schools. I believe they did this not only because our religious group affiliation was Catholic but also because we grew up during a time in which rampant segregation often meant that Black kids attending public schools in our community would be exposed to substandard educational experiences simply because of their racial group membership. My parents knew that their kids possessed at least a reasonable level of intelligence (e.g., I knew how to read books and multiply numbers by the age of four), so they probably wisely surmised that we might not receive adequate nurturance of many of our abilities and skills by enrolling us in a predominantly White public school in our hometown. I believe my parents were probably right in their decision in this regard. I think their commitment to ensuring that we were exposed to educational experiences that would affirm our racial group membership and challenge us appropriately has shaped so much of my life to date.

I first became aware of wanting to become a psychologist from watching early episodes of *The Bob Newhart Show* and from hearing many individuals in my life tell me that I had a natural curiosity about people and what "made them tick." I was only in elementary school when this realization occurred, and I began to seek information that could give me some sense about what psychologists did. I found out that that there were many different types of psychologists, but the general area in psychology to which I was most drawn was counseling. I found out that counseling psychologists tended to work with people who were struggling to find solutions to typical problems encountered throughout life. Thus, counseling psychology became my "dream career" during middle and high school, and I identified the goal of attending college to major in psychology. I was social and popular in high school, and I seemed to be someone that many of my peers came to because I was a good listener and gave good advice. Such descriptors strengthened my desire to pursue my avowed career goal. I graduated high school as valedictorian of my class and looked forward to entering college to pursue my educational and career goals.

Like everyone else out there, the story of my professional journey is one that is fraught with ups and downs, highs and lows, and rich fruitful discoveries about others and myself. Below I will explicate many of the experiences that have shaped my professional development as a multicultural counselor to date.

Undergraduate and Graduate School

During my undergraduate years at Xavier University of Louisiana, a predominantly Black private Catholic university in New Orleans, I majored in psychology and minored in English. New Orleans was located only two hours from my birthplace, and I chose Xavier because it was important that I stayed close to home to remain connected to my family and close friends. Although I entered Xavier with a full tuition scholarship, I definitely was not the most studious and diligent student. Living in New Orleans posed quite a few challenges to me in terms of balancing school and a social life. In fact, I partied quite a bit as an undergraduate student, partly because New Orleans is considered by many to be a party town and the legal drinking age at that time was 18. Despite my transgressions in this regard, I finished college in three years and then entered a master's program in business, industry, and social agencies counseling at Xavier.

While a master's student in the early to mid 1980s, I engaged in several experiences that significantly affected my professional life. For example, my first practicum as a master's student was at a battered women's shelter in New Orleans. At this shelter, I worked with women from a variety of racial, ethnic, and socioeconomic backgrounds. It was there that I began to get in touch with the fact that some of the information I learned as a master's student in terms of counseling approaches and modalities was not necessarily applicable to most of the women with whom I worked. I remember one client at that time who had disclosed to me that she had experienced extensive third-degree burns at the hands of her husband who had thrown a pot of boiling water in her face after an argument. My response to this client was, "How did that make you feel?" It felt so automatic to say something like this after the many role-plays of which I had been a part in my graduate courses. However, I knew innately that this response to the client was inappropriate, disingenuous, sterile, and just not me. I immediately regretted this question and vowed from that point on that I would have to get in touch with what my true feelings and thoughts were about clients' issues and disclosures and respond to them more genuinely.

My subsequent clinical genuineness seemed to serve clients well, both at the battered women's shelter and at a local psychiatric hospital, where I worked on an adolescent mental health unit for a couple of years. However, some of my practicum and work supervisors expressed a preference for me to offer more "cookbook" responses to my clients and their concerns. Even as an emerging professional in training, however, I was able to encourage some of my supervisors to understand the importance of moving away from "scripted" forms of counseling and therapy and responding to clients from a deeper and more authentic place. Moreover, I began to challenge both my supervisors and professors to resist conceptualizing clients of color and individuals from financially impoverished backgrounds as "disadvantaged" populations—a term that was featured prominently in many counseling and psychology textbooks during that time. These conceptualizations strongly tended to view these individuals from a pathological or a deficit perspective and failed to recognize the unique strengths inherent in every cultural group. I truly believed then, as I do now, that "different from" does not mean "less than." At this point, I also began to work increasingly in the local area as a volunteer consultant for issues pertaining to cultural diversity in mental health settings, and I was encouraged by the early professional writings of individuals such as William Cross, Derald Wing Sue, and Clemmont Vontress in this regard. I also began to study the works of social justice advocates such as Martin Luther King Jr. and bell hooks, a self-described Black woman intellectual and revolutionary activist, who shaped a great deal of my development in terms of beginning to integrate my professional and personal lives.

I finished my master's program at Xavier and then began working for the dean of the Graduate School there as a statistical consultant for a large project pertaining to academic achievement in Black school-aged children. I very much enjoyed analyzing data and reporting my findings to him. One day, the dean asked what my plans were for the rest of the day. It was early in the afternoon, and I informed him that I intended to go shopping and then go home to cook dinner. He asked if I would consider passing by the student union to attend Graduate School Day and gather information about possibly attending a doctoral program. I joked with him that I had experienced enough abuse as a master's student and that I did not plan to go back to school right away. He indicated that he would pay me for four hours of work to attend Graduate School Day to meet with various university recruiters. I happily agreed to attend, but I did not honestly have any serious intention of applying to doctoral programs at that time.

I entered the student union at Xavier and began looking at displays of various graduate schools and programs. I collected lots of literature from these schools and struck up conversations with several interesting college representatives. One particular individual, Dr. Hollie Walker Jr., was representing Memphis State University (MSU), and he asked me about my college background. He indicated that MSU had a doctoral program in counseling psychology and that I should apply for admission. Dr. Walker even wrote on the admission application that my application fee would be waived if I applied to the program. He then asked me for some contact information to follow up with me at a later date. I then left the student union feeling happy that I had just made money from my boss simply by walking around and talking to people about interesting things. At that point, I had no idea that such a serendipitous opportunity would influence my professional and personal life in many ways.

I forgot all about the graduate school applications and went on with life as usual. I received a follow-up call from Dr. Walker from MSU nearly two weeks later, encouraging me to apply there. I told him that I did not think I was going to apply to any school at this time. He encouraged me to send in the application anyway, just in case I would change my mind a bit later. I applied only to MSU and was admitted, but I also had just received news that my mother needed chemotherapy after the removal of malignant fibroid tumors. I was close to my family and felt that my parents needed me to be home with them, so I made the decision not to attend MSU. I informed my mother and Dr. Walker of my decision, but my mother assured me that she would be fine and she encouraged me to attend school. Dr. Walker also provided lots of support and encouragement at that time by offering me a teaching assistantship in the counseling program and finding me graduate student housing on campus. Thus, I made the decision to go to MSU.

My first year at MSU was challenging in several ways. First, I was flying home every month to help my mother deal with her chemotherapy treatments and help my father keep the household together. Second, I was working a couple of jobs to help put one of my younger sisters through college so that my parents would not have such a heavy financial burden. Third, I was attempting to adjust to an academic environment in which I was a numerical minority. Because I had attended predominantly Black schools in the past, I had not had much exposure to other racial and ethnic groups on an academic and social level. I did not find much support from some of my peers and many of the professors on campus. In fact, some of the faculty seemed to resent me openly, and one professor in particular characterized my admission into the counseling psychology doctoral program as an experiment. Specifically, he stated that I was a "guinea pig," as the first student of color admitted to the PhD program in counseling psychology at MSU, and that the success of my matriculation would determine whether other students of color would be admitted into the program in the future. Although his words and behaviors toward me throughout my doctoral program often angered me, they made me very determined to succeed as a doctoral student. Despite the fact that there were a few faculty members in the program who felt this way about me, there were several Black faculty and staff members there who were positively instrumental in my development as a counseling psychologist, including Joyce L. Young, Russell Thomas, and Rosie P. Bingham. My academic advisor, Burl Gilliland, also served as an important support person and role model to me during my days at MSU. I graduated from MSU in 1991 with a PhD in counseling psychology. Several Black students and other students of color were admitted to this program during the latter part of my matriculation there, and I'm happy that the doctoral program has since admitted and graduated many students of color who are making contributions to the field and to their communities.

Early Career Journey

After completing my predoctoral internship in 1990 at the University of Notre Dame's Counseling Center, my first professional job was at the University of Texas (UT) at Austin's Counseling and Mental Health Center. I had not yet finished my dissertation, but I was employed as a staff psychologist who provided individual and group counseling and outreach services to students of color on campus, particularly Black students. I finished my dissertation within the first year of my employment there, became a licensed psychologist, and opened a small private practice to supplement my counseling center income. I very much enjoyed my work with the students and staff at UT and the clients in the larger Austin community, but I found myself feeling unfulfilled about not nurturing the "scientist" part of me as a professional. The practitioner side of me was getting nourished in my work settings, but the need to engage in research activities was growing stronger by the minute.

I became involved in several research projects at UT and felt a strong draw in the direction of spending even more time engaged in these endeavors. I spoke with the counseling center director about applying nationally for academic positions that had a strong applied focus. He encouraged me to follow my heart in this regard, and I accepted a position as an assistant professor in the counseling psychology program at Temple University in Philadelphia. After spending the first five years of my professional life at UT, it was hard to leave behind many dear friends and colleagues who continue to serve as support persons today.

I arrived at Temple as a new assistant professor who was committed to having a balanced and successful academic life. I had heard from colleagues throughout the country that many pretenured academicians struggled, often unsuccessfully, to find time to play and enjoy life in the midst of working very long hours to publish so that they wouldn't perish. In order to combat the potential workaholism I'd heard about, I joined a wonderful church in Philadelphia and met several good friends with whom I worshipped and socialized. I also befriended several colleagues at my university, especially Nicholas Ladany and Portia Hunt. Nick and I collaborated on lots of research projects, and he mentored me in ways that few people have offered to date. I needed really Nick and other colleagues' support as I faced some difficult circumstances regarding sexism from a senior male administrator. I remember once trying to negotiate my salary with this administrator, and he stated that the salary for which I was asking was "a lot of money for a single woman with no children." I told him that what he was implying was probably illegal, and I got the sense that he would have been happy to meet my reasonable salary request if I had been a married (and perhaps White) male faculty member. After I'd been at Temple for almost three years, this administrator also gave me some feedback that I was "publishing too many articles" and "making a lot of senior faculty members look bad" because they were publishing comparatively less. I knew then that I might not be such a good fit for the program and the university at this point in my career. I was then courted by Teachers College at Columbia University in New York City to join their counseling psychology program, and I resigned my position at Temple to pursue this professional opportunity.

Middle and Current Career Journey

Teachers College offered me a pretenured associate professor position, and I was happy to be in an institution that valued the quality and quantity of my research. I was subsequently awarded tenure there and asked to serve as department chair. I resisted the invitation to serve as department chair because I did not ever have the professional goal of becoming an administrator and our department was fraught with interpersonal difficulties and conflicts that were historical and deeply entrenched. In fact, I was perfectly content serving as a "regular" member of the faculty by teaching two courses per semester, advising students, serving on committees, and conducting research. I do not consider myself to be a natural leader, although I have been told that I have good leadership skills. I am much more comfortable in a position where I am a "follower" who has some input into a given situation or process. In pondering the decision to serve as department chair, I remember a close colleague who remarked to me that sometimes people are needed to lead in situations that they might not want to because doing so might keep others who are potentially ineffective and destructive from serving in these capacities. Our college president and dean finally convinced me to serve as chair by offering some support to me to maintain my research productivity. I served as chair for a year, was given a yearlong leave without pay the following year to pursue another professional opportunity, and then returned to Teachers College as a full professor to resume the chair of the department.

My term as department chair thus far has been mostly good, but it has not been without its challenges. As a relatively young (i.e., early 40s), African American woman, I have experienced occasional sexism and racism in ways that would sound pretty unbelievable to most people who have not been in similar positions and who do not fall within these sociodemographic categories. The often surprising thing to me about some of this treatment is that the sexism and racism I've experienced comes not only from White men but also from women and people of color. It is surprising in the sense that I expect women and people of color to have a core understanding and awareness of oppression and discrimination and not to perpetuate these issues either consciously or unconsciously. Unfortunately, this has not been the case. It has been disappointing, for instance, to have found out that a female colleague circumvented me to go to a former departmental administrator to discuss a job offer from another university because she felt more comfortable dealing with and negotiating with men in positions of authority. She indicated to me that her behavior toward me was not personal, but that her social and cultural values dictated that men were likely to be more effective in meeting her needs in such instances. Moreover, I have had several departmental colleagues question my judgments, decisions, and authority in ways that they did not appear to do when a White male colleague served as department chair. I suppose this is part of the burden that many women and people of color bear when serving in leadership or administrative positions, but even this knowledge does not ease the occasional pain, anger, and sadness that I experience in this role when such blatant inequities occur. In order to maintain a constructive attitude during these adverse circumstances, I try to confront and challenge sexism and racism in ways that can make a difference in the lives of my colleagues and in my own future experiences as an administrator.

Having social support resources has been critical throughout my professional life, but especially in my role as department chair. I believe that without a network of individuals in whom you can confide your greatest problems, struggles, anxieties, and challenges, it would be nearly impossible for anyone to be effective in an administrative capacity. My network consists of trusted colleagues within and outside of my university, close friends from childhood and throughout my life, and some members of my family. This is the type of network that grounds me when I lose perspective about what really is important in life. Although I have been very satisfied with nearly all aspects of my professional life over the years, the thing that has brought me the most joy has been the important people in my life.

Work Style and Accomplishments

Some individuals have described me as having high expectations of both others and myself. I believe this characterization is very accurate, and I think it exists at both a professional and personal level. My work style is one in which I am dedicated to seeing tasks through to the end, and I believe that the work you produce speaks volumes about who you are fundamentally as a person. I have a high degree of persistence for many things, and I do not like disappointing others, although this sometimes happens. However, I have learned over the years to be accepting of many of my own limitations and the limitations of others. I always have enjoyed challenging myself to do my best work, and I like and value competent people. Furthermore, personal characteristics such as loyalty and trust are very crucial aspects of meaningful work relationships to me, and I believe these characteristics can indicate a lot about people on many different levels.

I am proud of many things I have accomplished to date. It is not in my nature to brag or be boastful about these achievements, but I do recognize that few accomplishments are realized without the help and support of others. Thus, it is difficult for me to take full credit for those things for which I have been recognized. One such professional area that has received some recognition by others is that of research and scholarship. Several individuals in my field have identified me as a prolific multicultural counseling scholar, and I have received several early career awards for my accomplishments. My scholarly contributions also have been noted in my appointment to several editorial boards in the field. For example, I have served as senior editor of the *Journal of Multicultural Counseling and Development* and as associate editor of both the *Journal of Black Psychology* and *Cultural Diversity and Ethnic Minority Psychology*. I have enjoyed conducting research related to the experiences of people of color and other marginalized populations, particularly with regard to their use (and avoidance) of counseling and other psychological services when they may experience problems. Moreover, one of my professional goals has been to examine the extent to which counselors and other mental health professionals possess appropriate levels of competence in working with diverse cultural populations when such populations do access mental health services. I received an Outstanding Research Award from the American Counseling Association for my contributions in this regard.

At times throughout my career, I have struggled with trying to balance my professional goals with personal ones. However, I must admit that I am very much satisfied with the direction my life has taken over the years. It is hard to regret the many blessings and rewards I have received from making conscious choices over the years to focus primarily on developing my career. My mother often has remarked to others and me that I have not experienced a shortage of marriage proposals, but I believe I have not been ready to pursue marriage with the same type of commitment and energy that I have directed toward my career. I think it would have been difficult to focus on developing my career while trying to attend to familial responsibilities, such as being an attentive and loving spouse and rearing healthy and centered children. I have great admiration for women academics and other female professionals who are able to "do it all" with seemingly relative ease. I am single currently and I am not entirely certain that I will ever choose to get married, but I do feel a strong need to be a parent and rear a child or children who will add yet another dimension to my already satisfying life.

Bridging Practice, Theory, and Science in My Development as a Counselor

Because of my spiritual background and beliefs, I believe that people are fundamentally good in their essence and spirit and that socialization in its many forms strongly shapes who and what we become throughout life. Many things influence these socialization processes, especially people and other living things. I acknowledge that there is an interconnectedness of beings that develops the basis for humans' ability to relate to other living beings and things. Similarly, there is an interconnectedness of practice, theory, and science in the field of counseling and in my own development as a counselor. Without clinical practice, which can provide counselors with a plethora of information about the personal and interpersonal functioning of a vast range of clients, initial theoretical formulations on which to integrate and synthesize the complexity of clients' concerns would not be possible. Similarly, without a strong theoretical foundation with which counselors can understand clients' issues, it would be difficult for them to formulate cogent questions that could be investigated empirically. In turn, it would be difficult to discern the etiology and extent of clients' concerns without engaging in some investigating (e.g., asking questions). In addition, as a person who engages in more research than theory-building or practice, I am convinced that both theory and practice inform my research questions and directions, and that one of the primary goals of counseling research is to identify means by which effective practice can occur. It is my ultimate hope that such research can have implications for the development of policy and practice in counseling. Hence, in my opinion, the interplay of practice, theory, and science in counseling is a virtual given.

Clients, professional peers, and supervisors have described me as a "relational" person. As a natural extrovert who has become increasingly introverted with age (much by design), I have gained a great deal of awareness about my impact on others. Although I do not perceive myself as a powerful person (in the "referent" or "expert" sense), I have been told that I have much personal power. I recognize that some individuals' perceptions of how powerful I seem to be often relate to their conceptions (and stereotypes) about the strength of Black women in general. As a person who tends to be more direct than indirect in relating with others, I strive to understand the needs and desires of others while expressing my own wishes in both professional and personal relationships. Although it would be wonderful to me if everyone liked and valued me, I am not overly concerned with pleasing others to the point that I would sacrifice myself unduly or "sell out." I have learned that it is important to be happy with myself despite my imperfections or "growth edges," because doing so is the key to self-acceptance, self-confidence, and self-love.

When working with clients who come in for counseling with problems that focus on interpersonal functioning, I believe strongly in using a relational approach to understanding their concerns and helping them to gain insight. I do believe that nearly all clients possess the ability to change and alter their ways of being, but many of these individuals are afraid to abandon their suboptimal ways of functioning in favor of optimal ones. I think it takes courage for clients and others to change things about themselves that are familiar and dear to their hearts, despite the fact that these things might be personally destructive or unhealthy. I applaud and encourage people who are risk-takers in terms of changing things about themselves that do not serve them well.

Journey to Becoming a Multicultural Counselor

There have been several other experiences that have shaped my ability to integrate cultural issues into my work as a counselor and researcher. As discussed earlier in this chapter, my journey to becoming a multicultural counselor began during my master's program, when I began to challenge both professors and clinical supervisors to resist viewing the experiences of clients of color and other marginalized populations from a deficit perspective. From reading much of the information contained in counseling textbooks related to the experiences of populations of color, I recognized that many of these books' authors did not truly understand what it meant to be a person or color, a woman, or even a person who came from a financially impoverished background. Most of what fell under "disadvantaged populations" within these textbooks is covered now much more extensively and appropriately under the heading "culturally diverse populations." The ability to conceptualize the experiences of marginalized populations from strength-based perspectives has helped the counseling profession move away from Eurocentric approaches to understanding human behavior and intervene with a wide variety of cultural groups. I am so happy to see this more affirmative and culturally sensitive approach to working with clients from diverse backgrounds.

Another important experience that encouraged my commitment to addressing cultural issues in the field of counseling occurred in the context of my training as a doctoral student. As a Black doctoral student in a program full of White peers, I often felt that some of my classmates were reluctant to speak out against blatant oppression and racism within the context of the program because of the privileges they experienced being a member of the White racial group. This was pretty isolating and discouraging to me. Although many of my peers were women, who I presumed had some understanding of sexism, I found that many of these women seemed more willing to buy into the status quo rather than challenge issues of gender oppression and inequity.

From viewing the behaviors of my professors, supervisors, and peers, I came to the realization that I would not be satisfied with standing on the sidelines and not working to combat social injustices such as racism, classism, sexism, and homophobia. Many of my experiences, such as those delineated above, have underscored my belief about the importance of counselors working to eradicate societal issues that adversely affect the mental health of both victims and perpetrators. It is clear to me that racism and other forms of discrimination do not just affect people of color. They affect Whites as well, albeit in ways in which many Whites are unaware. I believe it is part of my life's work to make our society one that perpetuates mental health at the individual, familial, and community levels.

Future Goals and Directions of the Field

Although I have achieved many of the goals I identified for myself earlier in my career, I would like to continue being a productive member of the counseling profession by continuing my research and clinical work, teaching counselors and psychologists about the importance of being culturally competent, working to eradicate oppression and discrimination at a broad level, and providing service to professional organizations in the fields of counseling and psychology. The work of becoming a culturally competent counseling psychologist does not end. The process is ongoing, and this is one of the things that I value most about being in a profession in which personal growth is encouraged actively over one's professional and personal life span.

I believe the counseling profession, as a whole, is in a wonderful place at this point in time. As counseling professionals, we have achieved much progress in our field in terms of addressing cultural diversity issues, but we must not rest on our laurels. There is much more work to be done, and the increasingly culturally diverse society that is the United States will continue to challenge counselors to work toward the valuing of cultural pluralism.

Words of Advice for Trainees and Young Professionals

Over the years, many students and young professionals have asked me for "words of wisdom" to help guide them through their career paths. I have offered many suggestions to them at various points, and below are some examples of the advice I have given.

1. This may be obvious to many people, but it is important to be your genuine self. There might be many people you encounter throughout life who would feel more comfortable if you were more like them. Without a true understanding of who you are fundamentally, it will be difficult to feel accepted by others for the person that is you!
2. There is nothing wrong with having high standards of yourself and others. Always strive to put your best efforts forward. Even if you fail after doing so, you will be able to rest assured that you've done your best.
3. Identify your strengths and limitations and surround yourself with honest people who can validate your strengths and help you to improve your shortcomings. These people can serve as reality checks for you throughout your life.
4. It does not take an inordinate amount of intelligence to succeed at most things in life. Persistence is the key to achieving many professional and personal goals, so do not give up on doing that which you truly love.
5. Remain connected to those individuals who mean most to you in your life. They will serve as a vital support system in both celebrating your accomplishments and providing nurturance during times of difficulty.

6. Work carefully to balance your professional and personal life. There is only one of you, so you must take care of yourself in order to take care of others effectively.
7. If much of your professional work focuses on issues of cultural diversity, find a network of supportive colleagues and friends to assist you with your work. There will be many individuals you encounter who will attempt to convince you that this work is too marginalized, too personal, too controversial, or too difficult to get published. Stay encouraged about achieving your goals and fulfilling your professional passions.
8. Question the status quo when warranted. Do not assume that all written words are the truth and that all policies and rules are fair and equitable. Oppression occurs in many forms, so it is important not to be brainwashed into assuming that what is "standard" or "the norm" benefits everyone. Strive for justice for all!
9. Be courageous in word and in deed! Most successful people have experienced both challenges and setbacks, but common characteristics that these individuals possess are courage and the ability to take appropriate risks.
10. Read literature written by laypersons in order to deepen your understanding of literature written by colleagues in our field.
11. The best way to develop sensitivity to issues of cultural diversity is to immerse yourself in opportunities (e.g., forming meaningful friendships and traveling) in which you are exposed to culturally different others.
12. In the field of counseling, I believe "the professional is the personal" in the sense that it is difficult to separate who counselors are personally from what they do. In fact, I believe that what I do as a counseling professional is a reflection of who I am, and I am proud to embrace a life role that has brought me much satisfaction and joy.

Chapter 11

Some Advice You Will Never Take
••

Jeffrey A. Kottler

Act 1, Scene 1

"Mom, open the door. Come on, let me in!"

I put my ear to the door and listened for any sound inside the room. Nothing. I tried the door handle again, but it was solidly locked.

"Ma, please open the door. It's me. It's just me. Come on, let me in." I banged with my fist to punctuate the urgency I felt.

"Leave me alone," the muffled voice behind the door said. I could just barely make out the words, but I could tell for certain that my mother was crying. Although only 12 years old, I was already an expert on the language of tears.

"Mom," I called out again, a little relieved that she had at least talked back to me. "Just let me in, okay? I'm not going to go away until you OPEN THE DOOR RIGHT NOW!"

I heard the lock click and then the sound of footsteps moving away. I opened the door a crack and found my mother in bed, the covers up to her chin. The room was completely dark, and the shades drawn and curtains tightly closed, even though it was three in the afternoon. I glanced at the nightstand and saw the tumbler of Chivas Regal. There was ice left but the scotch had been drained.

"Mom, you've got to get out of bed. Please."

I had just returned from school, a half hour ahead of my younger brothers, to find my mother barricaded inside her room. It was not at all unusual that she would spend long periods of time alone in her room or that she would be crying. I almost never remember seeing her without a glass of scotch on the table beside her. But it was highly unusual that she'd still be up there so late in the day, especially with the door shut.

My mother was crying continuously now, her back turned away from me. "What's wrong, Ma? Can I do something for you? Do you want something?"

"Just leave me alone," she said, or I think that's what she said, as her face was buried in a pillow.

"Please talk to me, Mom. Tell me what's wrong."

"You know what's wrong," she answered with sudden anger. "There's nothing more to say. I want you to leave the room, close the door, and give me some peace."

Yes, in a way, I did have some idea of what was wrong. Since my father had moved out a year earlier, my mother had become even more depressed than usual. She was never easy for me to be around with her mood swings, but now it was so much worse. She had asked me to come once to see her psychiatrist with her, thinking that I could use some help as well. But what I told the doctor when we were alone was that my only regret was that my father didn't take me with him when he moved out. He left me alone with my mother, to take care of my younger brothers. And now she was not only drinking more than ever but also frequently threatening to kill herself. Sometimes she told me that I was helping to keep her alive; other times she said I'd be the death of her. One time much later I asked my brothers if they'd ever had heart-to-heart talks like this with our mother, but they were too young to remember.

Act 1, Scene 2

"Doctor, this is Jeffrey Kottler. I met you once with my mother, Lois."

"Yes, Jeffrey, of course! What can I do for you?"

"Well, I found your number in my mother's phone book."

"Yes?"

Then it all rushed out of me. "My mom's in bed, Doctor, and she won't get out. She locked the door again."

"Again?" he said, confused by the torrent coming out of me through my own tears.

"Yeah. She locked it before but I got her to open it. Then I went in to see if she was okay, but she's not. She's really bad, Doctor. She's never been like this."

"What do you mean?" he asked. Initially, he seemed distracted and confused about why this kid was calling him on the phone. But now I had his full attention.

I hesitated, feeling disloyal, as if I was betraying my mother by asking an outsider for help. "I think she took some pills," I said.

"What kind of pills?"

"I don't know," I said, sobbing and struggling with my own tears. "Her voice doesn't sound right—it's kind of slurred."

"You mean from drinking?" The doctor already knew about my mother's scotch habit.

"I think it's something else," I tried to explain. I was desperate, and afraid he wasn't going to believe me. "There were some pills open on the nightstand. And her voice was weird. She said some things, some bad things. And I don't know what to do. Doctor, what should I do?"

Act 2, Scene 1

I know it might seem unlikely, but it seemed more serendipitous than intentional that I ended up studying psychology. In truth, I was originally enrolled in college as a business major, because that's what my father was, and what he wanted me to be. Both my grandfathers were businessmen, and it was expected that I would some day come into the family printing business.

But first I'd have to get through the first day of orientation, and so far, it was looking pretty bleak. I looked around the room and noticed that it was filled with earnest young men, all men as a matter of fact. Most of them were wearing collared shirts, some ties. I remember thinking to myself, "These are not my people. I don't belong here."

There was just no way that I was going to spend the next four years in the company of these lifeless drones with their dreams of climbing the corporate ladder. Besides, I much preferred the company of a more gender-balanced class.

I fled the business orientation only to find myself alone in the hallway. Now what was I going to do? I had no clue about what interested me, other than finding a girlfriend.

As it was, I had barely graduated from high school. I'm pretty sure I was not stupid, but I was not exactly well prepared for the rigors of serious study. Even today, as the author of over 50 books—some of them best sellers—I still can't tell the difference between the subject and object of a sentence, nor can I recognize an adverb unless it ends in *ly*. Algebra was even more tortuous for me. I remember the teacher asking me to come up to the board and balance an algebraic equation. I would stand there staring at the dumb thing and wonder why on Earth anyone would want to get some numbers from one side to the other. And what's with those *x*s and *y*s? I still have no idea what algebra is for, or why we are forced to study it.

The best explanation I can think of for why I was such an undistinguished student is that I couldn't see anything most of the time. It still amazes me that my parents never took me to get glasses when I used to sit about three feet in front of the television. They used to take me to Detroit Lions football games, and while everyone else was watching the action out on the field, I would look at the crowed around me. My father would yell excitedly, "Did you see that play? Did you see that guy make that run?" I'd just nod dumbly. In truth, I couldn't see anything of the field at all except a green blur.

I didn't know that I was half blind. I thought everyone saw the world as I did: blurry and indistinct. I was embarrassed about my poor vision, so I would memorize the eye chart at school and recite the letters from rote.

But this disability played havoc with any sense of accomplishment I desired. I could never see what was going on in class, so I lapsed into fantasy most of the time. I was exiled into right field on baseball teams, which was just as well because I could never see any ball that was hit my way. One summer I had a job as a caddy. The golfer would hit the ball and my job was to find it. The only way I ever found a ball was if I accidentally stepped on it.

Needless to say, getting glasses changed my life. For the first time, I could see the world relatively clearly. I was pretty far behind in school, but I began to realize that I was not as dumb as I (and my parents) had always thought I was.

I was admitted to college on probation, mostly because I was one of the few applicants who showed up for the interview without my parents. As an aside, the admissions officer who gave me that break and admitted me into the university with such a dismal academic record eventually became my colleague when I became a professor at that same institution 10 years later. We sat in a counselor education faculty meeting one time, and I confessed that we had a history.

Nobody really expected much from me in college. I was not particularly bright, talented, experienced, or ambitious. I remember sitting on the steps of the library one day watching students walk by. I wondered how to tell who was smart and who was not. I decided the smart kids carried books around, lots of books. It occurred to me that I could be smart too if I lugged books around and actually read them. I started doing that, and a strange thing happened—friends started treating me as if I was smart. They asked me for help with their schoolwork. I may not have been an athlete or a brilliant scholar or particularly good-looking, but I was going to work harder than anyone else. And I did.

Act 2, Scene 2

I am a junior in college, doing well academically and majoring in psychology. I am mostly enjoying my classes, but I'm far more involved in social activities, especially trying to work things out with the love of my life. Lately, it's been touch and go.

When my girlfriend decided she no longer wanted to continue to see me, I lost all semblance of control. I stopped going to classes. I went for long walks so that I could grieve in private. At one point, my pain became so intolerable that I had serious thoughts of suicide.

Although my mother did not actually kill herself with pills, she did die some years after that day she locked herself in her bedroom. The doctors said it was lung cancer, but I knew she had really died of her depression.

Now it felt like I had become like my mother: helpless, despondent, and with recurrent thoughts of suicide. I remembered her kindly psychiatrist, and although he had not really helped her much, I liked the wise, assured way in which he handled himself. It was time to see such a professional for myself.

Act 2, Scene 3

I had seen a psychologist at the counseling center on campus for a little over a year. She was psychoanalytically oriented, so I did most of the talking. She took notes, listened attentively, and occasionally offered an interpretation or two. I deliberately did and said things during sessions in order to get her to reveal more of herself, but I was mostly unsuccessful. I continued to talk and she listened.

The counseling helped a lot, and I greatly enjoyed the experience. My therapist was a bit aloof and cold (as befitting a proper analyst), not at all the warm and loving mother figure I most yearned for. Nevertheless, we covered a lot of ground, and I improved steadily.

I couldn't believe that people actually got paid to listen to and help others with their problems. As I was soon about to graduate, and had learned from a series of boring jobs that working really sucked, I was determined to stay in school just as long as I could. Graduate school in something—anything—was far preferable to holding a real job.

Mentors

One of my psychology professors invited me to do research with him on perception. I spent my extra time doing experiments on the autokinetic effect, a phenomenon in which people see moving light. I had a hypothesis that the direction that people perceived the light might reveal aspects of their personalities or life experiences. We never published the study, but it was the first time one of my teachers really believed in me. I also found that I enjoyed research.

I went to graduate school at Wayne State in Detroit at a time when it was one of the premier programs in the world. The whole field of guidance counseling was developed at a school right on the edge of campus.

My first teacher, in my very first class, was Wayne Dyer, who would soon become a best-selling author. It was an experiential group class in which we were expected to work on our personal issues and keep a log of the changes taking place. At the time I was engaged to marry a woman I did not love, but was fond of. I was also working in the family printing business, and I was miserable. I felt trapped but didn't see a way out.

I remember Dyer talking in his uniquely inspirational way about the possibilities of change that could take place in a group, if a person really wanted it. Before I could stop myself, I felt dizzy with the power of public declarations. I had seen how a group member could announce a goal or desire and then be held accountable to follow through, no matter how difficult and challenging that might be. Before I could even consider what I was saying, I abruptly announced to the group that by the following week I was going to be a changed man.

"How so?" someone challenged me. Dyer always required that goals be specific, descriptive, and attainable.

I said that during the following two weeks (spring break was coming up), I was going to end my engagement, quit my job, and start going to graduate school full time. Group members laughed because they thought I was kidding. I wasn't.

I booked a trip to Aruba for a week by myself. Besides a bathing suit, I took with me only counseling books and a tape series on counseling produced by Dyer and a collaborator, John Vriend. There were eight tapes. Every day for seven days I listened to one of the tapes twice, once in the morning and once in the afternoon. I sat under a divi-divi tree that overlooked the beach.

When I returned to the group, I announced rather proudly that I had followed through on my declared commitment. And then the real action began.

Dyer asked us to write a paper on the group experience, the sole basis for our grade in the class. It was to be called "My Behavior in Groups" and cover the history of our own group behavior in the various groups of our lives, including the class group. It was to be about 12 pages long.

I wrote a paper 70 pages long. I went absolutely nuts! I poured my heart out. I discovered my voice for the first time. This assignment so impressed me that now, 30 years later, it is still the final paper that I assign my group classes.

Dyer was also impressed with my paper, and he invited me to collaborate with him and John Vriend, another faculty member in the department, on an article they were working on.

Dyer soon left for fame and fortune, but John Vriend became my mentor during this early part of my career. Throughout graduate school I attended one of his counseling groups, and I still think that is where I honed most of my clinical skills. He invited me to join doctoral seminars while still a master's student, so I also got a tremendous vote of confidence. I think most of all, however, what John did was discover me as a writer.

At Vriend's urging, I began writing every day (and still do to this day). I started keeping a journal. We collaborated on articles and books, and while this produced little in terms of publishable products, he influenced me to begin thinking of myself not only as a counselor but as a writer.

One of the things good mentors do for students is not only teach them things but also open doors for them. John did this for me in a big way. We presented at conferences together (although often he did not show up). He introduced me to the shakers and movers in the field. He helped me do a reality check, confronting and challenging me all through our relationship. Most of all, he believed in me.

When it came time for me to move on, John found my next mentor for me, Bill Van Hoose, who was at the University of Virginia. By this time I was in a hurry to get out into the world. I didn't honestly believe I was going to learn much in my doctoral program; in fact, the politics were ferocious and the battles among the faculty were vicious. I just wanted to get the hell out of there as soon as I could, and I'm sure I set a world record for completing my program—14 months! I had actually written my dissertation before I began my program, and I had already accumulated doctoral credits while still a master's student. So, there I was, just turned 24 years old, and a newly minted professor.

What I Believe

I have never been able to separate the different professional roles I occupy as a counselor, a teacher, a supervisor, and an author, just as I haven't been able to do so between my personal and professional lives. I always thought it was the biggest gift of our field that we could use everything we learned in our jobs to make ourselves more fully functioning. Likewise, I have been a big fan of life experiences (especially travel to foreign lands) as a better teacher than anything found in books. Even though I plead guilty to being more responsible than most for contributing to the glut of counseling books on the market, I've learned a heck of a lot more from other sources. My secret confession is that I find most counseling and therapy books to be boring, repetitive, and without soul. They may inform me but they don't move me; they don't touch my heart. Of course, I can say this now, I suppose, because I spent the first 15 years of my career reading as many books in the field as I could. Now I would much prefer to read novels or nonfiction in other fields. I think most counselors and therapists are so parochial and narrow in their focus.

The other thing that has driven me to distraction is the obsession that writers and practitioners alike have with their favored theories. They have always seemed like religious wars to me, with each camp vying for more territory and wanting to debunk everyone else's ideas. I've been a psychodynamic counselor and done pretty well at it. I was a client-centered counselor in the best tradition of Carl Rogers and loved it. I was a raging fanatic as a rational emotive, cognitive therapist. I volunteered to be a client of Albert Ellis and then entered a training program on cognitive therapy. I have since been an existentialist, a behaviorist, and a constructivist (before I knew what that meant—or rather, I still don't know what that means).

I find it endlessly amusing when I read reviews of my books in which the authors label me as all of these, or they can't pin me down at all. In fact, when I was asked to do a video demonstrating my theory of counseling, I was more than willing to do so—except I wondered what the producer thought that was.

"Well," Jon Carlson said thoughtfully, "you're kind of existential, and a little cognitive, but mostly integrative."

"Exactly!" I agreed. "So what the heck do we call my theory?"

In truth, I'm not sure I have one. When I did that demonstration video, members in the audience counted interventions that I used as coming from 16 different theories. So I suppose that must mean that I am integrative, but my intellectual home is definitely among the existential humanists. I believe passionately in the importance of relationships.

It just amazes me how counselor educators and other educators—those who are supposed to be experts on human change—seem so clueless about following what is known about how this process takes place. No matter how interesting or entertaining, nobody listens to a lecture after the first 20 minutes. We all check out. Learning is all about relationships and creating meaningful experiences. That is why I think most courses in multiculturalism are ridiculous—as if sitting in class, reading a text, and having discussions is really going to impact anyone in an enduring, dramatic way.

That is why, in recent years, I've become intrigued with the metaphor of transformative travel. If you take inventory of the most significant learning experiences you've ever had—the ones that changed your life—I would be very surprised if they took place in a classroom. And I'd be shocked if they happened while reading a book like this.

I've been talking to people my whole life about the changes they've made, and the ones that have endured. In one way or another, most of these transformations took place during travel. I don't necessarily mean travel to another country (although this is probably the best way to do it) but travel in the sense of being transported to a novel environment that presents new challenges and opportunities to reinvent oneself. That's why listening to the tapes in my apartment would not have been as effective as doing so under a divi-divi tree in Aruba. It took me one year to pay off that trip as a starving student.

Following Orders

I'm supposed to talk about my development as a multicultural counselor, and I note that I am resisting this. I find this whole "requirement" in every conference and book to be more shallow and politically correct than truly authentic and meaningful. The bottom line is that counselors are not just about helping individual clients pursue their own particular (often selfish) goals, but also about working toward issues of social justice. This means challenging our own racist beliefs and prejudices, and it means taking a stand to become more honorable, loving, and respectful toward others.

Yet this whole multicultural thing reminds me of the McCarthy era, in which certain folks are monitoring what everyone else is saying and doing, making sure we toe the party line. As far as I'm concerned, this prevents a more frank and honest discussion of things. I believe everyone—even the most sanctimonious among us—is a racist. I believe that we all have preferences to hang out with people "like us" and avoid people "not like us." I believe that we all use our resources and power to help some people and not others, based on our personal preferences and biases. I believe we are all blind to some aspects of the ways we are hurtful to others, based on who they remind us of. I believe that race and religion and ethnicity are the tip of the iceberg; dominant cultures are just as often determined by socioeconomic class, hobbies, geography, profession, and a host of other factors.

So, where am I going with this rant? I have learned very little about multiculturalism from reading texts and books on the subject, studying the research in the area, attending workshops, and the like. As I mentioned, reading novels has taught me far more. But it is travel to new places that truly shaped most who I am and what I believe. I have lived in many, many places around the world (people have teased me for being flaky for moving around so much). I am hungry to read about people who live differently than I do, but I want to experience their lives. I have lived in rural Alabama, Southern California, Boston, Detroit, South Carolina, Virginia, and Las Vegas, each one a distinctly different culture. I have danced with the Bushmen of the Kalahari, practiced hula with my Native Hawaiian students, worked in Hong Kong, Singapore, Peru, Thailand, Nepal, Venezuela, Iceland, Australia, New Zealand, and a dozen other places. Each place I visit, I do my best to "join" the culture rather than sit on the outside as a tourist or visitor.

Advice You Won't Listen To

I have been asked to give advice to readers, which is an interesting paradox. I don't believe in advice. Nobody listens to it, or at least my advice. Just like you, I have strong opinions about what I think people should do with their lives. I see a client who is complaining that he doesn't have a love life and I want to say to him, "You want a love life? How about losing 40 pounds, getting contact lenses, changing your wardrobe, seeing a speech therapist to change that annoying sound you make, and then getting the hell out of your house so you might just meet someone?" I have this fantasy that the client will nod his head, say okay, and follow my instructions. But it never happens.

Same with self-help books. I can't figure out why anyone buys these things. Heck, I've written a half dozen of them myself and it seems futile. Same with diet books, which are always best sellers. If these things worked, why would we need more of them?

So, here I am, supposed to give you, the reader, some advice or words of wisdom that will make some difference. And this occurs in a context when you've already read a bunch of other narratives just like this one. So, for the 10 or 11 of you who are still with me, this is what I have to say to you: forget advice. It just flat out doesn't work. You won't any more do what people in this book tell you to do than any other bunch of advice people have given you your whole life.

I'm not saying that the collective wisdom of the "elders" represented in this book is not worth hanging on to, or at least paying attention to. I'm just saying that there is no sense of drama or ritual to accompany these words. And that's why it won't stick.

Go ahead, prove me wrong. I dare you.

Now that I have your attention, here's some advice you won't follow. You should also keep in mind that many of the other notable folks in this volume would strongly disagree with these bits of wisdom. So, here we go.

Counseling is not about content. Throughout your training you will have to pretend as if learning theories and research and such are important (and they do provide a foundation for what you will do), but they are small things compared to the relationships you develop—not just with your instructors but your peers. I think it's strange that students never take notes on what other students say, only the teacher (because it won't be on the exam).

That's another thing: grades don't matter. You will not take this advice either, but take it from a straight *A*, compulsive student: nobody will ever look at your grades again after you graduate. Employers won't care about them. Even doctoral programs consider other factors far more predictive of success.

Another piece of advice you won't listen to is that it is more important to be a counselor than to do counseling. Beginners are obsessed with technique—making sure you reflect feelings just so or proceed according to your treatment plan. But consider who impacted you in your life and how they did it. Was it with some amazing, fancy technique? I don't think so. It is not just what you do that matters, but who you are. That means that learning to be a counselor is not just about going to school; it is about walking a path. It is about practicing what you preach. It is about taking risks. It is about pushing your own limits. It is about living your life the way you would like others to lead their own—with integrity and honor and honesty.

As I said, this sounds good, but you won't do it; hardly anyone else does. Instead, we are obsessed with accumulating our continuing education hours, keeping the license up, obtaining degrees, and getting certifications, as if all that really matters in the big scheme of things.

A Confession

I know I'm on a rant here. But I'm taking risks with you because I am pretty sure I am going to erase this file and decide not to send in my chapter. Fred and Bob, the editors, are good friends of mine. We've had some adventures together. I feel indebted to them. So that's why I agreed to do this. But now I'm sorry I made that commitment.

Actually, right now it is Father's Day, and I'm on a plane to Orlando to do a keynote address at a conference. I am not with my family. I'm not with my father or my son. The truth is, I'm such a hypocrite. Here I am giving you advice, as if I have something to say, and I actually have the audacity to tell you to live your most cherished principles just as I am violating my own at this minute.

I would rather be surfing. I would rather be home. I'd rather be doing a lot of things other than what I'm doing right now—traveling across the country. I don't need the money. I don't need more recognition. I've written 50 books, and I'm producing an average of four more every year. What's wrong with this picture? Is this ambition gone haywire?

So, that's another reason to not take my advice. I can't deliver in my own life what I am asking of you. I am far too driven and ambitious and achievement oriented. I want to be known, and in my misguided, neurotic way I think that if only I write one more book or one more chapter like this, somehow I will feel good enough.

Sometime you might want to check out a dozen or two of my books, and you'll find a common theme running throughout all of them. I talk a lot about this journey we have chosen as counselors. I don't see it as a job or even as a profession, but as a calling. Our mission on this planet is to do good, to help people, to make a difference if we can.

I talk a lot about feeling like a failure, of coming up short. I was not able to save my mother, and I can barely save myself. I spend an inordinate amount of time thinking about my lapses, misjudgments, failures, and imperfections—I've written a dozen books on that subject alone.

I think I'm making progress. I'm almost at the point where I am ready to stop writing, or at least publishing. What more can I say that I haven't said before? That's why I want to delete this file. What is new in here that I haven't said before? Nothing.

What I like most about being a counselor (and I've said this a hundred times before) is that I feel a commitment to pushing myself to the next level, or dimension, of experience. I am a ferocious risk-taker. That's why, at age 52, I've taken up surfing. That's why I want to roam every inch of the globe.

That's why I want to try everything I can in the short time I have left. But most of all, like you, I want more love and to love more.

Questions, Answers, and Secrets

People frequently ask me how I manage to sustain such consistent productivity, turning out a new book (400 manuscript pages) every three months. It is perhaps ironic that for someone who is so self-critical and overly focused on mistakes and failures, I have a very supportive, fluid voice in my head when it comes to writing. I've been told that I write exactly as I talk, and that's true: I rarely have to rewrite anything or agonize over how I want to say it. These very words flow out of me, and I could write like this all day, every day. In fact, I do just that.

The truth is that I have to write. I can't help myself. I would just as soon write as do anything else. People ask me how I find the time to write, and I never understand that question. Why would I need to find time to do something I love?

The second question I'm asked most often that is just as puzzling to me is *when* I write, as if the time matters. I have written anywhere, any time, any place. I have literally written articles or chapters on menus and toilet paper. I write when I can't sleep (a not infrequent occurrence since I am "blessed" with needing little sleep). I write on airplanes. I write in between clients or classes. I write whenever I can.

I don't care what I write about either—I just love the process of creation. Right now I am working on a half dozen different books at one time. I do this because I hate waiting for others to do their jobs. I am always waiting for coauthors, editors, and production people to do their parts and get back to me. I start a book and send it in. Then I have to wait for someone else to do their job. So, while I'm waiting, I start another book. See what happens?

I was talking about my eclectic tastes. I am working on revising a few of my textbooks but I don't much enjoy these tasks—too predictable and routine. I am completing a book about research, trying to make the subject interesting. I'm sure you'd agree this is a very challenging assignment. I'm also working on a textbook on stress management, a huge project that involves covering the whole territory but in a way that makes the subject accessible to students.

Let's see: I just finished a series of four books with Jon Carlson in which we interviewed the world's most prominent theoreticians to ask them about their worst failures *(Bad Therapy)*, best sessions *(The Finest Hour)*, most unusual cases *(The Mummy at the Dining Room Table)*, and their most personally influential case *(The Client Who Changed Me)*. I am also working on a book about the connection between creativity and madness throught the lives of nine artists in literature, art, theater, and music.

What I mean to say by all this is that I am interested in everything. Being a counselor made me that way. Every client has a different story to tell, a different world for me to explore. I figure I've taught the group counseling class a hundred or more times, and it is always different. This year alone, I am teaching it not only twice at my university in Fullerton, but also in Nepal, Australia, and Hong Kong. And I keep learning so much about groups, and myself, in this process.

If I have had any sort of success in this essay/story/narrative/ confession, then I have developed some sort of connection with you—a relationship—even though we have never met.

So, here is my secret: In my teaching, in my counseling, and in my writing, I try to be as vulnerable, open, and honest as I can. I figure if I can model that kind of truth-seeking, then maybe that will inspire you to do the same.

Theory and Practice

Although I've been doing counseling, as well as teaching and writing about it for a long time, I still can't claim to understand the process very well. Furthermore, I don't trust those who say (or think) they do. I think the whole enterprise of helping someone is so complex and involves so many dimensions and factors that it is impossible to truly grasp what is really going on.

When someone is helped by some counseling encounter, we are left to wonder what really made the difference. Can we trust what our clients or the families report? Which extraneous variables may have served as a significant influence?

I know that we all have our favored theories. Every practitioner feels passionately that his or her preferred ideology is the best road to truth, but I've never been convinced that such theories were not more about the counselor's comfort and intolerance for ambiguity than truly about serving the client. I know theories help us to organize ideas, conceptualize what might be going on with a case, and even plan how we want to intervene, but it has always befuddled me how so many supposedly oppositional theories all seem to work equally well. I've written a lot of books on this subject—on the universal features of all helping systems—but I still struggle with the bigger picture of trying to explain how we can confront someone, or reflect their feelings, or dispute their cognitive distortions, or restory their narratives, or whatever, and have all these approaches be useful. The only, inescapable conclusion that I've settled on is that all good counselors really do essentially the same things no matter what languages they use, what they report they are doing, or what philosophies they espouse. I think all good counselors inspire people (even if we do it in different ways). I think we all offer support and safety. We all challenge clients to think or feel or behave differently. We all provide a structure for sorting things out and developing some action plan. We all facilitate some kind of altered state of consciousness in our sessions such that clients become more suggestible and more open to new ideas. We all promote basically the same ideas—that greater options and opportunities are possible, that it is better to have more rather than fewer choices, and that growth occurs with taking risks and experimenting with new behaviors. We all believe that change is possible with sufficient motivation, initiative, and courage.

I don't even think there are distinct theories any more; I think the boundaries have collapsed between them. Theorists who used to be cognitive theorists now call themselves constructivists. Humanists have embraced tenets from Choice Theory. Psychodynamic practitioners use systemic thinking in their work. Everyone uses the ideas borrowed from other frameworks such that the lines are blurred from one to the other. We may still persist in calling ourselves a particular sort of practitioner, but the reality is that in the privacy of our offices, we use anything and everything at our disposal, no matter where it originated.

So, where does that leave you, the relative newcomer to the field? Pick a theory, any theory, and stick with it for a little while. This will make your teacher, supervisor, or mentor happy and will give you a common language to speak. It also narrows considerably the body of knowledge and repertoire of practice for you to master, or at least familiarize yourself with. Then, slowly, gradually, incrementally, cautiously, and impulsively, start building on this foundation as you evolve and gain experience. Your clients will constantly challenge your current standards of practice, not to mention your abilities and skills. This is what will motivate you to learn more and familiarize yourself with other therapeutic systems that will provide additional options. Just as with our clients, it is good to have more options of what you can do in a given situation. This way you can co-create with your clients an individualized treatment plan that is maximally responsive to their needs, interests, situation, cultural context, and presenting issues.

My Work Style

Let me start off by confessing that in order to remain so productive, I play as hard as I work. I don't go anywhere to do a presentation or workshop unless there is some opportunity for adventure or discovery built in. I am off this week to Australia to teach for a few weeks, but then I will spend a week surfing and scuba diving. I go to Hong Kong soon thereafter to teach again, but only because I want to explore that part of the world.

When I used to teach the career class, I would define work as something you have to do and play is something you want to do. I still believe this. And it means that I rarely work in my life at all. I would do most of what I'm doing for free; I can't believe I get paid at all for what I do!

I also try hard to practice what I preach to others. I tell clients and students that the way we feel about what we are doing depends so much on how we choose to think and conceptualize these activities. When I catch myself resenting, resisting, dreading, or otherwise not liking a certain task, I remind myself I have several choices: I can decide not to do it, I can continue to whine and complain about it and feel sorry for myself, or I can change my attitude about it and make it into something fun and engaging. I almost always choose the last option. And I can teach this to others quite well because I am so skilled at doing it in my own life.

Chapter 12

Work Can Be Fun
• •

Marianne H. Mitchell

Born to Be a Counselor

I was born in Toledo, Ohio, to parents whose parents were immigrants to the United States. My father was also an immigrant, arriving from England when he was 15 years old. My maternal grandparents emigrated from Switzerland as young adults. I suspect that their backgrounds and also the fact that I still have many close relatives living overseas were an early influence on my tolerance and desire to understand peoples of all backgrounds and nationalities.

From the earliest days of my life, it was clear that I possessed the characteristics desirable for successful counseling. In the hospital nursery, I exhibited unconditional positive regard, I am told, smiling at everyone and anyone. I also showed a strong tendency for reflection of feeling by crying when anyone else in the nursery began to squall. As best as I can recall, my preschool years were relatively uneventful, although I am told that I did continue to develop my human relationship skills, often inviting all the neighborhood children home for dinner. Despite the lack of a counselor in my elementary school (elementary school counselors were very rare at that time), I did manage to survive and thrive. In fact, my work experience began in the third grade, when I took over my brother's paper route of more than 100 customers. I didn't break any glass ceilings, but I did manage to crack a few glass windows. In the sixth grade, I advanced up the career ladder when I was employed by a local bakery. Although the pay was minimal, I did get to eat all the desserts I wanted and my friends came in frequently to see me. My next job was as a soda jerk with the same fringe benefits (and same low pay). In these early jobs, I found that I enjoyed interacting with people of all ages and backgrounds, and they apparently enjoyed interacting with me.

In my adolescence and college years, I continued to engage in jobs that were people oriented, such as lifeguard and aquatic director at a YMCA. A characteristic of all my jobs was that they were fun. (This was probably the beginning of my philosophy that work or one's career should be something one enjoys doing.)

Warming Up—Even If I Didn't Know for What

My first thoughts regarding a lifetime career were pushed upon me when I entered DeVilbiss High School in Toledo, Ohio. My parents left no doubt in my mind that my education was not finished until I completed college. My commitment to their goals was enhanced by my educational experiences, from elementary school through undergraduate college, in which I was fortunate to have many outstanding teachers who served as role models, while encouraging me to achieve my potential. My 10th-grade English teacher particularly reinforced teaching as both an educational and career goal for which I should strive. She stimulated my earlier thoughts of becoming a teacher. While I engaged in the usual fun activities of high school life, I never lost sight of my career goal of becoming a teacher.

Mileposts Along the Way

After graduation from high school, I entered the School of Education at the University of Toledo and prepared to become a secondary school English teacher. Although counselor education programs were beginning to appear in numerous universities across the country at that time, there was no such graduate program at the University of Toledo. (Little did I suspect that six years later, I would become the first graduate assistant in the new Counselor Education Program at the university.) I enjoyed my undergraduate life at the University of Toledo. I joined a sorority and continued to participate in my synchronized swimming activities. (Synchronized swimming was new at the time, so I had to explain to my nonswimming friends why I was spending so much time acting like a fish in water.) This activity also enabled me to travel to demonstration and competitive meets, usually in warm weather places such as Florida. I had a great undergraduate experience, but like most of my class, was happy to finally graduate, and in my naïveté, I thought I had finished my formal education. I did recognize the necessity of getting a job, as my parents began to gently remind me, and they were really delighted when I secured a job as an English teacher at Toledo Woodward High School. (This is a school that today probably would be considered an urban or inner-city school.)

I enjoyed my high school students very much and also learned from them and their diverse backgrounds and cultures. Many of them came to me frequently for advice, and I often wished that I was more knowledgeable and skilled to provide them with the kind of assistance they needed. I began to think of going to graduate school to improve myself in this regard.

Testing the Water and Plunging In

As I discussed the possibility of graduate school with several of my friends, one of my close friends, who was a counselor in the Toledo public school system, encouraged me to enter the master's degree program in counseling at the University of Toledo. This was a new and developing program and had just been approved to offer the first doctoral degree program in the College of Education. I submitted an application for admission to the master's degree program in counseling and in short order was notified of my acceptance. I was both thrilled and uneasy as I began my initial course work, but these feelings quickly subsided as I found my fellow students, as well as the faculty, excited about these new developments and the opportunities they might provide.

When I completed my master's degree, the newly approved doctoral program in counseling offered its first graduate assistantship. Although the pay was minimal and the duties maximal, I applied for this position and was fortunate enough to be chosen. My timing couldn't have been better because the university had been among the early programs selected to offer National Defense Education Act (NDEA) institutes and was later chosen to be the only university to offer an overseas NDEA institute in 1962. As the only graduate assistant in the department, I found myself on my way to Weisbaden, Germany, in July 1962, along with four faculty and three volunteer assistants. My six weeks' experience in Germany plunged me into the waters of international teaching, research, and multicultural contacts. This was clearly a life-changing event!

Although unusual today and perhaps even then, the University of Toledo also provided travel monies for graduate assistants to attend national conventions. I attended my first national counseling convention in Denver, Colorado, in the spring of 1961. The university chartered sleeping coaches to take all faculty and graduate assistants to Denver and back from Toledo. This in itself was a grand experience. The convention was a source of constant awe and highlights for me. At that time, we had a unified counseling profession so that attendance of 10,000–12,000 members at the national convention was common. The sheer size of the convention ensured one of many options in program choice. A highlight for me was meeting many of the distinguished members of our profession. These experiences further reinforced my belief that I had entered the right field.

The University of Toledo also had a distinguished speaker series that enabled me to personally meet outstanding professionals in our field at that time such as Ed Williamson and William Dugan (University of Minnesota), Walter Johnson and Ray Hatch (Michigan State University), Ray Patouillet (Columbia University), and C. Harold McCully (U.S. Office of Education). In addition to these experiences, I was almost immediately immersed in funded research projects competitively awarded to the Counselor Education Department by the Ford Foundation and the U.S. Office of Education.

Enjoying the Swim

As I progressed in my doctoral program, I became more involved in the research activities of the counseling department (even though the number of graduate assistantships had now doubled and there were two of us!). I particularly enjoyed working on the Ford Foundation funded project titled "The High School Dropout Goes to College." In this project I became acquainted with a number of high school dropouts, again from diverse cultural backgrounds, who had been given a second chance and were now succeeding as undergraduate college students. The other influential research project in which I had a major involvement was a study funded by the U.S. Office of Education comparing the academic achievements of students in selected elementary schools in the United States and the British Isles. In this project, I traveled with a research team to various school systems not only in the United States but also in England, Scotland, and Northern Ireland three times a year. I became personally well acquainted with distinguished educators in these countries and have been honored to have them as professional colleagues for many years since.

Perhaps the biggest impression I made during these studies was not academic, but occurred when I made a running jump of approximately 10 feet from the wharf in Glasgow to land on the fantail of the departing Belfast Ferry. Crew members were astounded. One of my colleagues told the crew that I was a former Olympic broad jumper (not true, of course, but they treated me very deferentially after that!). My brief leap into fame was motivated by the fact that all of my research team was already on the departing ferry and waving me on! I also made another impression when at a lunch with distinguished British educators, I sat on the hat of Dr. P. E. Vernon (coauthor of the Allport-Vernon Scales), watched him search for it when he was getting ready to leave our luncheon, and finally discovered it when I got up to shake his hand good-bye!

Now to Work!

As I marched down the aisle to receive my doctoral diploma at the University of Toledo, it dawned on me that I now had to go to work for real. That spring I was interviewed at the American Counseling Association (ACA) San Francisco convention by, among others, Dr. Leslie Carlin at Central Michigan University. I was shortly thereafter offered a position as the initial counselor educator at Central Michigan University in Mt. Pleasant, Michigan. As a department of one, I felt somewhat overwhelmed on occasion and often wondered if I should put a few gray streaks in my hair, since nearly all of my students appeared to be older than I was! At least I could enjoy departmental meetings at my breakfast table or in my car while driving to work. Despite such perks, it made for a heavy workload, including teaching the majority of the required counseling courses offered (often five courses a semester) in the initial year of my employment. I enjoyed my several years at Central Michigan University and had the satisfaction of seeing my efforts rewarded by increased enrollment in the Counselor Education program.

In the spring of 1966, the ACA national convention was held in Minneapolis, Minnesota, where I met Dr. Paul F. Munger (he had attended my convention presentation). At the time, Dr. Munger was the chairman of the Department of Counselor Education at Indiana University. He invited me to apply for a position in their program (they were particularly interested in hiring a female). After a fun but exhaustive series of interviews, to my surprise I was offered the position before I left Bloomington, and I happily accepted on the spot. (With the exception of two years, I remained the only female faculty member for nearly 30 years.)

Enjoying the Ride on the Fast Track

Even though I had previous experience at several universities, including that of a student, my orientation to Indiana University was a delightful eye-opener. Here I was, ex-soda-fountain jerk from Toledo on one of the most beautiful campuses and most academically prestigious universities in the country, in a counselor education program consistently ranked in the top 10!

In the initial months I often felt a sense of exuberance at my good fortune. My delight was further compounded when I found that I was entitled to a graduate assistant. I promptly recruited one of my former students from Central Michigan University, who accepted the opportunity with enthusiasm to come and pursue her doctorate. This was the first of a long series of outstanding graduate assistants whom I enjoyed. My satisfaction didn't end when they graduated, however, as many of them went on to distinguished careers in counselor education. I am proud to say most of them have remained my close friends over the years, which is perhaps one of the greatest fringe benefits of my tenure at Indiana University.

In addition to teaching one or two courses a semester, I immediately became involved in the expected activities of professional writing and funded research. In this regard, I wrote periodical articles, authored a monograph, and then began a series of textbook writings with my current coauthor, Robert L. Gibson. I also continued my international research activities, which had begun at the University of Toledo in elementary school comparative studies; directed a study of pupil personnel services in the United States and selected European countries; codirected a study of common educational problems in the United States and the British Isles; and then became involved in comparative studies of secondary school students in these countries. These studies had large staffs of both faculty and graduate research assistants, so with at least three trips abroad each year, I began to feel somewhat like a travel agent! In this process I was able to continue the many close friendships with professional educators in the United Kingdom that I had formed earlier. I was also developing close friendships in the various school systems in the United States that were participating in these studies. Such friendships were a great fringe benefit that I had not anticipated when thinking of the old university adages of "publish or perish" and "research or rot." While my research activities both at home and abroad continued throughout my professional career, two significant and highly rewarding activities that grew out of these research projects were at the invitation of educational authorities in Scotland and Bermuda: the initiation of counselor training programs for their teachers. These programs continued for over 30 years. These were wonderful experiences in which I could really see counseling making a difference in the national educational systems of Scotland and Bermuda. These contributions were acknowledged in writing by prominent citizens in both countries, including the Premier of Bermuda and the Chairperson of the National Research Council of Scotland.

From the university's standpoint, these programs were a smashing enrollment success, since in many summers the number of enrollees in both the Bermuda and Scotland programs exceeded the number of enrollees on the Bloomington campus (and our campus enrollment was always substantial). An additional benefit to the university was that unobtrusively we recruited a significant number of advanced-degree students in counselor education from these countries. The many friends and former students I have in these countries led one of my colleagues to remark that I could never rob a bank in Bermuda or Scotland because too many people would recognize me as I walked out in my ski mask.

Another of the many highlights of my experiences in these countries was the opportunity to chair (ably assisted by my good friend and professional colleague Margaret Jarvie, then at Moray House College of Education in Edinburgh) the International Convention of the American Counseling Association in Edinburgh, Scotland, in the summer of 1992. In addition to counselors representing 13 countries, I was particularly pleased by the large number of our former Scottish students who took advantage of the opportunity to hear the many distinguished speakers on the program.

Throughout my career, I also enjoyed and benefited tremendously from my professional service activities. Within the university, perhaps my most interesting and challenging service responsibility was as chair of the Indiana University Athletic Committee and Indiana University's Faculty Representative to the Big Ten and National Collegiate Athletic Association (NCAA), positions I held for nine years. In this role, I had the privilege of becoming acquainted with such outstanding coaches as Sam Bell (track), Doc Counsilman (swimming), Bob Knight (basketball), Bill Mallory (football), and Jerry Yeagley (soccer) at Indiana University and meeting many other well-known coaches from other institutions, as well as university presidents.

My professional service activities beyond the university were centered almost entirely on my professional field of counselor education. My initiation into the elected offices of my profession was when I was elected president of the Indiana Counselor Educators and Supervisors Association, followed by my election as president of the North Central Association of Counselor Education and Supervision. In 1988–1989, I was elected president of the Association for Counselor Education and Supervision (ACES). One of the highlights during my presidency of ACES was planning and conducting the first national convention of ACES, which was held in October of 1988 in St. Louis, Missouri. This initiated the scheduling of national conventions for ACES on a regular basis.

I was later elected to serve as national president of ACA in 1991–1992. Among the highlights of my term of office was an emphasis placed on governmental relations—an emphasis that saw many of our members visiting their Congressional representatives in Washington, DC, prior to the ACA national convention in Baltimore to acquaint them with the interests and activities of our profession. It was at the ACA Baltimore national convention that the name of the American Association for Counseling and Development (AACD) was changed to the American Counseling Association. One of the distinct benefits to me of my national presidency was the opportunity and privilege of meeting with fellow professionals all over the United States. I was truly impressed with the remarkable accomplishments and dedication of our association members and the positive effect their services were having on the populations they served. It made me proud to be a counselor and a counselor educator.

Continuing with my international opportunities, I had the pleasure and privilege of visiting Hong Kong as well as Beijing and Xian in the People's Republic of China in the fall of 1992. I especially enjoyed the time spent with my good friend and fellow counselor educator Man-Ping Lam, PhD. A delightful residual of this visit was to occur eight years later when Dr. Lam and 10 of her doctoral students from the Chinese University of Hong Kong visited Indiana University and participated in a research seminar with students enrolled in Indiana University's PhD program. All participants, as well as many observers, agreed that this was one of the most stimulating occasions in their recent academic experiences. An outgrowth of this conference has been a continuing dialogue across cultures with many of the participants.

As I approached retirement, it seemed that somehow I had forgotten to take my foot off the accelerator! I was not only serving as the director of Indiana University's master's degree program in counseling but was also still involved in Scotland and Bermuda, teaching two classes per semester, revising one text and writing another, and serving on various university and student doctoral committees. I envisioned myself arriving at the academic finish line breathless! In the summer of 2001, I joined the "over-the-hill" gang.

Joining the Over-the-Hill Gang

I quickly found out that retirement was not the stuff of daydreams of the past in which one sits in a rocking chair on the front porch and dozes the day away. Initially, it seemed as though I had retired to go to work! I was still busy advising students, serving on committees, teaching sections of classes, and writing and researching professionally, in addition to the fun stuff (i.e., Bermuda and Scotland programs). I found out from some of my colleagues who had joined the over-the-hill ranks earlier that one has to learn to retire. It does not happen automatically when you are listed in the faculty directory as retired. I found out (as I had been advised) that this was really hard work. When one has worked most of one's adult life and enjoyed it, as I did, it is sometimes hard to let go. So, it has been a gradual process for me, easing into true retirement. I suppose the committed professional never truly retires but continues to look at ways to make a contribution but still enjoy increased leisure time. In the latter, I have increased my leisure travel time and my visits to close friends and family members, and I even sleep in occasionally in the morning.

In retrospect, I can't imagine having any more fun and satisfaction than I've had in my work as a university professor. The opportunity to work on beautiful campuses, both at home and overseas; the opportunity to work with enjoyable and stimulating colleagues; and the opportunity to contribute to the education of bright and aspiring students and assist them in becoming professional counselors have been rare privileges and great joys. As I am involved in the current writing of a career counseling text, I have suggested that for individuals to have success in their chosen careers, they must (a) like what they do, (b) like where they do it, (c) enjoy with whom they do it, and (d) be satisfied with the outcomes of their efforts.

Highlights of My Career as a Counselor Educator

Since retirement, I have frequently been asked about the highlights or most fulfilling moments of my career. I must confess that I have had so many that as I list them, I am sure I will leave some out. Obviously, one of the highlights, probably common to most college faculty, would be my promotion to a full professor with tenure at Indiana University. At the time of my promotion (1978), this was perhaps more of a highlight than it would be today, as there were very few women full professors in many of the major research institutions. Of course, the major funded research projects that I directed or participated in were a major positive consideration in my promotion to full professor and, at the same time, were very fulfilling to me because of the opportunities to meet distinguished educators and travel worldwide. I was conscious of the traditional publish-or-perish syndrome that exists on most university campuses; however, I must admit that the authoring or coauthoring of textbooks and monographs was very satisfying. At the expense of repeating myself, I must also again mention the immense satisfaction derived from the establishment of counselor education programs in those delightful settings of Bermuda and Scotland and the wonderful, close personal friendships that resulted from the more than 30 years.

I would also have to identify these international experiences as major influences on my personal and professional life. Without question, these experiences broadened my cultural concepts, increased my understandings of individuals from diverse backgrounds, and enhanced my knowledge of human relationships and human development. I also cannot forget the great fulfillment and pride I enjoyed in my various professional elected positions. To be elected by my professional peers to serve in local, state, regional, and national presidencies has to be among the most rewarding and fulfilling of my professional lifetime experiences. All of these moments presented many—almost constant—challenges, but I must conclude that the outcomes and rewards far outweighed the anxieties, and sometimes uncertainties, associated with the challenges.

These memoirs would be incomplete if I did not mention the constant, ongoing rewards resulting from watching the progress of my many former graduate students as they advance in their professional careers. I would not run the risk of listing some of my distinguished former graduates for fear I would overlook (unintentionally) some of the others who are equally distinguished. They have made me proud and the university proud and the profession proud. What more could one hope for?

Highlights of My Journey

As one reminisces about one's lifelong commitment to a career, I suppose it is normal—at least I hope it is—to ask, "What were the highlights or major events shaping my profession during my working years?" Although I am certain that I will overlook a few, the following are the ones that come to mind as I write this.

The National Defense Education Act of 1958

This act had as its centerpiece provisions for the training of counselors for school settings. These provisions were the result of a major lobbying effort by the leadership of what was then a unified counseling profession. Although the training of the thousands of counselors resulting from this act is well documented, I personally benefited by my experiences first as a graduate assistant and later as an instructor in several of these institutes.

Increased Attention to Elementary School Counseling

The last third of the recent century saw a tremendous increase in attention to and provisions for the employment of counselors in our nation's elementary schools. From a personal standpoint, this led to the initiation of an elementary school counseling training program in Bermuda. This program had some unique aspects, such as a 12-credit-hour block of social work courses and courses in special education and behavioral management. (It also resulted in two lifelong personal friendships with distinguished educators involved in these programs.)

A Series of Movements Designed to Strengthen the Counseling Profession

These activities included the licensing movement and the formation of the National Board of Certified Counselors (NBCC) and the development of the National Counselor Examination (NCE). By the end of the 20th century, the NCE examination was used by 33 states for licensing purposes. Also during this period, the profession established the Council for Accreditation of Counseling and Related Educational Programs (CACREP), an accreditation body for approving programs of counseling and counselor education. CACREP is a corporate affiliate of ACA.

The Globalization of the Counseling Profession

During my years as a professional counselor educator, there has been an ongoing and increasingly recognized movement to stimulate the international growth of the counseling profession. Counseling organizations sprung up around the globe, and international conferences initiated by ACA and other counseling organizations were increasingly well attended.

The National Organization Played the Name Game

I initially joined the American Personnel and Guidance Association (APGA). This later became the American Association for Counseling and Development (AACD), which more recently became the American Counseling Association. I am pleased to say that I belonged to all three of these associations.

The Development of Computerized Career Assistance Programs and Other Technologies

Although such computerized career assistance programs as DISCOVER and SIGI are now commonplace, the profession is now debating the efficacy and ethics of online counseling and the granting of degrees by educational institutions offering degree programs online.

The Decision of Some Divisions of ACA to Separate Themselves From ACA

I personally regretted to see this development, because I have always believed that there is strength in numbers and that speaking with one voice was more effective. For example, when I was ACA president visiting the U.S. Congress, representatives and senators were much more inclined listen to an individual representing 60,000 members of a professional organization, rather than a president representing an organization of 5,000 members.

The Future

Although reminiscing about the past is usually pleasant and conjures up happy memories, presently my thoughts are more about the future than the past. I have always been a futures optimist and have enjoyed planning and preparing for the years ahead. At the present, I envision my future activities centering on the major activities of my preretirement life, namely, travel (both professional and leisure), professional writing, some research, and a bit of consulting. I do plan to spend more time enjoying my personal relationships.

I have always enjoyed travel, and I plan to continue my travels to both Bermuda and Scotland, where I will combine consultation with extended visits to my close friends living in those countries. I hope to spend increased time with my family in California and my relatives in Switzerland. I also hope to visit my personal friends in Australia and return to New Zealand, one of my very favorite spots. I hope to make first-time journeys to Hawaii and Nova Scotia. Being retired will also give me the option of spending more time in all of these locales. I will continue to swim and snorkel as long as I can!

As for professional publications, somehow I find it difficult to just lay the pen down! So, as long as my coauthor is willing, I anticipate in several years doing the seventh revision of our *Introduction to Counseling and Guidance* textbook (Gibson & Mitchell, 2003), plus a long-overdue third edition of our program development text (Gibson, Mitchell, & Higgins, 1983). Also, as the itch for inquiry has not yet subsided, I currently am developing two research proposals.

I intend to retain my professional memberships and attend selected state and national conventions. These give me the opportunity to renew old and dear friendships, make new friends, and rejuvenate my professional knowledge.

Some of my friends have suggested that I should find a hobby. I believe I already have one—my profession—which has given me a lifetime of opportunities, challenges, and wonderful experiences and friendships. I am hopeful that in the future, I will continue to enjoy such opportunities, challenges, and friendships.

References

Gibson, R. L., & Mitchell, M. H. (2003). *An introduction to counseling and guidance* (6th ed.). Columbus, OH: Prentice Hall.
Gibson, R. L., Mitchell, M. H., & Higgins, R. E. (1983). *Development and management of counseling programs and guidance services.* New York: Macmillan.

Chapter 13

Reflections of a Multicultural Road Warrior
● ●

Courtland C. Lee

I have the honor, privilege, and good fortune to be a professional counselor and counselor educator. For the past 25 years, my life has been committed to the profession of counseling. The majority of my time and efforts over those years has been devoted to promoting the discipline of multicultural counseling through my writing, teaching, and leadership positions. I have traveled thousands of miles, both in the United States and abroad, advancing concepts related to the theory and practice of counseling across cultures. The road has not always been easy, but I think that I and others who have traveled it with me have made remarkable progress in raising awareness, imparting knowledge, and expanding skill levels to meet the needs of increasingly diverse client populations. At this point in my life and career, I consider myself to be a multicultural road warrior, molded by years of fighting the good fight for the important cause of counseling across cultures.

As I reflect on my personal and professional experiences, I find that my life has become an interesting story of growth and change. The purpose of this chapter, therefore, is to tell my story. Why tell this story? In considering this question, three important reasons emerge. First, I have become very interested in generational diversity as a construct and its influence on the development of professional counselors. I believe that what one experiences in life as a member of a particular generation has a profound impact on his or her perspectives as a counselor. Second, in hearing my story you will have an understanding of things that have contributed to who I am as a person and as a professional counselor. Third, in the United States, as an unfortunate rule, African American men who have PhDs, are full professors at prestigious universities, and have served as the president of a national, predominantly White professional association such as the American Counseling Association (ACA) are a rarity.

So, who am I, how did I get where I am, and what is the message in my story for professional counselors? Here, by year, are some of the defining moments and significant events of my life. These are the things that I use to grade my existence. These are moments and events that have profoundly influenced my worldview, both as a person and as a counselor.

Past Influences

1949

I was born in 1949, which makes me a baby boomer. I belong to the most indulged and studied generation of the 20th century. It is significant to note that in 1949, Jackie Robinson won the National League batting title. This is important to note because in 1947, Robinson had broken the color barrier in Major League Baseball. As the first Black man to play in the major leagues, he suffered the effects of racism and discrimination at every turn. Still, he prevailed and became a pioneer for civil and human rights for scores of Black Americans, including me. Jackie Robinson is one of my heroes. I know that I would not be what I have become if not for his racial trailblazing in the late 1940s and early 1950s.

1954

In 1954 I turned five years old. In October of that year, the U.S. Supreme Court ruled that the country could no longer have segregated schools in the landmark *Brown v. Board of Education of Topeka, Kansas* decision. This decision effectively began the Civil Rights Movement. It signaled the beginning of the end of formal institutional apartheid in the United States. This event also signaled that my life was going to be much different than my parents' lives had been. It implied that opportunities that past generations of Black Americans had only dreamed about would be open to me. That event in 1954 is another major reason why I am who I have become.

1961

As an 11-year-old schoolboy in January of 1961, I watched on television as John F. Kennedy proclaimed, "Ask not what your country can do for you; ask what you can do for your country." I remember a sense of collective empowerment in the air as I watched the first U.S. President born in the 20th century being inaugurated.

1963

On a hot day in August of 1963, I remember sitting in front of my television and watching thousands of people marching in Washington, DC, for civil rights. About 5:30 that afternoon, Dr. Martin Luther King Jr. stood in front of the Lincoln Memorial and gave his famous "I Have a Dream" speech.

I was 13 years old and was thoroughly transfixed and moved by Dr. King's words. Watching this speech was one of the most significant events in my life. When King finished, even though I was only 13 years old, I realized that I had just experienced one of the greatest moments in human history. King made me a lifelong believer in his dream that afternoon.

Then on November 22, 1963, the defining moment for my generation occurred. As a 14-year-old high school student, I remember my history teacher, with tears in his eyes, informing my class that the President had just died in Dallas.

There was life before November 22, 1963, and there has been life after. Things have never been the same since that event, in ways large and small every day, for anyone who remembers exactly where he or she was when they heard the news that Kennedy had been assassinated. The late Senator Daniel Patrick Moynihan, at that time an aide to President Kennedy, was asked at the President's funeral, "Will we ever laugh again?" He replied, "Yes, we will laugh again, but we will never be young again."

1968

In the span of two months in my first year in college in 1968, Dr. Martin Luther King Jr. and Senator Robert F. Kennedy were shot and killed. I remember sitting up all night in my college dormitory with friends, both Black and White, trying to make sense out of King's death and what was happening in the world. I remember having my first meaningful cross-cultural dialogue that night.

That was also the night that I decided I wanted to make a difference in the world. I made a commitment to find a career that would allow me to help people.

I also stood by the railroad tracks in my hometown of Philadelphia in June of 1968 when Robert Kennedy's funeral train passed through on its way to his burial in Washington, DC. As the car with his casket passed by me, I remember seeing his brother, Senator Edward Kennedy, waving to the crowd and thinking, "Maybe there is still hope!"

That thought was dashed later that summer when I watched on television as police officers beat up people my age on the streets of Chicago for protesting the war in Vietnam at the Democratic National Convention. The contrasting images of flag-waving politicians in the convention hall and club-wielding police on the street were just too much. It was then that I developed a suspicion of and cynicism about both politicians and police officers, which I carry to this day.

1969

July 20, 1969, was probably the most exciting day of my life. To this day, it is hard to describe the feeling when I heard "Houston, the Eagle has landed" and "That's one small step for a man, one giant leap for mankind." Since I was a small boy, I have been fascinated with space and space travel. I religiously followed NASA and the space program as a child. For me, Neil Armstrong setting foot on the moon is the greatest event in human history. I had a feeling that day and during the entire Apollo 11 mission that the world really was one large human community.

If landing on the moon was not incredible enough, the New York Mets won the World Series in 1969. This event was almost as significant as the moon landing, because the Mets had been the operational definition of *loser*. Their dismal record had given new meaning to the terms *marginalized* and *oppressed*. However, when these underdogs became world champions, the event made me a firm believer in the concept of human empowerment. Ironically, cynics had said that the Mets would win the World Series when man walked on the moon.

It is important to note that all of the events in this period took place against the backdrop of the Vietnam War. The Vietnam experience, like any war experience, changed my life and the lives of everyone in my generation, whether we went to Vietnam or not. As history continues to reveal, our government lied to us and betrayed us. The Vietnam experience made me question values like patriotism, duty, and honor. Why do for your country, when your country screws you?

I was fortunate; I didn't go to Vietnam. In late 1969, as part of my opposition to the war, I took part in a massive antiwar demonstration in Washington, DC. My images from that march are thousands of people, all ages and colors, feeling empowered; soldiers with bayonet-fixed guns on top of government buildings; and the smell of tear gas in the air.

Vietnam is still with me. I lost a cousin to drug abuse related to wounds he suffered in the war. Additionally, it is very difficult for me to visit the Vietnam Veterans Memorial in Washington, DC, because I knew some of the people whose names are etched on that wall.

1972

In 1972 I became a professional for the first time. After graduating college, I got a job as an elementary school teacher in the Bedford-Stuyvesant section of Brooklyn, New York. At the time, Bedford-Stuyvesant was one of the largest African American and Puerto Rican communities in the United States, as well as one of the most economically disadvantaged. My leadership skills began to develop at this early stage of my career when my colleagues and I threw out the Board of Education's curriculum, which was not meeting student needs, and developed new and creative ways of teaching these extremely poor but bright and resilient children. The issues of poverty and diversity that I encountered on a daily basis formed the foundation for my views on counseling clients from diverse cultural backgrounds.

Because I was the only African American male teacher in the school, the other teachers would send their problematic boys to me in hopes that interacting with a male teacher would be helpful. The school's counselor noticed that I had a skill for connecting with these students and suggested that I might make a good counselor. She convinced me to enroll in a counseling graduate program and pursue my master's degree.

1974

As a 24 year old studying for a master's degree in counseling, I met my mentor, Dr. Alfred B. Pasteur. Dr. Pasteur was one of the founding fathers of the discipline we know today as multicultural counseling. He was a prolific writer and a noted lecturer. Dr. Pasteur's area of scholarly expertise was the psychology of people of African origin. He explored the dynamics of Black personality and behavior from its origins in Africa to its manifestations throughout the Diaspora. His scholarly work presented a holistic overview of the major aspects of Black mental health.

I was inspired by Dr. Pasteur's lectures and his writings. He would constantly challenge me with new ideas and concepts. His way of looking at counseling, from the vantage point of a person of color, completely shattered every notion that I had been taught previously about psychology and education. He gave me the courage to question many of the Eurocentric ideas that I had been taught. He showed me that as an American of African descent, I had a valid alternative view of human personality.

It was Dr. Pasteur who encouraged me to pursue my doctorate in counseling and guided me to my first faculty position in counselor education. As my mentor, he has left me with a very rich legacy. My mentor and my friend, he is the major reason why I became a counselor educator. He also kindled my passion for the discipline we know today as multicultural counseling.

1976

In 1976, as I was studying for my PhD, I remember watching a news story on television about Black school children rioting in a place called Soweto in South Africa. I had been fascinated with South Africa since reading Alan Paton's classic novel *Cry, the Beloved Country* in high school.

The pictures of dead children in Soweto horrified me, but I was also encouraged to see that people were beginning to stand up to apartheid. This was the start of my awareness of the issues of civil and human rights on a global scale. I remember signing a petition to free a South African political prisoner named Nelson Mandela about this time.

1979

In the fall of 1979 I began my career as a counselor educator as an assistant professor at the University of North Carolina at Chapel Hill (UNC-Chapel Hill). This was an extremely challenging time in my life. I came into an institution and a training program that had little experience with cultural diversity. During my years at UNC-Chapel Hill, I began to develop my line of research, although my interest in studying people of color did not really resonate with my senior colleagues. However, while there, I began to achieve a national reputation for my work with African American mental health issues. It was this national reputation that helped me to get promoted to associate professor and receive tenure at UNC-Chapel Hill.

1988

In 1988, as an associate professor at the University of Virginia, I got my first home computer. It changed my life in ways I am still assessing. That computer cost a small fortune and took me four years to pay for. This started me thinking: What about those people, now and in the future, who do not have the resources to afford rapidly emerging technology? Will they fall further and further behind? The Digital Divide became very real for me at this time.

1989

In November of 1989 I sat in a hotel room watching CNN. I was watching citizens of Berlin tearing down the Berlin Wall. I could not believe I was watching this event and the end of one of the great scourges of my lifetime: Communism. For me the destruction of the wall was particularly significant, because I remembered when it went up in the early 1960s and all of the fear that surrounded its construction. As I watched the deliriously happy Berliners chip away at the wall, it gave my hope that perhaps a new world order was emerging.

1993

In late November of 1993, I took my first trip to South Africa. My trip took place in the waning days of apartheid. I had the surreal experience of conducting workshops in Soweto, in areas that I watched on television as burning killing fields back in 1976.

During my stay, I had the opportunity to visit a squatter camp outside of Johannesburg with a worker from a South African social welfare agency. The camp was set up behind a school and provided temporary housing for thousands of people from throughout South Africa who had been displaced by the violence that led up to that country's historic 1994 election. The camp had one source of fresh water—an open spigot in the middle of the camp—and the only toilet facilities were several open pits.

Many of the families in the camp were living in crowded temporary classroom buildings. In one such building that my companion and I visited, there were at least 15 large families living together in hot, cramped, and extremely unsanitary conditions. The male members of these families were off either looking for work or doing low-paying jobs in Johannesburg. It was lunchtime when we arrived, and the women were tending to the children who were eating a meager meal of rice, beans, and cabbage out of small plastic bowls. Most of the children looked severely malnourished, and many had open sores on their faces.

The image that is most vivid in my memory is of one small girl who, while running with her bowl, tripped and fell. As she did, the contents of her bowl spilled onto the ground. At that moment, at least five other children rushed up with their spoons trying to scrape up spilled rice. The social service worker remarked to me that this accident was very costly because food was scarce, and this would, no doubt, be the only meal that the children would eat that day.

This image and the worker's statement struck me hard. Soon I would be returning to my comfortable accommodations in Johannesburg and looking forward to a nice dinner. I would also be leaving South Africa in a few days to celebrate a joyous Christmas with my family in the United States. However, these children would still be in the squatter camp. Christmas Day would be just another day of hunger and misery for them.

This dichotomy between my reality and that of those children made me feel both guilty and angry. Guilty that I should have so much and they so little, and angry that political and social circumstances would affect the lives of children in such a cruel fashion, I vowed that as a professional counselor and a human being, I would take some type of action.

When I returned to the United States, I made the following proposal to my colleagues in the counselor education program: rather than hold a faculty holiday dinner at an expensive restaurant, which had become our custom, we make a donation to the relief agency that was working in South African squatter camps. My colleagues eagerly agreed to this, and we sent a sizable contribution to the relief agency.

1994

In the spring of 1994 I connected to the Internet for the first time. My life since then has never been the same. The Internet is the greatest single innovation in my life since television. I was now personally interconnected globally. However, I continued thinking about those people, particularly young people, who did not have access to the Net: Will they fall even further behind?

As I became more Internet savvy, I began to argue that the issues of access and privilege that have traditionally divided people into the "haves" and the "have-nots" must not be allowed to stifle the vast network technology. I concluded that all people, regardless of their socioeconomic realities, should be able to find the "on-ramp" to the information superhighway.

It was also in 1994 that I was promoted to full professor at the University of Virginia. I was proud that my accomplishments had afforded me this honor. I subsequently came to learn that I was one of only five African American counselor educators in the country who had achieved the rank of full professor.

2001

On Tuesday, September 11, 2001, I was on a bus in New York City working its way downtown from the Bronx. Sitting with a friend of mine, I looked out the window at the Manhattan skyline and saw billowing black smoke against a brilliant blue sky. A few minutes later the bus driver told us that he had just heard on his radio that an airplane had crashed into the World Trade Center.

That is a day that will live in infamy. It has altered our future. I think that the events of that day are a transforming event for my generation and the defining moment for members of Generation X. That generation has finally lost its innocence.

As a cynic from the Vietnam era, most of my disdain for police and politicians evaporated. I no longer questioned values like patriotism, duty, and honor. It is hard to be cynical and question your country when you see jet planes smashing into buildings and killing thousands of innocent people.

1997

On July 1, 1997, I became the 45th president of ACA. My presidency had historical significance in that I was the first African American man to hold this office in ACA. I was sworn in almost 50 years to the day after Jackie Robinson broke the color barrier in baseball. Given the historical significance of my presidency and its alignment with the anniversary of this important event, I dedicated my presidency to the legacy of Jackie Robinson.

When I assumed the presidency that day, I thought about who I was and all that I brought to the role:

- I am a member of the first generation of Black Americans to benefit from the civil rights struggle.
- I am a person who came of age in the 1960s, when we discovered that if we organize and educate, we can become empowered to bring about massive social change.
- I am a person who grew up with television and is growing old with a computer.
- I am a person who has seen major shifts in global economic, political, and social paradigms.

Because of these milestones and events in my life, there were some important ideas, concepts, and principles that were very meaningful to me as I assumed the presidency: access, equality, empowerment, social action, and diversity. All of these words underscore who I am as a professional counselor. They are the foundation upon which I stand. These words anchor my counseling practice.

These words provided the impetus for my theme as ACA president: "Empowerment Through Social Action." These words were also the inspiration for my book, coedited with Dr. Garry Walz, *Social Action: A Mandate for Counselors* (Lee & Walz, 1998), which was published in conjunction with my presidency.

Four words provide the anchor for who I am as a counselor, and they form the context for my assumptions about the practice of counseling: passion, advocacy, commitment, and empowerment (PACE). PACE is about getting beyond talking the talk to actually walking the talk when it comes to putting our mission as helpers into practice. PACE is about facing the challenges and opportunities that I feel confront our profession. As we do so, I think it is important that we stop and reflect on some simple truths about our profession, regardless of our work setting:

- Counseling is more an art than a science.
- Our profession is part of a centuries-old, worldwide helping and healing tradition.
- As such, we are all inheritors and guardians of a timeless wisdom.
- People look to us to use this wisdom to help them solve problems and make decisions.

Given these truths, it is important to remember, as my story suggests, that we have always assisted our clients against a backdrop of rapid and substantial change. This change shapes clients' values and their views of the world.

The events of the last few years suggest there is a major shift in global social and cultural perspectives, bringing with it a new set of human challenges. In this new century, we as counselors need to rethink our views on human development and refine our methods for promoting it. It is time for us to move from gatekeepers to advocates! Traditionally, counselor energy and skill have been focused on helping individuals resolve problems and make decisions. Yet often the origin of problems and impediments to effective decision making lie not in individuals but in an intolerant, restrictive, or unsafe environment.

Social Action: A Personal Perspective

Within the context of my story, I would like to share with you some thoughts and ideas on social action and its role in counseling. The concept of social action provides a conceptual basis for the role of counselor as social change agent.

For me, social action refers to two important interrelated concepts. First, it involves our ability to intervene not only into clients' lives but also into the social contexts that affect those lives. Second, from a preventive perspective, social action encompasses the professional and moral responsibility that we have to address the significant social, cultural, and economic challenges that have the potential to negatively affect human development. This second aspect relates to our sense of social responsibility. It involves our taking stands on social issues and working to eradicate systems and ideologies that perpetuate discrimination and disregard individual rights.

In order to fully understand the role of social action in counseling, three concepts must be considered. The first concept is empowerment. As a term, empowerment has certainly been over-used in counseling. For me, empowerment is a process in which people, particularly those who have been marginalized and oppressed in some manner, become aware of how power works in their lives and develop the skills to effectively address power and gain control over their lives. Remember the '69 Mets! I think it is important for us to remember that we do not empower people. People empower themselves. We as counselors merely provide the facilitative conditions that allow people to become empowered.

The second concept is advocacy. Advocacy refers to the process or act of arguing or pleading for a cause or proposal. An advocate, therefore, is an individual who pleads for a cause. As advocates, we are called on to help clients challenge institutional and social barriers that impede human development. When necessary, we need to be willing to act on behalf of marginalized or disenfranchised clients and actively challenge long-standing traditions, preconceived notions, or regressive policies and procedures that may stifle human development.

The third concept is the counselor as an agent of social change. The concepts of empowerment and advocacy provide the basis for the role of counselor as social change agent. A counselor who is a social change agent works with and for clients in a variety of ways. For example:

- Participating with clients in an AIDS walk to make a statement to the government and the public about his or her commitment to fighting the AIDS epidemic.
- Working to ensure that affirmative action and other equity issues remain central to policy and procedures in both education and the work world.
- Speaking truth to power. For instance, speaking out at legislative forums and hearings about how cutbacks in school counseling programs have the potential to negatively impact the academic, career, and personal–social development of young people, particularly poor youth and children of color.
- Working with the business community to find ways to make computer technology available to economically disadvantaged young people.

Conceptualizing our mission in a social action context may require a re-thinking of our profession and of ourselves. Questions we need to consider include the following:

- What do we do, and why do we do it?
- How do we do it?
- For whom do we do it?
- What do we believe about our clients?
- What do we believe about ourselves?
- What are the results of our efforts?
- How can we improve?

Social action, be it on a local or a global scale, will require a counseling philosophy that believes all people have the following:

- the right to life, liberty, and security of person
- the right to work
- the right to leisure
- the right to a standard of living adequate for the health and well-being of self and family
- the right to an education
- the right to freely participate in the cultural life of one's community.

These rights were included in the Universal Declaration of Human Rights adopted by the United Nations more than 50 years ago. They are the basis of a social action philosophy of counseling for the 21st century.

As professional counselors, we can and should be agents of both individual and social change. We can employ our diverse expertise to both help people and resolve the profound social, cultural, and economic dilemmas challenging the world. Through our own social action, we can help to empower people and to foster a healthy society.

From This Point Onward

As for how the rest of my story goes, I am currently professor and director of the Counselor Education Program at the University of Maryland. I have become a senior scholar and leader in the profession. I plan to continue writing, hopefully inspiring students and junior faculty members to be all that they can be as professional counselors and educators, and to offer my services to the profession as a leader and consultant, both in the United States and on the international counseling scene.

I have no plans to retire but rather transition into a phase of life in which I can continue to write, mentor, and consult on issues I am passionate about—but at a less frenetic pace.

Lessons Learned

To conclude my story, I would like to share five lessons learned from my journey:

- *Lesson 1: Strive for balance.* While you work hard, it is also important that you find time to play hard. Make sure that in the midst of focusing on developing a professional life, you do not lose sight of your personal life. It is vitally important that you work to balance your professional and personal worlds. I have learned, sometimes the hard way, that it is really important that you nurture your personal life. Take time for yourself and the significant others in your personal life. Although there are times when the demands of your professional life can consume you, it is important to put those demands in perspective and consider what and who is really important in the broad scheme of your life.
- *Lesson 2: Adopt a holistic perspective.* Along with working for balance in your life, it is important that you take care of your body, mind, and soul. Physical exercise is an imperative. It is also crucial that you continue to stimulate your mind. Always remember that learning is a lifelong process. In addition, discover what is truly sacred in your life and ensure that whatever this is, you cherish it and ensure that it enriches your spiritual well-being. Your sense of spirituality should be the essence of how you approach living and dying.
- *Lesson 3: Reach behind you.* As you experience success and achieve professional stature, it is imperative that you reach back and extend your hand to those who are coming behind you. Always take seriously your potential position as role model or mentor to the next generation of professionals. Never hesitate to take time for a student or a new professional. Actively pursue ways that you can mentor those who are following you.
- *Lesson 4: Give back to the profession.* As the profession rewards you, make sure that you find ways to give back. Whether with time, effort, or money, find ways to return your good fortune to the profession. This was important to me when I donated the royalties from a book I published to establish a multicultural counseling excellence fellowship through the

American Counseling Association Foundation. The counseling profession has been very good to me, and I feel that through this gesture I have been able to repay it for all it has contributed to my development as a professional and as a person.

- *Lesson 5: Think globally, act locally.* Being a multicultural road warrior has taught me that in these challenging times, it is important to extend thinking and action beyond national boundaries. To be a professional counselor today means being a true citizen of the world. It is important to adopt a global perspective on your work as a professional counselor. While you are thinking globally, it is imperative that you become a force for positive change in your own community. Commit yourself to linking internationally with colleagues to collaborate on addressing common human challenges. Use the knowledge gained from your international collaborations to promote the empowerment of those in your local community. As the bumper sticker suggests, I would urge you to anchor your counseling practice in the concept of thinking globally and acting locally.

I end my story with a quote that strongly underscores the message in my journey. It comes from a famous U.S. citizen whose social action helped to change the face of America—my hero, Jackie Robinson. Robinson reflected on his achievements with the following statement: "A life is not important except in the impact it has on other lives." This quote is the credo for my life and work as a multicultural road warrior.

Reference

Lee, C. C., & Walz, G. (Eds.). (1998). *Social action: A mandate for counselors.* Alexandria, VA: American Counseling Association.

Chapter 14

Living With Change: A 50-Year View

Allen E. Ivey

My first serious encounter with change occurred after graduating as a psychology major from Stanford University in 1955. Stanford certainly gave me a fine education, but I was soon to learn that the orientation of their outstanding psychology faculty was incomplete. After graduation, I was fortunate to receive a Fulbright scholarship for a year of social work study in Denmark and had the good fortune to work with Poul Perch, major advisor to the Social Ministry. From Perch and Denmark, I learned several new lessons:

1. Psychology in the United States was and is deeply encumbered and mired in an individualistic orientation with little awareness of relational and environmental contingencies.
2. The positive psychoeducator model is an alternative approach to treatment. Perch was one of the first in the world to advocate a teaching model for the social worker and psychologist. Almost 20 years later, we were able to introduce the psychoeducator model to our profession in a special issue of the then *Personnel and Guidance Journal* (Ivey & Alschuler, 1973).
3. Moving institutionalized populations to a supportive community and away from closed hospitals and institutionalization can work. Twenty years ahead of the United States, Denmark in 1955 was eliminating large, closed institutions for delinquent youngsters (those with mental and physical challenges) and psychiatric hospitals. But they also provided extensive preventative and supportive community resources to help these people return to society—something that we have completely failed to do in our "open" society.
4. A mixed capitalist/socialist economy works for the good of all. This was a very different message than I had learned in college and continually still receive through the media. I'm still not sure that our excessively individualistic culture could ever cope with socialism, as certain cultural attitudes of cooperation, collective spirit, and esteem for others (as well as self) are necessary ingredients.
5. Most important, I learned that my elementary, high school, and university education was incomplete and sometimes biased. This knowledge has helped me challenge the status quo of our field from time to time.

In short, I learned firsthand the importance of the person-in-environment. I learned that community support could make a significant difference in people's lives. I learned that other countries may have ideas superior to those in the United States. I learned how to question established practices in psychology and the helping fields. Denmark was a wonderful preparation for living with change throughout my career. In effect, I had to change before I even started a career.

In this chapter, I'd like to share over 50 years of living with the helping professions. Guidance and counseling were in their infancy as I entered the field and the changes have been vast.

Early Recollections: How Allen Became Committed to a Multicultural Approach

Both my parents were born in poverty or near poverty at a time when there was no social safety net. My father's parents had emigrated from Cornwall, Great Britain, at the turn of the century. Cornwall was then and remains now under the thumb of the English crown, whose "majesty" is founded on Cornish tin (approximately 30% of Cornwall is controlled by Prince Charles). My grandfather died when my father was nine, leaving my grandmother as sole support of the family. She literally took in washing to support the family and made Cornish butter from her few cows to sell to homes near a local mill. One day when she went to sell butter, the people refused to buy any more. She eventually found out that the mill owners required them to buy everything at the company store. At one point, the situation was so desperate that my father and his brother were almost sent to a foundling home.

On my mother's side, my grandfather inherited the local paper, founded by my great-grandfather; but he soon lost the paper playing cards. As a compulsive gambler, my grandfather left my mother with no money for shoes for school or for the required books. From my parents' painful experiences in childhood, I gained some sense of economic oppression and injustice.

The Great Depression was in full force when my mother and father were to be married in 1930, and dad lost his rather good job with Standard Oil the week before the wedding. They still got married and rented a very small gas station in rural Mt. Vernon, Washington. I grew up in a small house attached to the store. A quarter mile south was my mother's family farm and a quarter mile west was my dad's family farm (after my grandfather's death, my grandmother married his brother—a common practice at that time).

All this makes for a very small world, oriented to family relationships and the need to work together for mere survival. A mile away was a two-room school, which was to be my learning base until finally I was the only person in the eighth grade. The teaching practice at that time was for each class to go to the teacher's desk and read the assignment aloud. This was true whether it was language, reading, social studies, or math. I recall reading all the books I was to read in the next several years early in the second grade. I anticipated a boring time ahead, and I was right!

One of the lessons in school focused on capitalization, and the teacher taught us that the names of all peoples were to be capitalized. A few days later, presenting the history of the Civil War, she wrote the word *negro* on the board. Being the type of child a teacher hates, I immediately raised my hand and pointed out that she had just taught us to capitalize the name of peoples. She was flustered and angry. I don't recall her exact response, but it was something like, "Well, I guess they are not that important and are not really a people." I was not satisfied with her answer and have always capitalized *Negro* and *Black* ever since.

My hero during early childhood days was Tandy Wilbur, manager of the Swinomish Nation eight miles down the road. He always made a fuss over me. I was very impressed that he was a "manager," and he always dressed in a suit and tie. In high school, his son Tandy Jr. was an outstanding basketball player for nearby LaConner High, and he became a hero as well. Later, I played my accordion for dances at the Swinomish Hall and got to know Tandy in a new way.

In the 1960s, the Bolt Decision in Washington state court validated the fishing treaties signed in the previous century between the U.S. government and the Native American tribes in Washington, which had been ignored to this point. The decision returned 50% of salmon rights to Washington nations and tribes. Needless to say, this caused quite a conservative outcry, which has not died down fully even today. Tandy Jr. became quite active as a spokesperson for Native American Indians. He was found murdered in a bathroom in SeaTac Airport at the high point of resistance to the decision. His murderer has never been found.

In the summers, Native Canadian Indians came to our area to pick strawberries and do other farmwork. Dad used to take our pickup truck to camps around the area and sell groceries off the truck. One day, he came home looking sad. I asked what had happened and he said, "The farmers want a kickback from me. If I sell groceries there, I'd have to raise the price to the Indians." Dad wouldn't pay the kickback, even though the economic loss was important to our family.

At school, I endured frequent teasing and was called many anti-Semitic names that I'd rather not repeat in print. As a Baptist, I did not even know what a Jew was, but the names certainly were not fun. I suspected that my "friends" did this because they learned those words at home from their parents, who likely were referring to my merchant father running a small store in a farm community. The stereotype of the Jew exploiting the gentile seems to have taken hold in this small corner of America. Nonetheless, I had to smile at those parents when they came into the store, and I never shared this story with my own parents. Later, when teaching Jewish students at Boston University, I found that several of them had had experiences similar to my own in school. They also did not share their stories of oppression with their parents.

Out of this rural childhood, I learned to hate oppression in all forms. And fortunately, my parents' value system of standing up alone for right gave me a foundation for understanding and supporting multicultural issues. After I went to college, a Swinomish child was named Miriam after my mother, and my parents were invited to participate in community powwows, including the exchange of gifts.

There were also many strengths that helped pave the way to the future. Most of all was the support of a closely knit family. My Sunday school teacher was incredibly conservative and fundamentalist, but was a wonderful person and model. He guided me toward becoming an Eagle Scout, and I enjoyed working for several years as a Junior Assistant Scoutmaster. Now, of course, I am very disappointed with the Scouts' attitude toward gay issues. Music was central in high school and there I had many successes and developed friendships that have lasted over the years. I am particularly thankful to my high school speech teacher, George Hodson, who did much to bring me out of my shell, likely due to the challenging rural elementary school experience. High school was an almost perfect total joy compared to those early years!

College and University

My Baptist orientation and rural experience certainly did not prepare me for sophisticated Stanford. I went to college believing that one drink would make a person falling-down drunk! My two roommates did little to change that impression, as they flunked out after only one term. I liked the academics at Stanford and was particularly impressed with introductory biology, where I learned that environment and heredity deeply affect one another. I've always been puzzled with the nature–nurture arguments that go on endlessly, even today when the evidence for an interactional effect (person–environment) is so immense. And introductory biology was a challenge for my Baptist roots. Graham Regnery and David DuShane were superb teachers and did much to open my mind. (How many of us recall our introductory biology teachers' names?)

The anti-Semitism continued at Stanford. I lived off campus and worked in dining rooms to help pay my expenses. I felt I was able to afford a campus dormitory in my senior year and asked my friends if they could find me a room near them. They did, but three of them came to me together to ask if I was willing to room with a Jew. I remember being shocked at their comments, but at that time I said nothing. I still had not learned to stand up against prejudice. Of course, I enjoyed the time with my new roommate, perhaps because I had more in common with him than I knew at the time.

I didn't know what to focus on, so I started as a piano major. It was great fun, but my talent clearly was not up to the challenge for a long-term career in music. I visited the campus counseling center, and when the interviewer asked me what I'd like to do with my life, I replied, "What you do looks like fun to me." Needless to say, he glanced at me a bit dubiously.

Leading me in a new direction was introductory psychology, taken with the famous Ernest Hilgard (president of the American Psychological Association [APA]; he was a learning theorist who made the study of hypnotism respectable). Richard Alpert, later to become famous for LSD studies with Timothy Leary at Harvard, was a teaching assistant in that course. He gained even more fame as Baba Ram Dass, an important New Age philosopher and teacher. Stanford's psychology department at that point was one of the best in the nation, with many famous professors and soon-to-be-famous teaching assistants. I most appreciate the way that they taught me how to read psychological literature and criticize research design. It was a fine education, but I was soon to learn that it was incomplete.

Robert R. Sears, another APA president and a famed child psychologist, was another hero at Stanford. As an undergraduate, I took a graduate course in child development and learning theory, perhaps unconsciously preparing for my work in developmental counseling and therapy. What I remember most from that course was Sears's words to me as I talked to him about graduate school. His comment "Get out as quickly as you can and learn something!" was incredibly helpful to me in understanding and working with the complexities of graduate school.

The University of Copenhagen, Denmark, came next, and its influence has already been described. Stanford had given me the ability to read and think critically about the literature. But I very soon learned to criticize what I had learned there. While in Denmark, I applied to several graduate schools. I still recall the delight that came with my first acceptance—a letter from Ralph Berdie, head of the University of Minnesota Counseling Center. An assistantship there would clearly have been a wonderful experience, and I've valued my colleagueship and friendship with many Minnesota PhDs. But Harvard University offered a fellowship that was sufficient to pay all my expenses and the choice was made.

Harvard did two main things for me. First, it made me very humble and fully aware of my limitations. Doctoral work was not easy for me. Paradoxically, Harvard does another thing—it shows you what you can do under pressure, and the demand for excellence is unending (and unnerving!). I was lucky enough to have Ray Hummel and David Tiedemann as my advisors. Ray was patient with me in my early clinical fumblings, and David was a great teacher and model who helped me focus on developmental issues in counseling. They were endlessly demanding, but also supportive. I was also very foolish. I finished my master's and doctorate in three years and worked full time the second year in the Guidance Department of Boston University. I would not recommend this for anyone who wants a life.

Bucknell and Colorado State University: Professional Foundation

At the age of 25, I had my doctorate and was named director of the Counseling Center at Bucknell University—far too young, but somehow I survived. I visited Penn State and Don Ford at his innovative Division of Counseling two or three times yearly. There, I saw the several campus prevention and outreach programs developed by the outstanding staff, which included the likes of Hugh Urban, Sam Osipow, and William Snyder. Don and various Penn State people have been important influences throughout my career.

My next move was to Colorado State University (CSU) as director of the Counseling Center. This was to be my place of growing up. I was lucky to assemble an outstanding staff over the years, including Gene Oetting, Charles Cole, Dean Miller, James Hurst, Cheryl Normington, and Wes Morrill. With Dean of Students Burns Crookston, we expanded on Penn State ideas, renamed ourselves the Student Developmental Center, and built a major campus outreach program. After I left CSU, Morrill, Oetting, and Hurst in 1974 developed the influential cube model outlining the many possible interventions.

I wrote a grant for a major statewide research/action project with the Fort Logan Mental Health Center in Denver, a large inpatient psychiatric facility. Our goal was to stop the "revolving door" of recidivism in the hospital. Our first effort focused on vocational counseling and job placement. The grant also funded our Student Development Center and led to the hiring of Gene Oetting, who was later to take over direction of the project. He also became an important mentor to me. We soon discovered that basic counseling and placement services were not enough, so we moved to helping employers prepare for the patients and counseling patients and employers on the job. This improved things, but still was not quite enough. Just as we started to explore changing the nature of the work environment, the funding for the project was canceled. This experience obviously built gradually on my earlier experience in Denmark and highlights the importance of institutional climate and institutional change if we are to help individuals in any significant way.

In 1966, we received a grant from CFK Ltd., a division of the Kettering Foundation, to explore the behavioral skills of counseling via the then new medium of television. Out of this came the now well-known microcounseling (Ivey, Normington, Miller, Morrill, & Haase, 1968). A second grant from Kettering focused on the behavioral skills of teaching. There I applied microcounseling research to the teaching process. One of the six basic skill areas of the project was focused on understanding racism—my first serious study of issues of multiculturalism and oppression.

Thus, multicultural issues became embedded early in microcounseling thought. I've been pleased with the growth of the microskills over the years; over 450 empirical studies have been completed to date (Daniels, 2003). I first met Tom Daniels as a graduate student and eventually served as external examiner for his PhD at Dalhousie in Canada. His scholarship and friendship have enriched me and expanded the microtraining tradition. It is exciting to see our ideas used in so many areas of training, including medicine, management, nutrition, library work, county extension services, the UNESCO AIDS training program, and refugee counseling.

But as others have picked up the ideas and language of microcounseling, it makes me very sad to see how very many of these people fail to cope with multicultural issues, which are closely allied to skills training. At times, this leads me to wonder if the skills approach (without multicultural awareness) is more problem than solution.

At this point in my career, I realized that I no longer wanted the pressure and responsibility of administration. I also found it particularly terrifying when it was time to write a new grant: Could I and our group write it well enough so that 50 people and their families would not be disrupted? Through microcounseling and our multicultural experiences, I knew that teaching and writing were where I wanted to head. But my heart has always remained with CSU. I miss my close friends there, the walks for coffee in the student center, and the bowling team practice at lunchtime.

University of Massachusetts: Expanding Multicultural Awareness

The year 1968 found me in a new and exciting setting. Dwight Allen had just been named dean of the School of Education at the University of Massachusetts (UMass) and had been given an unlimited number of hiring slots by Provost Oswald Tippo. The goal was no less than to revolutionize education. Dwight brought in over 20 new faculty members plus a large number of perhaps even more innovative graduate students. We all climbed on a chartered airplane for a week in Colorado for planning. All courses in the School of Education were eliminated, and we started afresh. It was an exciting time, but there was also an immense amount of wheel spinning and confusion. Nonetheless, many good ideas and programs came out of this. Unfortunately, over the years many of these innovations slowly disappeared. Universities don't like change.

But there was consensus on the importance of innovation in education and fighting against racism, sexism, and oppression in general. That became a theme of the school and highly influential in my own thinking. Within two years of my arrival at UMass, I was coteaching a group-counseling course, "Black and White in Helping," with Norma Jean Anderson. Work with Norma Jean and the diverse students in the class became my most significant personal lifetime learning experience. Later coteaching the multicultural course with Ernest Washington in the "Ernie and Al show" helped me integrate my earlier learning with Norma Jean. Norma Jean and Ernie have taught me the importance of taking multicultural ideas and theory into practice.

As I had already written on issues in fighting racism and sexism, I considered myself a nonracist who was fighting to become less sexist. But through teaching the "Black and White in Helping" course, I learned much more about myself and institutional racism. I learned about White privilege and that regardless of how well-intentioned I might be, I will always benefit from a racist society and that inevitably all White people are infected with racism, including myself. This was a difficult and humbling journey for me. And despite my best efforts, I still find myself engaging in thoughts or actions that to me represent vestiges of internalized racism. I find myself both amused and angered by White people who claim that they are not racist. They are asking for the impossible.

In 1974, I founded Microtraining Associates with Norma Gluckstern. This small educational publishing company began with *Basic Attending Skills* (Ivey & Gluckstern, 1974), a video program supplemented by a training manual. Here the basic listening sequence was introduced, and the skills training program has gone through several editions. The first cross-cultural video-tape for counseling training in the nation was developed six years later (Ivey, Shizuru, & Pedersen, 1980). Lanette Shizuru demonstrated to me for the first time how collectivism—a "we" orientation—could be brought into the counseling profession. Work with Paul Pedersen over the years has brought me a wonderful friend, colleague, and coauthor. Since that time, the Microtraining Associates video list has grown, and now we have the largest list of skills-oriented and multiculturally focused videotapes in the nation. The company remains small, but somehow has survived now for over 30 years.

Counseling and Psychotherapy: Skills, Theories, and Practice (Ivey & Simek, 1980) was written because I wanted a textbook that focused on taking theory directly into practice in which students could identify specific things that they could do by the end of the course. The theory–practice orientation has always been important to me. Also, this was the first counseling theories text to bring multicultural issues to the fore. The latest edition continues to focus on how traditional theory can be enriched by multicultural practice (Ivey, D'Andrea, Ivey, & Simek-Morgan, 2002).

However, there is a lot of focus and pain that go into writing. My then-wife commented to me as I started writing the theories of counseling text, "If you write that book, we'll end up in divorce." She was right, and there was more pain and difficulty in that book than I expected. At the same time, she was completing her PhD in engineering, and we all know that many divorces occur in the process of doctoral degrees. Whether caused by the book or the PhD, we separated. But we had many good years and produced two wonderful boys, with whom we both remain close.

Elected president of the Division of Counseling Psychology in 1980 (now the Society for Counseling Psychology), I appointed Derald Wing Sue to head the Professional Affairs Committee with the charge of making recommendations for multicultural practice in our field. Derald's committee report introduced the multicultural competencies to our field. I recall how disappointed I was that the Division Executive Committee specifically voted not to endorse that report but merely to accept it. Approval of that report did not occur until 20 years later!

Mary Bradford Ivey and I met after my divorce, and we were married in 1982. I'm lucky to have such a friend, scholar, and coauthor as a lifelong partner. She's a great cheerleader, but also knows when to comment and criticize. She is sometimes known as the heart, while I'm known as the head of our dual-career marriage. My work has greatly improved since we've been together. The multicultural journey has expanded and become enriched. She, however, agrees that I am not always the most pleasant person when in the middle of a difficult writing challenge; perhaps that is why she has joined me on so many complex journeys in both writing and lecturing.

In the early 1980s, I felt academically restless and needed a new challenge. My colleague George Forman was then president of the Jeanne Piaget Society, and I decided to sit in on his basic course. For the final paper of that course, I wrote the first draft of a book that was to be finally titled *Developmental Therapy: Theory Into Practice* (Ivey, 1986). I remain impressed and fascinated by the power of neo-Piagetian cognitive–emotional development in the interview. I'm particularly pleased and proud with the latest edition of *Developmental Counseling and Therapy: Promoting Wellness Over the Lifespan* (Ivey, Ivey, Myers, & Sweeney, 2005). In a sense, Developmental Counseling and Therapy (DCT) is based on the year of Fulbright study in Denmark. It is a positive, contextual model that brings developmental psychology into concrete practice. The wellness ideas of Tom Sweeney and Jane Myers have been incredibly helpful, and it has been great fun to write with them. And it has been exciting writing new chapters on spirituality, multiculturalism, and a positive developmental approach to the *Diagnostic and Statistical Manual of Mental Disorders*.

Mary and I were especially enriched by two teaching assignments in Australia and additional visits for workshops. Through David Rathman, then-CEO of Aboriginal Affairs in South Australia, and Matt Rigney, we experienced in depth the meaning of person–cultural context and spiritual foundations of counseling. Matt could take us to the grove of trees from which his forebears came into the world and where he would return. David took us to the Murray River where he grew up and worked in early years. We learned some of the richness and meaning of traditional Aboriginal culture. We began to understand the deeper role of connectedness and spirituality in personal development. Needless to say, we also encountered new and complex issues as we experienced Australia's form of racism and discrimination.

Equally important was work with Machiko Fukuhara, president of the Japanese Microcounseling Association. Mary and I have visited Japan frequently over the past 20 years, and each time, we come away with a new respect for cultural difference. Microcounseling and DCT have led to invitations throughout the world, and our books have now been translated into at least 17 languages. We like to think that it is the precision of the microskills model, plus the constant attempt to maintain multicultural awareness, that has made this possible.

The final phase at the UMass focused on a concentrated look at spiritual dimensions of counseling, and we've conducted several workshops and have begun to write in that area. (You may note at this point that I've shifted from *I* statements to *we* statements, for there is very little I do now that is not influenced deeply and profoundly by Mary.) We invited a student, Sister Rita Raboin, to teach with us. Sister Rita has since become our spiritual guide and inspiration. She is currently working in the Amazon

Delta seeking to improve the material and spiritual lives of all with whom she comes into contact.

I've been asked why we bothered to teach a new course on spirituality in the last two years of my life at the UMass. If you look back over my years at four institutions of higher education, there has been a constant change in emphasis and interest, but with a set of core interests carrying through. Each new change was really an amplification of some part of me (and now Mary) that always was there, but perhaps needed new emphasis and clarification. Coming into contact with Sister Rita and the spirituality course was an integration of all that had come before and an indication of what was to come. All we can say is that this work has been special to us, and we are appreciative of the new challenges work in the area of spiritual counseling offers.

Moving to the Future: Is There Life After Academe?

I left the UMass five years ago so that I could spend more time on writing and working with our small firm, Microtraining Associates. The first thing that I learned was that I lost an excuse to say no, and Mary and I have gradually learned that we need to prioritize our lives. Opportunities for speaking, writing articles or chapters, and of course, the ever-present books and conventions more than keep us busy.

The first year after leaving UMass, Mary and I completed over 125,000 miles of travel, catching up on national and international lecturing invitations. We returned to southern Australia to teach again. On this trip, David Rathman arranged for us to speak to all the judges in Adelaide about cultural issues, including how Aboriginal people could be approached in a culturally respectful fashion. We loved our year, but when we counted up the 30 days of air travel, we realized clearly that it would be wise to have more modest travel schedules in the future.

Particularly satisfying was being elected in 1995 to the Executive Committee of Division 45 of APA, the Society for the Psychological Study of Ethnic Minority Issues. (In 1966, I had been named a fellow of the Society for Counseling Psychology.) There I was able to develop a deeper understanding of multicultural issues. It was particularly joyful in Chicago when we adjourned to watch the final APA Senate vote on the Multicultural Guidelines, which were passed unanimously. Nadya Fouad and Patricia Arredondo had done the extensive work that resulted in the final wording, and their full report was published in the *American Psychologist* (APA, 2003). What a change from 1981 when, after debate, Division 17 only accepted the Sue committee report on Multicultural Competencies. The Multicultural Competencies have been a long road with many people contributing. However, the real challenge is still ahead—will we implement the competencies in teaching, research, and practice? I've learned over the years that guidelines are not always implemented.

The books and chapters continue, and as I write this life review chapter, I can report on another lesson. Watch out for overcommitment. I participated in the completion of four books in a six-month period, plus three book chapters. And I no longer need them for the annual faculty report! Just like our 125,000 miles of travel, balance is needed.

I'm also excited about work with two publishers as a consultant/editor. I've been contacting younger faculty members throughout the country and internationally to write books for our field from a multiculturally sensitive base. This brings me into contact with the future of our field, and I find myself very optimistic as I work with this group. We need a full set of textbooks written from a multicultural base, rather than simply adding multiculturalism on to existing texts. Let me know if you'd like to write. I'd love to be in touch with you.

A very important part of our life is our multicultural family, who together form the National Institute of Multicultural Competence (NIMC). Mary and I get together once or twice yearly with Patricia Arredondo, Michael D'Andrea, Judy Daniels, Don Locke, Beverly O'Bryant, Thomas Parham, and Derald Wing Sue. At the NIMC meetings, we review what we have been doing personally to further multicultural issues and seek ways in which we can work together to support further change. A summary of our work may be found in the *Handbook of Multicultural Counseling* (D'Andrea et al., 2001).

Mary and I have become deeply involved in St. Boniface Episcopal Church here in Sarasota. We have been attending monthly meetings of FOCUS, a two-year educational program to facilitate discernment of one's life mission. Several people in our group are planning to enter the priesthood in late career. I've found that what I really want to do is continue what I've been doing all my life—serving and working with helping professions and also expanding my knowledge and writing in spirituality. The FOCUS experience has been helpful in finding a new balance in life—and what I have learned through the program will likely filter into my future writings on the integration of counseling and spiritual concerns.

Currently, the Episcopal Church is in strife over the appointment of Bishop Robinson of New Hampshire. The Bishop is in a committed gay relationship, and this has led to possible division in the Church. We have joined with others in an effort to recognize and support diversity in the Christian Communion. I am sure it will surprise some to learn that my Baptist roots have been helpful in this. The Baptist tradition, originating with Roger Williams in New England, is one of independent thought and respect for each person finding her or his own answer. Many in the Baptist denominations have fallen away from these origins, but I learned independence of thought and openness.

Personal Reflections on Working Style and Accomplishments

Frankly, I would not recommend that anyone spend as much time at the computer keyboard as I have over these past years. I would not recommend working full time while completing a doctorate in three years. I would not recommend traveling as much as we have at some points. I would not recommend becoming overburdened with writing assignments. I realize that I am a workaholic, and that side of me still needs balance with more play.

Mary, however, makes me laugh. We love being together, whether it is writing, a conference, travel, or some other adventure. Sarasota is a blessing to us with its many cultural activities and interesting people—and, of course, superb weather. But we will admit we escape to Lake Sunapee in New Hampshire for the summer where all our children and grandchildren are within two hours. And just as the leaves start to fall, you'll find us back in Florida, where they visit frequently. We are thankful for laptop computers and cell phones for our mobile life so that we can live with the changing seasons.

As I look back on what I've written above in terms of accomplishments, I'm particularly pleased with four contributions that might last over time.

1. *The Student Development Center of Colorado State University.* What a magnificent group of colleagues I had. I think we made a difference in counseling center development, but today we seem to have returned to the traditional medical model. We need more prevention and less remediation.

2. *Microcounseling.* I was lucky to be there when the video recorder first appeared on the scene. Our group at CSU developed the basic microskills. I've added a few on my own, and many others have contributed concepts and completed research on the model. It is particularly gratifying now to realize that the original research work has developed in courses taught at many universities and appears to have influenced the extensive development of skills training textbooks.

3. *Multicultural learnings.* I say "learnings" because I started in this area in 1966 from a very low knowledge base. So very many people have contributed to my development in this area. I am happy that I've been able to be a part of the development of the multicultural competencies for 25 years. Also, through Microtraining Associates, I have had the pleasure of helping key figures in multicultural counseling and therapy reach the classroom through videotaped presentations. I've done what I can in my writing to support multicultural counseling and therapy as the core of all helping approaches.

4. *Developmental Counseling and Therapy.* DCT integrates positive wellness and developmental concepts into the here and now of the interview. It is not necessarily an easy theory. It is integrative and requires knowledge of traditional theory and strategies and the willingness to think about these concepts in a new way. For those professors and students who make the effort, I am delighted with the results and their feedback. I find it amazing that all books that I have written since 1970 remain in press or are currently in redevelopment. These have been translated into at least 17 languages. I've been fortunate to meet so many people and make friends around the world through my professional efforts.

A question that the editors of this book posed to us is, "What is the 'secret' of your success?" Looking back at this chapter, I am particularly struck by the importance of colleagues in my development. All my so-called accomplishments came in relation to others. I was lucky enough to be there during some critical times, but I really do think that what has made the difference is the excellent mentors and colleagues I've had over the years. When I look back at the names cited above, I feel very humbled and appreciative to those with whom I've been associated over the years. I'll admit that the Protestant work ethic is a part of this—working and contributing are fun for me.

The day after we visited Auschwitz in Poland and viewed the Holocaust Memorial, Mary and I flew to Vienna where we met with Viktor Frankl. It was a fascinating discussion, and when we asked him how his work related to Freud and what he thought of Freud, Frankl commented, "We all build on the shoulders of giants." What little I've done in my career certainly depends on super giants such as Frankl, Freud, Skinner, Rogers, and Ellis, but it also depends on friends and colleagues who are giants in their own right. We can do very little alone. We are persons-in-relationship, people-in-context, and people-in-community.

Some Thoughts on the Future:
Thoughts and Advice to Other Professionals

Mary and I will continue to read and write, attend conventions, and maintain contacts with as many people as we can. We are eager to work with younger professionals as they take over the field. We also plan to take some time to ourselves and enjoy our eight grandchildren, who are now becoming the devoted skiers that we have long been.

For the profession, we anticipate that a more multicultural future lies ahead. The foundations of our future theory and practice need to be fully attuned to diversity of all types. We worry about an increasingly individualistic government and society that does not seem to care who is left behind in the general prosperity. Currently, we personally know three families only a step away from homelessness, and we worry that this type of thing will increase. Our anticipation and prayer is that counseling and therapy will increase people's awareness of socioeconomic oppression and start research and teaching on how we can make a difference in this most challenging area.

Technology is clearly going to be central. We wonder about the future of some colleges and universities as online courses and programs become more central. Perhaps we should worry more about professors as the need for full-time staff is clearly decreased as technology provides new alternatives. We are at the point that more than textbooks can be written by authors—full courses can now be delivered in readily applicable form. How personal and amenable to change will these new modes of delivery be?

Counseling will be an important part of our global village. We have the knowledge and skills to help communication between and among peoples, but those in the United States and Canada have a special obligation to start learning languages and the multiple ways in which cultures solve the many problems and issues of life. The American Way is not the only way. We need to help people in Western countries realize that other ways of organizing the world have validity and that we need to pass on our ideas to others with sensitivity and care.

For incoming professionals, I've been asked to share advice, based on my own experience. First, Mary and I know that advice is often not useful unless the recipient asks for it. So with that caveat in mind, read the following and select any ideas that seem useful to you.

1. Consider developing your work style consciously as a person-in-relation rather than as a competitive, totally autonomous individual. The U.S. culture in particular leads us easily to think that we work alone. In each of the ideas with which I've been associated, I've had wonderful mentors and colleagues. When you get into those inevitable arguments and differences with your coworkers, remind them and yourself of the need for a community of scholar–practitioners.

2. Realize that much of the education that you are currently receiving will soon be out of date—and some of what you are learning is just plain wrong. The challenge will be to separate the wheat from the chaff. The things that stand out for me in my education were learning how to read literature at Stanford, discovering in Denmark that what I learned at Stanford was incomplete and just plain wrong at times, and encountering many people at Harvard who were a lot smarter than I am, but that I could still survive. Continuing education, keeping up with journals, and constant reading are essential. Otherwise, you will become a "drone" professional, and we have far too many of those.

3. Learn from your errors. My plumber once said, "It's not the mistakes you make, but your ability to fix those mistakes that is the sign of a true professional."

4. Constantly learn more about yourself and others in a multicultural context. Read and attend plays and community events and volunteer. Explore and become an active member in the community in which you provide services.

5. Recognize that you are part of the future. You can make a significant difference in the lives of your clients and of the counseling profession as a whole. As part of your professional practice, attend conventions and work actively with others for the long-term vitality of counseling at the local, state, national, and international level. The key secret to moving ahead in an association is actually doing the job for which you volunteered. Many people seek committee work, as it looks good on their faculty report or in their credentials. I'd estimate that 90% of the work done by committees is actually done by only 10% of those on the committee. Those who do the work are eventually recognized, and their influence gains over time.

6. Recognize yourself as a multicultural being and define multiculturalism broadly to include race/ethnicity, language, gender, sexual orientation, spiritual/religious background, level of mental or physical ability, economic status, age, and other factors. For each of these categories (and others), recognize that privilege and power are accorded to some but not to others. Social justice and action in the community to change the status quo is increasingly being recognized as important in our society. Effective counseling and therapy demands that you give some time in our world to produce institutional change in our communities.

7. Take care of your health and include wellness counseling as part of your therapeutic strategies. Meditation can be as effective as or more effective than medication with some clients. Walking and jogging help those with depression. Eating correctly, getting sufficient sleep, taking time for one's family, and keeping a spiritual center are critical if you are indeed going to help others.

Counseling is a great profession. Given another life to live, I'd do the same thing. I'd avoid some of my many mistakes, but likely I'd make a whole batch of new ones. Welcome to the journey of change!

References

American Psychological Association. (2003). Guidelines on multicultural education, training, research, practice, and organizational change for psychologists. *American Psychologist, 58,* 377–402.

D'Andrea, M., Daniels, J., Arredondo, P., Ivey, M., Ivey, A., Locke, D., et al. (2001). Fostering organizational changes to realize the revolutionary potential of the multicultural movement: An updated case study. In J. Ponterotto, J. M. Casas, L. Suzuki, & C. Alexander (Eds.), *Handbook of multicultural counseling* (pp. 222–254). Thousand Oaks, CA: Sage.

Daniels, T. (2003). A review of research on microcounseling: 1967–present. In A. Ivey & M. Ivey (Eds.), *Intentional interviewing and counseling: An interactive CD-ROM.* Pacific Grove, CA: Brooks/Cole.

Ivey, A. (1986). *Developmental therapy: Theory into practice.* San Francisco: Jossey-Bass.

Ivey, A., & Alschuler, A. (Eds.). (1973). Psychological education: A prime function of the counselor [Special issue]. *Personnel and Guidance Journal, 51*(9).

Ivey, A., D'Andrea, M., Ivey, M., & Simek-Morgan, L. (2002). *Theories of counseling and psychotherapy: A multicultural perspective* (5th ed.). Boston: Allyn & Bacon.

Ivey, A., & Gluckstern, N. (1974). *Basic attending skills: Participant manual.* North Amherst, MA: Microtraining Associates.

Ivey, A., Ivey, M., Myers, J. E., & Sweeney, T. (2005). *Developmental counseling and therapy: Promoting wellness over the lifespan.* Boston: Lahaska/Houghton-Mifflin.

Ivey, A., Normington, C., Miller, C., Morrill, W., & Haase, R. (1968). Microcounseling and attending behavior: An approach to pre-practicum training. *Journal of Counseling Psychology Monographs, 16*(2).

Ivey, A., Shizuru, L., & Pedersen, P. (1980). *Cross-cultural counseling: Clinical case examples* [Video]. North Amherst, MA: Microtraining Associates.

Ivey, A., & Simek, L. (1980). *Counseling and psychotherapy: Skills, theories, and practice.* Englewood Cliffs, NJ: Prentice-Hall.

Chapter 15

The Personal/Political/Professional Journey of a Social Justice Counselor ●●●

Judy Lewis

Aristotle said that justice is "more admirable than morning star and evening star." That idea resonates with me because in my own personal and professional life, the concept of justice is actually what serves as my guiding star. I know that a lot of people think antioppression work is just one aspect or one brand of counseling, but that's not the way I see it. I believe that counseling is one way, among many, of working against oppression. The counseling profession is the vehicle that I've chosen. I could work for social justice in some other way, but I couldn't be a counselor if it meant that I had to put social justice on the back burner. To me, a person's professional orientation is inseparable from his or her politics. I don't think that's a commonly held view among counselors (at least not yet), but let's remember that there was a time, not so long ago, when we actually believed we could separate our counseling from our values. We know better now.

The idea of counseling as antioppression work is a theme that connects my personal life, my professional life, and my theoretical framework, so I will keep coming back to that theme as I talk about my journey. As I think about my life experiences, I can see that my political orientation has influenced my professional work. But it's a circular process. My experiences with students and systems have had a huge effect on my politics by helping me see firsthand the insidious nature of oppression as it plays out in the lives of the people I've wanted to help.

As I talk about my journey, I'm also going to have to talk about oppression in my own life. The form of oppression that's created the most barriers in my career is sexism. I started out in counseling in the 1960s, and at that time, sexism was blatant and direct. When I was a student, I had to listen to one of my professors, a counselor educator, warn me that I should try to write my own papers rather than having my husband write them for me. Gee, thanks for the advice. As a new professional, I heard a counselor educator tell my then-husband that, "Judy is a wonderful ground for your figure." Aaargh! My practicum supervisor said I was "nonassuming." Yuck! When I wanted to move into counselor education, I heard, "We do have an opening, but we're not looking for a woman."

Yes, I know what you must be thinking: "This was 40 years ago and you still remember these things word for word? As a professional counselor, shouldn't you have worked through this by now?" Well, it does still make me angry and it does still hurt, not in the sense that it's been constantly on my mind, but in the sense that my stomach begins to churn as I write about it now for the first time. And it's not just an emotional reaction. This sexism has affected the trajectory of my career. For instance, as I think about the places that I've studied and worked, I realize that I've always had very close peer relationships but I've never had a mentor.

Many people think that because there are now women in key leadership roles in the profession, discrimination against women must be a thing of the past. I'm happy that sexism in the profession is not as direct as it was in the old days, although it's too late for me now that ageism has kicked in, too. Women still have to fight hard just to be visible in the profession if they're not young, White, straight, good-looking, native English speakers, and a tad deferential.

Sounding this angry isn't good for my career, is it? But I think I should hang on to the anger anyway, don't you? In fact, I hope that you, the reader of this book, will get on board with me. Okay! Here's the journey.

Past Influences

I grew up in Detroit in an extended family home. My parents, my brother, and I lived upstairs. My aunt and uncle and two older cousins, Lyle and Bob, lived downstairs. My parents and my grandparents were all in the laundry business, and my father worked about 14 hours a day in the store. My dad had been brought up mostly in foster care after his father had died, and he was tremendously proud that he had graduated from high school and that he owned a business. When my brother and I were kids, we always heard the same thing when we wanted to buy something or when we asked why our family car had to be a laundry truck. "We're still paying off the loan." The loan must have been money that was borrowed to open the business. I'm guessing now that it might be possible that it was my grandfather—my mother's father—who had loaned them the money. I wish I could ask!

My mother worked in the store sometimes but was mostly at home with us. It was from my mother that I got interested in writing. She used to write musical plays that she and her friends would put on to entertain the people in the "old folks home." She also used to sing around the house. I still know the words to all of the popular songs of the 1930s and 1940s. Don't ask me about anything more recent than that.

I was not much of a student in elementary school, in junior high, or in high school. I was a shy, quiet kid who wouldn't be noticed much. (Okay, I was unassuming.) In high school, I took a lot of typing and shorthand classes. In the 12th grade I was one of the kids in the retailing cooperative program. We left school at noon every day to go to work in a department store. My parents wanted me to go to college, but they thought I should know about typing and shorthand and retailing just in case. I don't think anyone had great hopes for me as someone who would do well academically or have a serious career.

It was some kind of miracle that I got into the University of Michigan. I know I was accepted because I tested well, but it's a wonder they let me try with grades that were not Michigan caliber. This was one situation in which the timing was fortunate. Michigan is very selective now, but at that time it was easier for in-state students. Of course, the tuition was $100 a semester, too.

The first semester at Michigan I got two *A*s, a *B*, and a *D*. The *D* was in the astronomy class that was supposed to be really easy as long as you had copies of old tests, which, of course, I didn't. I remember it being fun when the post cards came with my two *A*s. (I knew the *D* was coming, but that was later.) I didn't get any more *D*s after that. I was okay. I even started to think I might be intelligent.

The years at Michigan were great. I had a group of close friends in the dorm. In fact, the six of us went on a reunion trip to Washington a couple of years ago. We were good kids and just a little bit mischievous. I remember the time we wrote a letter to the editor of the *Michigan Daily* suggesting that women students shouldn't really have to be in by the 10:30 p.m. curfew if we could prove that whatever damage might occur in the late evening had already been done. The letter was a big hit, but female students—not male students—still had to be tucked away in the dormitory by 10:30.

I was a political science major and had kind of planned to get a doctorate in that field. Then my Uncle Jack, the one who lived downstairs, sat me down for a serious conversation over the summer before my senior year and told me that it was very important for me to get a teaching certificate so I would always have a job to fall back on. I think he was chosen to represent the family because he was an accountant and wore a tie to work. Anyway, I got the message and followed through. Who knows why. I still had time to take my ed school classes and beef up my English minor so I'd have a subject to teach. I did it.

There have been times in my life when I regretted that decision, but I think I made the best of it and came out okay. Years later, I found out something interesting. According to Uncle Jack, I had to be a teacher. But my male cousins also had conversations with Uncle Jack. My cousin Lyle had to go to law school even though what he really wanted was to be a history teacher. My cousin Bob was pretty good in science, so he had to go to medical school even though what he wanted to be was a pharmacist. My brother Bill was the youngest so nobody hassled him, and he got to go in the Peace Corps. At any rate, this family story reminds me of what my friend Mary Arnold always said, "Oppression hurts everyone—not just the victims but the perpetrators as well."

Experiencing the Journey

After I graduated from college, I did teach in junior high and high schools for several years. I wasn't able to get a job in a city school district, so I went to work in South Redford, a working-class suburb near Detroit. The most interesting thing that happened to me there was that I was attacked by the John Birch Society. The John Birch Society is defined by the MSN Encarta dictionary (John Birch Society, 2004) as "a right-wing political organization formed in the United States to combat communism." The society isn't as well known now as it was in the 1960s, but it still exists and is working now on issues like getting the United States out of the United Nations. At the time I was teaching in 1964, the society used students to keep diaries of things that took place in the classrooms of teachers who were viewed as too progressive. In my case, I was accused of being in favor of racial integration, socialized medicine, and the separation of church and state. A local, ultraconservative newspaper put all of this in screaming, front-page headlines. (Separation of church and state sounds a lot different when you frame it as, "Teacher says God has no place in government.") I was also identified as one of a group of 37 teachers who were guilty of having meetings with the Redford Township Council of Human Relations.

I must say that the Board of Education came through with flying colors. I've just gotten my clippings out of mothballs, so I have the exact words of the resolution that the Board passed. Here is one passage:

> If Mrs. Lewis is guilty of anything, it is in motivating her pupils to think. Learning is a hard job, and often requires much more effort than the students are willing to put forth. It is the teacher's task to lead and guide the students to the facts not as either the teacher or the students would like them to be, but as they are. This, the Board believes, Mrs. Lewis has done and hopes she will continue to do.
>
> While your Board of Education regrets having personalities involved in such a discussion, it takes this opportunity to reaffirm its position in support of academic freedom in our public schools. If students are to be free to learn, teachers must be free to teach, without fear.

What particularly strikes me about this statement is the affirmation of academic freedom. Reading this again after many years reminds me that academic freedom was once considered central not just in universities but in elementary and secondary schools. We've lost a lot of ground on this issue over the last four decades. Today's school boards are much less likely to affirm the idea of academic freedom and, I'm afraid, less likely to take courageous stands.

After receiving such wholehearted support from the school district, I knew that I should stay at least another year in the same position, but I wanted to move into the counseling profession. During my teaching years, I had been working part time on my master's degrees at Eastern Michigan University. I finished my counseling master's in 1965 and decided to accept a counseling job in another district near Detroit.

Being a School Counselor

My experience as a high school counselor really opened my eyes to the counselor's role as a change agent in the school. As I worked with each and every 11th-grade student in the school, I couldn't help but notice how many of them were affected by inequities, poor learning environments, punitive school policies, and differing expectations based on economic class. One of the reasons I've been so taken with the Transforming School Counseling Initiative of the Education Trust is that its approach fits my personal experience as a school counselor. I did do a lot of individual counseling, but that served as kind of a needs assessment to let me know what learning barriers were present in the school. I knew that I had to work on the environment if I wanted to be helpful to those kids.

I began my doctoral program at Michigan at about the same time I became a school counselor. When I had finished all of the PhD requirements but the dissertation, I moved to Chicago and began working as a high school counselor at Niles North High School. By this time, the Vietnam War was raging and a lot of the students were active in the antiwar movement. I wondered whether these high-school-aged protestors were just emulating their older, college-aged brothers and sisters or whether their own characteristics led them in this direction. That's when I decided on my dissertation topic: *A Study of the Characteristics of a Group of High School Student Activists as Compared With the Characteristics of a Group of Peers Not Associated With the Activist Movement.* I compared a group of activists who belonged to an association called the Student Coalition with a sample of nonactivist students attending the same high school. The results were astonishing. The activist group had significantly higher academic ability and achievement as measured both by grade point average and by test scores. The antiwar students were activists not just on this one issue but across a broad range of activities. They were more involved than their peers in all types of extracurricular activities with the exception of athletics. The personality differences were especially interesting. I used the Sixteen Personality Factor Questionnaire and found significant differences in several of the personality factors. What was really striking was that there was an overall score for creativity that had been developed through a study of artists and scientists. The activists fit that profile.

Because the antiwar students and nonactivists differed on so many variables, I believed that the activists would continue in their vigorous political involvement. I was as wrong as I could be! Luckily for me, however, I was Dr. Lewis before the bottom fell out of the student activist movement. I should mention that at the same time I became Dr. Lewis, I also became a mother. My son, Keith, was born while I was doing my dissertation. When I turned in the final copies, they were stacked around him in the baby carriage. It worked out well.

Having an "Aha" Moment

My first job after finishing my doctorate was in a school system in Florida that was in its first year of court-ordered desegregation. I was leader of a team of school–community consultants under federal funding. Our role was to avert crises, resolve conflicts, and engender communication and collaboration. That sounds like an unrealistically difficult job. In fact, however, what was really most surprising was how easy it was to avert crises, resolve conflicts, and engender communication among students. The hard part was working with the adults.

I remember the first time we were called to a junior high school that was experiencing a student walkout. We were very anxious as we drove there, especially when we got stuck in the traffic behind a house that was being moved. When we arrived and started working with the students, we found that they wanted to talk, that they were thrilled to find some people who wanted to listen, and that they could communicate effectively with one another when the process was skillfully facilitated. In all of the schools, however, adults were behaving as though they wanted to make sure that student-to-student collaboration didn't happen. There were the teachers who let the Black kids and the White kids sit on opposite sides of the room and then kept their backs to the Black students when they were teaching. Then there were parents like the one who said that Black students shouldn't be allowed to carry combs because they could be used as weapons, but made sure his son always went to school with a can of Mace. There were the administrators who never showed any inclination at all toward facilitating healthy school climates.

While I was doing this work, I happened to have a conversation with an organizational consultant who was much smarter than I was. She was working in another district and told me that she would never work in any system unless she had a definite commitment toward positive change from the people at the top. I knew that she was absolutely right. I knew that organizational development experts have always said that's what you need. But at that moment, I took a different fork in the road. That was the moment when I knew what kind of professional I wanted to be. I never expect people in power to be committed to positive change, and I'm not willing to make their victims wait until they are. As a counseling professional, I'm going to take part in advocacy to change systems from within whenever it's necessary. Aha! That's social justice.

Staying on Message: Educator, Writer, Leader

While I was in Florida, I coedited *Counseling and the Social Revolution,* a special issue of the *Personnel and Guidance Journal* (now the American Counseling Association's [ACA] *Journal of Counseling & Development*). While still in Florida, I also started work on another special issue, "Women and Counseling," which was published in 1972. Those special issues meant a lot to me because they represented vehicles for wide dissemination of ideas about new ways of looking at the counseling profession.

I've always tried to stay "on message" as I've moved into various roles as educator, writer, and leader. What I mean by staying on message is that I've encouraged students, counselors, and readers always to see human development in the broadest possible context. My first counselor education position was at Loyola University of Chicago. While I was there, I worked on the first edition of *Community Counseling* (Lewis & Lewis, 1977). I'm proud of that book because it presented a counseling model that hadn't really been out there very much before. The idea that counselors should not limit their practice to direct service but should also be active environmental change agents is widely accepted now, but it was considered pretty radical when the book first came out in the mid-1970s.

After I'd been at Loyola for a few years, I accepted a position as director of Community-based Education at the University of San Francisco. I directed several externally funded projects including an ACTION program, in which students did volunteer work in community settings; another project that trained community agency personnel to carry out effective evaluations; and, on a completely different note, a training program for female employees of the Bank of America. I learned a lot in that job, especially how to be a whiz at grant proposal writing, but I think it took me too far away from my central focus in the counseling profession. I was glad to get back into counselor education after a few years.

A good friend of mine, Roger Aubrey, was chair of the counseling department at Vanderbilt University. At that time, the program had an overseas component, offering a master's and doctoral program in England. I taught in England for a year and had a great time. My son was nine years old then, and he loved going to school in Cambridge. I was invited to go back to the home campus as a visiting associate professor, so Keith and I went to Nashville for a couple of years. I was only at Vanderbilt for a short time, but those few years were very meaningful to me. The friends that I made there are still very much part of my life today. In fact, several of my recent books were written with people who were part of my Vanderbilt connection. Loretta Bradley and I edited *Advocacy in Counseling: Counselors, Clients, & Community* (Lewis & Bradley, 2000). Robert Dana, who was a student at Vanderbilt when I was there, is a coauthor of *Substance Abuse Counseling* (Lewis, Dana, & Blevins, 2002). Michael D'Andrea is a coauthor of the new editions of *Community Counseling* (Lewis, Lewis, Daniels, & D'Andrea, 2003). Michael was just finishing his doctoral program when I taught at Vanderbilt, and I used to take my classes on field trips to his mental health program at Meharry. That's how I knew that Michael understood the community counseling model. I saw him practicing it. Over the years, Michael D'Andrea has often brought together sizable groups of people who are interested in saving the world, beginning with ACA. Sometimes the meetings have been at ACA headquarters, and more frequently, they've taken place at conferences. I once joked that someone walking by in the hallway looked in at the group and thought it must be a 12-step group for people with oppositional disorder. I just love folks with oppositional disorder. Maybe that's why so many of my closest counseling friends are people I've met in those meetings. We haven't saved the world yet, but I think ACA is in pretty good shape.

After Nashville, I came back to Chicago, where I've been ever since. I guess I've been at Governors State for 20 years. It's flown by. I've had a chance to do a lot of special things like creating a telecourse on multicultural counseling that attracts hundreds of students every year, working with Jon Carlson on video projects, teaching antioppression and multicultural family counseling workshops with Mary Arnold, and now developing expertise in online teaching. My years at Governors State have also coincided with my most active involvement in ACA.

My professional life has included ACA-related activities over the last 30 years. In general, the kinds of activities that I've been involved with have been content oriented rather than governance-oriented. I've always been attracted to journal editorial boards, media committees, conference program committees, human rights committees, and of course, those save-the-world get-togethers. I was never on the Governing Council until I became ACA president-elect.

I became actively involved in the International Association of Marriage and Family Counselors (IAMFC) when I was recruited by my colleague Jon Carlson. At that time, ACA committees were much larger than they are today and included representatives of each division, so I became IAMFC's representative on the ACA Human Rights Committee. Being on that committee was one of the best professional experiences I've had. ACA had just gone through one of those frequent reorganizations we used to have, which meant that the newly formed Human Rights Committee replaced task forces and interest groups that had been focused on a number of separate forms of oppression. Under Michael Hutchins's leadership, the Human Rights Committee quickly got past the threat of warring agendas and coalesced into a strong, collaborative, and active group.

I ran for president of IAMFC because I hoped it might be possible to increase the diversity of the leadership group, to develop among members a broader view of what it means to be a family, to infuse a multicultural perspective in the media materials disseminated by the association, and to strengthen the association's connections with the counseling profession as a whole. During my term, we did make progress toward these goals, a process that was made easier by the fact that one success would build on another. For example, we moved toward collaborations not just with family therapy organizations but with other ACA divisions. At the time I was president of IAMFC, Patricia Arredondo was president of the Association for Multicultural Counseling and Development, so we were able to collaborate on a presentation by Jose Szapocznik, a family therapist with a strong record of multicultural research. During the same time period, the IAMFC video series, which is always filmed at the ACA annual conference, highlighted the work of family counselors with feminist and multicultural perspectives as well as counselors with expertise in working with gay and lesbian couples. The clients who took part in the demonstrations were also drawn from more diverse groups than they had been in the past. Having this visible a commitment to diversity of all kinds made it possible for the association to earn the interest and participation of multiculturalists seeking an organizational home.

As ACA president, I continued to emphasize counseling perspectives. There were just a few basic ideas that I hoped would interest the members. I wanted to encourage counselors to:

- Emphasize their clients' strengths and resources, not just their problems or diagnoses.
- Use developmental and preventive skill-building methods.
- Increase their multicultural competencies.
- Be courageous in confronting harmful social environments.

The division presidents and region chairs worked with me in developing the theme, "Counseling at Its Best: Celebrating the Human Spirit," which built on those four points. These ideas found their way into my presidential columns and were reviewed in a video that was produced with funding from the ACA Foundation. The content of the annual conference also built on these ideas. The conference was in San Antonio, so that was a perfect setting for "Celebrando el Espiritu Latino," a set of programs celebrating Latino cultures.

But the ACA leadership experience couldn't be just about counseling content. There was governance. To tell you the truth, I had heard horror stories about the Governing Council being a hotbed of conflict, so I was a little bit scared to go there. I was really happy to find out that it was possible to create a governance environment that was warm, light-hearted, collaborative, and effective. Our process observer said we were a functional group. Now that's what I call high praise.

I found also that it was important to be able to pay attention to details, to get tasks done, to listen to everybody, and to remember everything. There's a lot of detail that's necessary to bring about structural changes that can last. I'm really proud of some of the things that we were able to do, like improving relationships with divisions; developing the new leadership training to increase the diversity of ACA's pool of leaders, with Bob Conyne as lead trainer; bringing student representatives to the Governing Council and committees; offering new professionals a year of membership at student rates; and having public policy and legislation training for division and regional leaders. All of these activities are still going on.

The ACA experience was great for me. I'm still close to the people who were in leadership positions at the same time I was. I've gone on vacations with Donna Ford, who was president before me. I've also gone on vacations with Loretta Bradley, who was in office before Donna, but we've been doing that for years. My relationship with Jane Goodman, who came after me, was warm, easy, seamless, and invigorating. We never had a disagreement, whether we were talking about a bylaws change, the budget, or where we should go to dinner.

It was a wrenching experience to come back home to my old job after having had an experience in which every day was new and unusual. I had to do a lot to keep myself entertained. I joined the union negotiating team (not having predicted that it would go on for a year and end up with all-night mediation sessions). I Web-enhanced all of my courses. I became department chair. I adjusted.

Connection Between Theory and Practice

I began this chapter by saying that the idea of counseling as antioppression work was a theme that would permeate my reflections, and I think that's what has taken place. My theoretical perspective has expanded over the years, but it's always remained consistent. I think my ideas about empowerment present the clearest way for me to explain my point of view. Years ago, Bree Hayes and I used to do ACA workshops about counseling women. One of the things we talked about was the fact that women often get mired in self-blame until they begin to understand how powerfully their lives are affected by factors like limited gender roles. I've become increasingly more certain that all of our students and clients—not just women and, in fact, not just members of identifiable oppressed populations—should gain awareness of the social context that affects their lives.

I make a distinction between nonbiased counseling and empowerment counseling. A nonbiased counselor tries to avoid racism, sexism, and other forms of oppression in work with clients. An empowerment counselor, in contrast, helps clients recognize the impact of social, cultural, economic, and political factors on their lives. A nonbiased counselor encourages clients to consider a wide range of choices, but an empowerment counselor helps clients explore the degree to which their perceptions of their choices may be based on internalized oppression. A nonbiased counselor avoids using overtly biased assessment instruments, but an empowerment counselor doesn't pat himself or herself on the back because the Strong Interest Inventory no longer comes in pink for women and blue for men. The empowerment counselor includes analysis of gender and cultural issues as a component of all assessments.

A lot of these ideas fly in the face of what we were taught and what students are still being taught in graduate school. It sounds logical when someone tells us that we should keep clients focused on those aspects of their lives that they have the power to change. A lot of counselors have learned to steer clients away from discussions of environmental factors over which they have no control. My own approach—illogical as it may be—says that people do need to explore environmental factors before they're ready to make changes in the ways they adapt to life. I've come to believe this because of the experiences I've had in my own development and because of what I've learned as a teacher and a counselor.

I also believe that counselors are uniquely qualified not just to help clients become environmentally aware but also to bring about environmental changes on our own. When we work with students and clients, we learn about the barriers that impede their development. With this knowledge in place, we can use our strong interpersonal and problem-solving skills to make a difference. Recently, I worked with Mary Arnold, Reese House, and Rebecca Toporek on the development of the ACA Advocacy Competencies. We could all see that counselors have a strong role in advocacy at all systemic levels. We could also see that it is possible to have an advocacy orientation when we do direct counseling work with students and clients. I don't believe we have to choose between counseling and advocacy work. I know they fit together because that's what I've experienced in every professional role that I've played.

Development as a Multicultural Counselor

I think I might have come to multiculturalism from a different direction than other people. A few years ago, Mary Arnold and I coauthored a book chapter on the counselor's transition from multiculturalism to social action (Lewis & Arnold, 1998). Here's something we said in that chapter:

> Most counselors today are very much aware that multiculturalism must play an integral part in any work that we do with our clients. . . . We have learned that multiculturalism involves more than an acquaintance with the customs of distant populations, more than tolerance of differences, and even more than expertise in cross-cultural communication. Multicultural counseling is built on an understanding that all of us— counselors and clients alike—are cultural beings. . . . It is a short step from becoming aware of the impact of the cultural milieu to noticing the role of oppression in our clients' lives. Once we begin to notice systemic oppression, it is just one more step to accepting our responsibility for social action. (p. 51)

Clearly, we were addressing people who understood the value of multiculturalism, who even saw themselves as multicultural counselors, but who might not yet have accepted the responsibility to take part in social action. We assumed that counselors might typically move from lack of awareness of cultural issues to multiculturalism and, finally, to social action.

The reason I say that I might have done this backwards is that I self-identified as an antiracist, a feminist, and a social/political activist before I self-identified as a multicultural counselor. For as long as I can remember, I've participated in marches and rallies for equal rights and against war. And for as long as I've been a counselor, I've seen social action as closely integrated with my professional role.

Maybe it's because I've been around too long, but I remember the era when people thought multicultural counseling was about studying other ethnic groups, especially groups that were far away from one's own community. That just didn't fit for me. Once the Multicultural Competencies (Sue, Arredondo, & McDavis, 1992) were published, more counselors began to understand multiculturalism more as a process, as a way of being in the world, as a bottom-line necessity for every practitioner. As multiculturalism has become more sophisticated, the lines between the study of culture and the study of oppression have become blurred. Now it's clear to me that I've always been a multicultural counselor. It just depends how we define our terms.

Work Style and Accomplishments

Some people assume I'm a workaholic, but I'm far from it. I hang out a lot. I was just thinking about this past week, the week that I'm finishing work on this chapter. Here's some of the nonwork stuff that I did from a Tuesday to the following Tuesday:

- Saw a movie: *Barbershop 2.*
- Saw *For You Were a Stranger,* a play about a Muslim woman and a Jewish woman who meet three times over a 4,000-year span.
- Went to a Foreign Affairs Council lecture.
- Saw *The Moliere Comedies.*
- Attended my University of Chicago adult education class where we're studying Aristotle and Herodotus (hence the Aristotle quote that opened this chapter).
- Got a group of six people together and bought tickets for a performance of *Free Man of Color.*
- Read *Nickel and Dimed* on time for a discussion group at the library.
- Complained to the manager of my health club that they don't have enough step aerobics classes and that yoga is not at all the same, and I have workout machines in the building where I live and I don't want to pay extra dues for this club just because they have tennis courts and a boxing ring.
- Babysat my 10-month-old grandson.

Here's what I think when I look at this list:

- Most of the events on the list included going to dinner so each event took longer than what it might look like.
- It's no wonder it's taking me so long to finish this chapter.
- If I'm going to call myself a nonworkaholic, shouldn't I cut down on the leisure activities that require homework?
- I really need to live in a big city.
- I really need to change health clubs.

The times in my life when I'm most productive—like writing a whole book in less than a year, say—I manage by concentrating on one project and one project only. I don't multitask. Whatever the single thing is that I'm working on, I think about it all the time. I make sure to have lots of open time to work on the project, never trying to squeeze in an hour or two here or there.

At this time in my life, I don't feel like doing that. For one thing, I have a lot of different projects going on at the same time, all of which are important. For another thing, I'm not at a time in my life when I want to stay home with my computer. It works better for me now to let myself bask in culture. I can do that if I take on more short-term projects. I have one major book to finish (luckily, with great coauthors), but then I'm not going to start any new ones. (Well, check back with me when Bob and Fred do the next edition of this book and I'll let you know how things have gone.)

My Future Journey

Even though I don't plan to take on any new book projects, I am feeling energetic, enthusiastic, and very far from retirement. I'm optimistic about the direction in which the counseling profession is going, and I want to continue to be right in the middle of it.

One thing that makes me happy is the growth of Counselors for Social Justice (CSJ). We started that ACA division just a few years ago, and we've now grown to almost 600 members at a time when division membership as a whole is shrinking. I interpret the CSJ phenomenon as an indication that we now have a critical mass of counselors who believe that working for justice is part of their professional responsibility and who want to connect with others who feel the same way. When you look at conference sessions and new publications, there's just more good stuff out there. ACA has endorsed the Multicultural Competencies (finally) and the Advocacy Competencies (immediately), school counseling models are being transformed, and I'm beginning to see a subtle shift among community agency counselors. For a while, many counselors seemed to be caught up in a situation in which they had lost confidence in the developmental, preventive, strength-based approaches that have historically characterized the counseling profession. I think that confidence is returning.

Advice for Younger Professionals

Here are just a few suggestions that I think might enhance the satisfaction you obtain from your career:

1. Join and stay active in your professional counseling associations. In 2002, ACA past presidents put together a video to celebrate ACA's 50 years of excellence. As they came before the camera, one by one, so many of these venerable leaders said that ACA had given them a sense of community, a professional identity, a stimulus for learning, and a lot of good friends. This kind of experience is important from the beginning to the end of a career. The counseling associations provide a source of support that is at once emotional and very practical. The people you meet can help you get access to cutting-edge ideas, to resources, to mentorship, and even to jobs. You might be surprised to know, by the way, how open counseling associations are. It's easier to move into positions of leadership and influence than people sometimes expect.
2. Read outside of your own discipline. I've personally found it important to have an expansive reading agenda. Especially when you're a student or a new professional, it may seem as though you don't have time to read anything beyond what's required. I'd suggest, though, that reading poetry, fiction, and all kinds of literature across disciplines will give you a breadth of vision that enhances your understanding of your own field.
3. Don't assume that you have to choose between a technological perspective and a multicultural perspective. I think the technology to which we have access now is thrilling. Online teaching, in particular, is growing so steadily that I don't think the counselor educator of the future

will be able to get by even minimally without some expertise in this area. Some people assume that technological and multicultural perspectives are somehow in opposition, but I don't think that has to be true. Cyberspace might force us all into higher levels of multicultural competency. Without visual stimuli, we may be less likely to depend on simplistic or stereotypical generalizations based on clients' race, ethnicity, gender, age, physical disabilities, and other characteristics. Instead, we'll have to ask probing questions about the role that culture has played in the individual's life.

4. Get in the publishing habit. My first publications were articles that were based on papers I wrote in graduate school. I don't like the idea of spending hours and hours writing something that only one person will ever read. So think of yourself as a writer rather than assuming that your work isn't publishable. This suggestion might seem on the surface to be more applicable to counselor educators than to professionals in other settings, but to tell you the truth, we all need to read more work by practicing counselors.

5. And if I haven't sold you on it yet, here's my one last try. View yourself as an advocate for your students and clients, and see your profession as a force against oppression.

References

John Birch Society. (2004). Retrieved November 14, 2004, from http://encarta.msn.com/dictionary_/John%2520Birch%2520Society.html

Lewis, J. A., & Arnold, M. S. (1998). From multiculturalism to social action. In C. C. Lee & G. Walz (Eds.), *Social action: A mandate for counselors* (pp. 51–66). Greensboro, NC: ERIC/CASS and American Counseling Association.

Lewis, J., & Bradley, L. (Eds.). (2000). *Advocacy in counseling: Counselors, clients, & community.* Greensboro, NC: ERIC/CASS and American Counseling Association.

Lewis, J. A., Dana, R. Q., & Blevins, G. A. (2002). *Substance abuse counseling.* Pacific Grove, CA: Brooks/Cole.

Lewis, J. A., & Lewis, M. D. (1977). *Community counseling: A human services approach.* New York: Wiley.

Lewis, J. A., Lewis, M. D., Daniels, J. A., & D'Andrea, M. J. (2003). *Community counseling: Empowerment strategies for a diverse society* (3rd ed.). Pacific Grove, CA: Brooks/Cole.

Sue, D. W., Arredondo, P., & McDavis, R. J. (1992). Multicultural counseling competencies and standards: A call to the profession. *Journal of Counseling & Development, 70*(5), 477–486.

Chapter 16

It Takes a Village to Raise a Leader: Meet Mark Pope

●●●●●●●●●●●●●●●●●●●●●●●●●●●●●●●●●●●●

Mark Pope

I grew up as a poor gay Cherokee boy in rural southeast Missouri. This was how I described myself when I accepted the American Counseling Association's (ACA) Kitty Cole Human Rights Award. I wrote that one sentence as I sat there minutes before receiving the award, but that has now become my life descriptor. I have come to wear each of those individual descriptors like a badge of courage. I am proud of who I am, proud of each of those various facets of my personal cultural identity. It is impossible to fully separate my sexual orientation, my native Cherokee ancestry, my lifelong disability, my rural upbringing, and all that constitutes my personal cultural identity from any of the other facets.

Identity Development

When I turned 50 in 2002, my fellow tribal members welcomed me into Elderhood within our St. Francis River Band of Cherokees with the presentation of a beautiful handmade quilt. Each panel was fashioned by a different tribal member and was hand-sewn together by members of our Women's Council. I mention that quilt because my identity is similar to such a quilt. Each part of my cultural identity is distinct, yet truly part of a whole that has developed over these past 50 years.

Beginnings of a Personal Identity as a Leader

Early in my life, I never thought of myself as a leader. My first elected position came as a sophomore in high school; I was elected to the position of parliamentarian of the Fisk-Rombauer (Missouri) High School Library Club. (Hey, after a fast start like that, I was sure that I could accomplish anything in my life.)

But it probably wasn't until Karen Cunningham had a long talk with me that my personal identity began to include the role of leader. Now, Karen and I were classmates, and she had been elected the state president of the

Missouri Chapter of the Future Homemakers of America (FHA). (Earlier in our lives, during our fourth grade, she and I had been elected as prince and princess of our elementary school for our annual yearbook, *The Pirateer*. I was the prince.)

You have to remember that I grew up in a small town with a total population of 498 people. We had 65 people in my graduating class at Fisk-Rombauer High School in the boot heel of southeast Missouri (the part near the Mississippi River that hangs down into Arkansas), and that was the largest graduating class in the history of the school. People from my town and my school just didn't go on to be state anything, let alone a state officer in a big national association.

Karen's long talk consisted of telling me that I was going to run for state vice president of the Missouri Beta Clubs (Beta Club is like the National Honor Society for small schools). She had already talked with Mrs. Patricia Hall, our advisor, and they had both agreed. I thought about it for a while and finally agreed to do it. Abraham Maslow talks about "peak experiences"—something that happens in your life that changes your path. This was one of those kinds of events. And I even knew at the time that it was just that. I just felt it. And I felt real good that someone would think that I could do something like that.

So I ran for election at the state convention in St. Louis that year with the theme "There's Hope with Pope," and I won. It was a big honor for my little school, and the beginning of a revised personal identity for me. I was a "Leader" with a big *L*. Later, I was even elected vice president of my senior class and president of my high school student council, along with being selected as the "most talented" and "most likely to succeed" by my senior classmates. I learned early that I delighted in receiving such positive reinforcement and that I had certain natural relationship skills that were useful in a leader.

Family Influences on Identity

Fisk, Missouri, has been our family's ancestral home for at least six generations. We can even trace the roots of our tribe (the St. Francis River Band of Cherokees) to the early 1700s, when the first Cherokees migrated across the Mississippi River in search of better hunting. Like any good Southern family, my family is filled with characters. For example, one of my grandfathers was a Baptist minister and one was a bootlegger, who worked "contrary to law."

I grew up on a small farm near Fisk, Missouri, on the St. Francis River. My mother was an elementary school teacher and my father was a factory worker and barber. Every Sunday we all would get up and go to our local Presbyterian church for worship services. For me it was always more of a social gathering than what I thought of as worship. I went there to be with my friends, learn about the history of our Calvinist brand of Protestantism (Sunday school), and sing in the church choir. After church was over, all of our family would pile into our car and head for my grandparents' home in Bernie, Missouri. It was a 30-minute drive, but it always seemed like an eternity because I couldn't wait to get there. When we got to Grandma and Grandpa Ray's house, we would get to see our big extended family of grandparents, great aunt, uncles and aunts, and cousins. We all came together each Sunday for dinner (the noon meal of the day) and socializing. Me, my brothers, and our male cousins would all go outside (weather permitting) to play football in our grandparents' front yard or sit around in the living room listening to the grown-ups talk about how the weather this year was the worst in the last 20, how Aunt Thelma had decided to can 40 jars of tomatoes from this year's harvest, who had attended church that day and who hadn't, how Naomi Wiggs's health was doing. Nothing of world-shattering importance, just good old down-home talkin'. It was a good way to grow up.

My family also has unusual names. Remember that I grew up in a predominantly French and Cherokee area of the country (southeast Missouri). As a direct result of that, my family has unusual names (for which, as with all adolescent trauma, I blame my mother), like my brothers' names—Isom and Dolen—or my mother Ethyle (pronounced "ee´ thil"). Or my "real" name, Markel LaVern Pope, which I quickly shortened during early adolescence to Mark.

Now you have a flavor of how I was raised and some of my early values. Values like the Golden Rule (you know, "Do unto others as you would have them do unto you") and the Ten Commandments. And good old-fashioned salt-of-the-earth values like respecting your elders and addressing them as "ma'am" and "sir" and being polite. These are values that my family is now socializing our daughters and sons, nephews and nieces to have. It was truly a good way to grow up, and southeast Missouri was a good place to be from.

Forming a Cultural Identity

I have always been interested in social justice issues even before I realized I am one. I was always interested in the underdog and helping right the ills of this society. I was always the kid who stood up for the littler kid who was being bullied. As the oldest of four sons, I learned quite early from my mother and father that I had to take care of my younger brothers. It was the role of the eldest to do that—it was just expected, and I gladly conformed because it also fit into my blossoming worldview. There are people out there in the world who will take advantage of people and call them names and hurt them. I am someone who was born to not let that happen.

Some of the previous generations of my family were secret Indians. I really do not know if my father and grandmother were ashamed or afraid or very introverted or just modest, but neither one of them talked very much about our heritage. It was only when he was dying that he talked openly about it. "We are Cherokee," he said and died. Maybe it was that introverted personality type, eh? Then my brothers and I began to explore our heritage. Yes, it is just as he said, "We are Cherokee," and on both sides of the family. But where I come from, no one knew that piece of our identity until the last 25 years or so. My Native American identity has been growing over the past few years and came out when I volunteered some time at the American Indian AIDS Institute in San Francisco. They liked me so much that they made me director of psychological services. I also play a mean reed flute and drums. It is something that has helped me explore my spiritual side.

Now, my spiritual nature was an early victim of organized religion. When I was just coming out as a gay man during college, I was also beginning to explore my spirituality. I went to talk to my hometown minister about my budding sexual orientation. Now, I am not a meathead—there were reasons for me to believe that he would have been more tolerant. None that I will go into here, but (I know you see this coming) he quickly told me that I was destined for a life of sin and depravity, as he had spent the summer in Washington, DC, ministering to street youth, some of whom were teenage male prostitutes. He seemed to say that I was going to go that way, too, if I did not renounce this perversion. I—who he had known for 15 years, who he had baptized, who he had sang with in the choir, who was the valedictorian of the high school, who was student council president, who was state honor society vice president . . . How could he say such a thing to me? I was shocked by his attitude. I was only gay. Nothing else had changed.

I decided right there and then that organized religion, which for me at that time represented spirituality, was casting stones without enough ammunition. I knew that I was okay and, therefore, this part of me that was attracted to people of my same gender was okay, too. All I wanted was to be loved by and to love a special person. I decided right there that if Reverend Coates could be wrong about this, he could also be wrong about other things, too, like the existence of God. If this was how people who were gay were treated by religion, then I wanted no part of it. I could never imagine myself being wrong on my sexual orientation, because it had taken so much energy and time and study to accept myself, to get there. Strong identity formation is good and sometimes you just know. I was not evil. I was good. So I got a good taste of what it is like to feel discriminated against, misunderstood, and treated badly at a very early age, and it helped me to develop much empathy for those who have been pushed to the margins of our society.

Forming a Strong Professional Identity

In 1968 I was a student at the University of Missouri at Columbia majoring in political science and sociology and headed for law school, followed by election to the U.S. Senate from Missouri, and eventually President of the United States. I had big plans. As a product of the 1960s, the anti-Vietnam War movement, President Nixon's invasion of Cambodia, and the killing of protesting students at Jackson State and Kent State, I had helped lead a student and faculty strike that had shutdown our campus at the end of 1970. Ah, the good old days.

I went on to become involved in student government and was elected student body vice president at the end of my sophomore year. Along with a cabal of like-minded student politicos, we took over the student government and ran it for the next five years as the Individual Coalition Party—a coalition of individuals seeking our rights as students in an unfair and unjust system (i.e., the university). I was headed for law school, but was exposed to something called "student personnel work" through my involvement in student government. I had never considered a career in student affairs in my whole life. I first wanted to be a cowperson, followed by physician, and eventually narrowed down to pediatrician, but after extensive career counseling at the university's Testing and Counseling Center and receiving my results from my Strong Vocational Interest Blank, I had decided that law was my goal and political science was my path. I wanted to be a civil rights attorney—not corporate or criminal—a civil rights attorney and help the downtrodden masses.

Really, I was headed for law school when I had another of Maslow's peak experiences. The assistant to the chancellor at the university sat me down one day and told me that I should not waste all of the experience and knowledge that I had gained through my service in student government. He said that I should think about making a career in the student affairs area and told me that most people who worked in that area got their master's degree in counseling and student personnel services, and lucky me, we had one of the top programs in the country right in our own backyard. I could get my master's degree in student personnel work, and along with my law degree, I could be a dean of students someday. I was immediately intrigued. I thought about it awhile, and instead of applying directly to law school, I applied to graduate school in counseling and personnel services to get my master's degree.

As part of my graduate school experience, I met three men who changed my life. Those three men were John McGowan, Bob Callis, and Norm Gysbers. All three were my professors in the Department of Counseling and Personnel Services in the College of Education at the University of Missouri-Columbia.

I was assigned to Dr. Robert Callis, who was my advisor, and he scared me. Anyone who remembers Dr. Callis can verify this. He was a tall, swarthy University of Minnesota graduate who had been dean of students on our campus a while ago and had authored or coauthored several inventories. He had lots of doctoral students but only three of us who were his master's students. He had a long history of involvement in both professional counseling and counseling psychology, and he had been president of the American College Personnel Association (one of the founding Divisions of the American Personnel and Guidance Association [APGA] now known as ACA), as well as holding an office and several leadership positions in Division 17, the Counseling Psychology Division of the American Psychological Association (APA).

Then there was Dr. John McGowan, who was a Creighton University graduate. During my undergraduate career, I served as one of two student members on the Chancellor Search Committee. Dr. McGowan was the dean of extension then, a very powerful position at a state, land grant university. I had become very close to Dr. McGowan. He became my friend and mentor, and I blame much of what has transpired since then on him. He too was a faculty member in the Department of

Counseling and Personnel Services, and he had also held important leadership positions in our profession, including president of Division 17.

Then, during my first semester in my master's program, I was required to take Occupational and Educational Information—"Occ and Ed," as it was lovingly referred to by those of us who were being "forced" to take this required and, we thought before we took it, boring course. Hey, we thought, we'll never need this career counseling stuff, we're here to be deans of students or personal counselors not (yech!) career counselors. (Ironically, as you may already know, I later went on to be president of the National Career Development Association [NCDA].) Well, anyway, that course in occupational and educational information turned my life around and was taught by Dr. Norm Gysbers, who was a serious, methodical professor and graduate of the University of Michigan. I found out that he had been president of the National Vocational Guidance Association (now National Career Development Association) and then later was president of the American Personnel and Guidance Association (now American Counseling Association).

I was impressed. Three of my professors were not just exceptional professors but they were also leaders in the counseling profession. The message that I got from them was that it was your responsibility to be involved in your profession through service in your professional associations. This is a lesson that I have taken to heart (according to my partner, Mario, too much so). All three of these men were bridges to both professional counseling and counseling psychology. They felt a responsibility to belong, but much more than belong, to help lead our whole profession. They saw the profession as broader than one association, one kind of degree, or one anything. They felt a responsibility for where we were heading at all levels of our profession. This has had a profound effect on my developing professional identity.

Then I also began to come to grips with my amodal sexual orientation. Okay, so this was something that I had been trying to cope with for a while. I had tried to get out of it by marrying my high school sweetheart, by bargaining with myself that I could not be gay because I wanted children, by talking to my local Presbyterian minister who then proceeded to tell me that I was going to hell. Let's just say that these were not strategies that were very effective in the long run. However, with the acceptance of my gay identity came a whole host of other realizations, including that I was probably not going to be President of the United States. Hey, call me crazy, but in 1973, it did not exactly look like this career path had a high probability of success. So, I began to focus my political work toward changing the view of my new profession on issues of sexual orientation.

I attended my first American Personnel and Guidance Association Convention (now known as the American Counseling Association) while studying for my master's degree. I met Dr. Joe Norton, who had founded the Caucus of Gay Counselors in APGA, and I was hooked. My emerging professional identity and cultural identity had found a home—together. I became the third male chair of the National Caucus of Gay and Lesbian Counselors in APGA.

Later, I moved to San Francisco for love and became involved with the California Career Development Association. I worked my way up through the ranks of the California Career Development Association until I was elected president in 1993–1994. In 1991, David Jepsen, from the University of Iowa, who was the immediate past president of NCDA and chairing the nominations and elections committee, asked me to run for an office in NCDA. I was elected secretary of NCDA and served for two years, then treasurer for three years, and then president of NCDA in 1998–1999.

I ran for president of ACA in 2001. I was elected and took office in 2003, following Donald Super, another past president of both NCDA and ACA, by exactly 50 years (he was the second ACA president and I was the 52nd). I am proud of this for many reasons, not the least of which is that I have always followed my mentors in the profession—Callis, McGowan, and Gysbers (another NCDA and ACA president)—who saw themselves as bridges to both professional counseling and counseling psychology. I proudly carry that banner. Each enriches the other. Then in 2002, I was elected to fellow status in both NCDA and Division 17, the Counseling Psychology division of APA. It has not always been easy for practitioners or minorities (people like me) to get into such a "club" in psychology as Division 17.

Firsts

I have a lot of firsts as part of my résumé. Always have. I am an innovator with a vision as large as the Grand Canyon. But I'm not just one of those "great vision, does nothing" people. I make things happen. I started the first student council ever at my high school. I started the third student lobby in the country and the first one in Missouri. I founded the first gay and lesbian peer counseling program in the country as part of the Chicago Gay Community Center. I was the first openly gay man to be elected to the Illinois American Civil Liberties Union Board of Directors.

In our profession I have continued my pioneering work as I wrote one of the first articles (and my first article) on sexual behavior in older gay men; organized the first symposium on lesbian, gay, and bisexual (LGB) issues in career counseling; edited the first LGB section in a major career counseling journal; served as the first openly gay president of NCDA; and then served as the first openly gay president of a major mental health professional association, ACA. I want to provide some context for each of these.

I have been a pioneer and scholar on LGB issues in counseling and psychology since 1978. My first national conference presentation on LGB issues was at the ACA conference in 1978. During that time, the session rooms were often full because the program was one of the only ones on LGB issues. Almost no one was "out" at the conferences, and those who attended felt very vulnerable to be openly LGB. LGB conference attendees' choices about whether to be seen at such a program were agonizing. Amidst this climate, I was out there doing these much-needed presentations. I just couldn't imagine not doing this.

My first publication was the culmination of a rather long and rocky road. It began in 1978 when I had initiated my doctoral studies at Northwestern University. I had been working at Northwestern's Institute of Psychiatry as a mental health worker on its Adolescent Unit. As part of my doctoral program, I took a course in gerontology that required proposing a research project. I proposed a project to survey a group of aging gay men about their level of sexual behavior, to see if there were any changes from one age cohort to another. My professor liked my proposal so much that he funded it. So I contacted a group of older gay men in Chicago called Maturity, and they allowed me access to their mailing list of over 200 members. I received over 100 completed responses. I was in heaven. This was great. My very first research project, and I was already a success. I submitted the manuscript to the *Journal of Homosexuality*, the premier journal in this area of research, and waited. It seemed as if it took forever (only four months, by the way), but when I received the letter with the return address of *Journal of Homosexuality*, I was excited. It was my first submission, and I was not prepared for a no, which was unfortunately what I got. Not even a "revise and resubmit." It was just a flat "no" with lots of comments. I was quite devastated. I put aside the letter, reviews, manuscript, and data for 10 years. Let's just say I was deeply hurt by this incident.

Later, during my doctoral work at the University of San Francisco, I thought of the manuscript and the data and decided to return to them. I knew that it was going to take the right editor to see how important these data were. I revised the manuscript based on the reviews and decided to resubmit it to the *Journal of Homosexuality*. By now it had been eight years since my rejection (notice how I say my rejection, not the manuscript's). But I was determined! I believed in these data and their importance in the research on aging gay men. About six months after my submission of the revised manuscript, I received another letter with the return address of *Journal of Homosexuality*. I was hoping that the editors did not remember that I had previously submitted the manuscript, for I was sure they would reject it again. As I opened the letter, I had tears in my eyes when I saw that my manuscript had been accepted. I had learned a very important lesson from this journey—that persistence is the key to success. I believed in my work so much that I persisted. It took me a while to work out the feelings of rejection and hurt, but I did. I came back to my truth, and I persisted, and I was rewarded. It was truly a great lesson for me, one that I have never forgotten. Here's the reference that is one of the most important in my career: Pope, M., & Schulz, R. (1990). Sexual behavior and attitudes in midlife and aging homosexual males. *Journal of Homosexuality, 20*(3-4), 169–178.

Also, I am one of the parents of what is being called in the literature LGB career counseling and vocational psychology. Through the mentoring of Mark Savickas (then the editor of *The Career Development Quarterly*), I organized a symposium on gay and lesbian career counseling held at the 1994 NCDA national conference. This led to a special issue of *The Career Development Quarterly* on this topic in 1995. These were absolutely the first pieces of multiwork scholarship in this area. Before these pioneering pieces, all that there was in the literature were isolated studies and practice pieces. There was no sense before this symposium and special issue of building a body of LGB career-related knowledge. Now, any text on career counseling must address these issues or be considered incomplete.

I have also had a variety of leadership roles in the counseling profession, culminating with my elections to two of the most prestigious associations. There have only been 53 people elected to the ACA presidency and 90 to the NCDA presidency. I have compiled the demographics for the ACA presidents just to give you a flavor: men (31, 58.5%); women (22, 41.5%); 15 (93.8%) of the first 16 presidents were men; 12 (75%) of the last 16 were women; 3 (5.7%) of the 53 were African American; 0 were Asian; 0 were Hispanic. Only one ACA president was openly gay, only one was Native American, and only one had a major physical disability at the time of service. Those last three statistics are me. Breaking into such a small group takes perseverance, hard work, vision, some talent, and luck. There have only been a very few openly gay or lesbian leaders who have been able to attain these offices in the counseling professions.

I wrote in my second president's column in the ACA newspaper, *Counseling Today*, in August 2003, of the recent U.S. Supreme Court decision that overturned the sodomy laws in this country. The headline of that column was "First We Were Sane, Now We Are Legal." The first part of that headline refers to the removal in 1973 of homosexuality from the *Diagnostic and Statistical Manual of Mental Disorders (DSM–II*; American Psychiatric Association, 1968). By a vote of the Board of Directors of the American Psychiatric Association, millions of gay and lesbian citizens of the United States were made "sane" overnight. Wave your magic wand and you are no longer mentally ill. Get it! Do you understand the power we have to affect people's lives? We who are gay, lesbian, or bisexual were judged mentally ill because of the prejudices of the dominant culture. We who are in the mental health arena have responsibility for that. That is why my election to the presidency of one of the largest mental health organizations in the world is so important. In the December 9, 2003, issue of *The Advocate*, the world's largest gay and lesbian newsweekly, the headlines proclaimed "A Big Step for Mental Health" (Bull, 2003). Exactly 30 years after homosexuality was removed from the American Psychiatric Association's *Diagnostic and Statistical Manual of Mental Disorders*, the first openly gay person was elected to the presidency of a major mental health association. As the first openly gay man elected to such a position, I represent a final and total repudiation of that past. I think that if I died tomorrow, I would be fulfilled. My life would have meant something to a very important group of people in the world.

Career Detours or What I Did for Love

A career is what you do over your lifetime. It's sometimes misunderstood popularly as a job. I have had a great career, a great life. I have lived it fully.

I have wandered when I needed to. I have listened to my heart and truly followed my passion in all things. I am a better counselor because of that. I have three most favorite political buttons: "A woman without a man is like a fish without a bicycle" (catchy, eh?); "Republicans are people too: mean, selfish, greedy people" (even my Republican friends appreciate that); and finally, "Don't die wondering."

I lived in New York City back in the early 1980s. I was not a practicing counselor then. I had burned out working with heroin addicts on the Southside of Chicago and needed a break, so I came to New York looking for fame, fortune, fun, and love. I lived in Chelsea, 15th Street and 8th Avenue, just across the street from The Village. And I paid an exorbitant amount of rent for a two-room studio there (so what else is new for Manhattan). And I worked as a pipe fitter at the Brooklyn Navy Yard and took computer programming classes at night at New York University. Yes, I was really burned out.

While working at the Brooklyn Navy Yard, I hurt my back very badly. When the physicians took X-rays of my back to find out what had happened, they found that I had a substantial amount of bone missing from my spinal column. I was diagnosed with spina bifida occulta, a congenital birth defect. Now, this type of spina bifida is the best type, but it was the first time that I was aware of my condition. My mother tells me stories of how I would complain of my back hurting when I picked cotton on our farm in southeast Missouri, but she just thought I was saying that so I would not have to go back to the cotton fields the next day. This diagnosis, however, meant that my days working in the Navy Yard were over. When my back had healed as best it could and I was once again able to sit upright, I enrolled in computer school at Control Data Institute on 42nd Street in New York City. I enjoyed computer programming. I had a quick mind, and the part I liked best about it was the designing of a computer–human interface that was easy to use, the human factors part of this process.

During my computer education, my partner of three years at this point decided that we should live apart, and I decided that I was not going to wait around in New York City for him to come to his senses. It was another peak experience as I took control of my life interpersonally. I had been following Steve around for all of those three years. I had given up my doctoral studies at Northwestern University. I had lived in poverty in San Francisco. And I had moved to New York City and worked as a pipe fitter (not that there's anything wrong with that). All for Steve, and I was tired of it and tired of Steve, and I was going back to San Francisco. So, I transferred my computer schooling to the Control Data Institute in San Francisco, where I completed my computer studies and got a certificate in computer programming. I now had expertise in COBOL, FORTRAN, RPG II, IBM 360/370 Assembly Language, and Basic. I was hot!

I found a job very quickly after graduating from computer school. I had previously learned a computer programming language while attending New York University in the evening (DEC PDP 11 Assembly Language), and with my knowledge of Basic acquired through my studies at Control Data Institute, I was hired immediately. I was hired as a computer programmer by an insurance company (Pacific American Insurance Company) with offices in a newly built complex on Van Ness Avenue in San Francisco. I was in heaven.

Then I met Shahri Kadisan. He was from Malaysia, and he was my "type." You know. He met my physical compatibility requirements. And he met my emotional compatibility requirements. He was perfect. Well, not really. See, he was from Malaysia. And he had gone to school in the United States for his BS and his MS, and he was now working as a waiter at a restaurant in San Francisco. I was already in love with him when he told me that he had to return to Malaysia. I was devastated but vowed to wait for him until he could return. We had been together for only six months when he left for his home. See, he had promised his family that he would return. They were dirt-poor farmers living in a small village in southern Malaysia, and they were basically waiting for him to return and save them. Because Shahri was bright, he had been able to get government scholarships and attend the best secondary schools in his country. He then was able to parlay that into additional scholarships for his overseas education, but he was expected to return and work for two years as repayment for his educational scholarship.

And we both knew that in order to keep our relationship going we would have to have regular communication with each other. We missed each other greatly. Shahri wrote to me every day, and I telephoned him once a week. Our telephone calls were not short either, as that would serve no purpose. We needed to keep current on each other's life so that we could maintain our feelings. When I had completed computer school, I took a trip to Malaysia to see him. My intention was to find a job there so that we could be together. I got my first passport. I got on the plane. And I traveled 18 hours in the air to Kuala Lumpur to be with the one I loved. I did not have any Malaysian money. I just got on the plane and went. I had studied the Malaysian language a little from books. I remember flying into the airport in KL, as Kuala Lumpur is called, and seeing the red tile roofs and white billowy cumulus clouds floating just above the roofs. I landed and there he was to meet me. I was in tears when I saw him, tears of supreme happiness. I cry even now as I write this as the intensity of feelings comes rushing back to me.

I lived with Shahri in Malaysia for three months. You could do that on a U.S. passport as a tourist without getting a special visa from the government. And I looked for jobs. I looked everywhere. I approached the DEC computer office in KL. I looked in the newspapers, at least the English language ones, for computer programmer jobs. I got interviews, but because of my lack of computer experience, I was not a hot commodity. And there was another political reality. Any company that tried to hire me would have to open its books to the government, and most of the smaller ones refused to do that. I was trapped. So, at the end of three months, I was forced to return to San Francisco alone.

Once I was back in San Francisco, my plan was to get a computer programming job at an international company with offices in Malaysia and then transfer to Malaysia. Seemed like a good plan, but I did not really know how big international companies operated. Anyway, with my love reinforced by my three months with Shahri, I tackled the problem with great energy. I applied for jobs at Bank of America, Wells Fargo Bank, Transamerica Insurance, and finally, Bechtel Engineering, where I was hired as a computer programmer almost immediately upon my application. I had tried to get hired at Bechtel when I had originally completed my computer training, but because I had no experience, I never heard from them. This time was different. I had a year's experience with DEC computers, and they just happened to have a position open for someone who had DEC experience. I worked for Bechtel for a couple of years and during that time, I tried to get a transfer to Malaysia, but I was now in charge of the computer system that produced the management reports for the executive officers and the board of directors of the company. They were not about to let me go to Malaysia.

Anyway, Shahri was able to get back to the United States and so I did not have to go, but I was ready. With Shahri's return, I was able to think about my long-term career. My interest in business and computer programming was waning. I was sick of it, to be honest. I was not getting enough human interaction, and I missed helping people in more meaningful ways. I also had wanted to complete my doctorate in counseling that I had started at Northwestern University six years earlier. It was now 1984 and I wanted to get back on my chosen career path, so I looked for university programs that would meet my needs. The most important and pragmatic was that I be able to work and attend school so that I could afford it. That also meant that I was limited to the San Francisco Bay Area for my schooling. I wanted my degree to be in counseling, not clinical psychology or industrial/organizational psychology or any other aspect of psychology. I was a counselor and committed to working with people and their life transitions—that was my professional identity that had been drummed into my head during my schooling at the University of Missouri-Columbia.

I applied to the University of San Francisco doctoral program and got an interview. At that interview, three events happened that changed my life. During the dinner that evening with the faculty and all of the candidates for admission, the people I was setting with began to talk about "I'm an *E*" and "Oh, I'm a *F*." I had never heard this type of talk before. I waited, not wanting to appear ignorant of this professional subject that it seemed everyone else knew about. My dinner partners continued and talked about the Myers–Briggs Type Indicator (MBTI) and the codes you received as your results from that inventory. I was intrigued. I had graduated with my MEd from the University of Missouri-Columbia, which was a big testing school, but had never been exposed to the MBTI, and this was very interesting to me.

The second event occurred during our group introductions at the beginning of the interviews. One of the candidates introduced himself and "came out" as a gay man, right in front of the faculty and all the candidates. This was a big event for me. You may not know it but the University of San Francisco is a Jesuit institution of higher learning. Catholic. For a guy who grew up in a Baptist and Presbyterian household, we did not know the nuances of Catholic organizations. A Catholic is a Catholic, whether they were Jesuit or Dominican or Franciscan did not matter to us because we did not know what that meant. They were all religious. And this was a religious institution, and I knew that none of them liked those of us who were lesbian or gay. I learned a lot about the faculty and the institution that day, because everyone responded positively to the candidate who came out. Everyone. I was happy for him, but even happier for me. His trial balloon had opened the way for me to be out too, not then but after I got my letter of acceptance into the doctoral program and in my first classes. We even formed a gay and lesbian support group, as there were three gay men and one lesbian in our cohort, and we found each other quickly and held on.

The final experience occurred just after the two days of interviews. I was sitting around with several of the other candidates, and we were talking about how we had each been away from school for a while and that coming back and talking about counseling with others who were also so committed and focused on our profession was wonderful. We each had a very intense emotional reaction to this. I realized that my decision had been the right one. I was finally home professionally.

A year into my doctoral studies I was still working at Bechtel Engineering to pay the bills. As I was looking through the help-wanted section of the *San Francisco Chronicle* one day, I saw an advertisement that immediately piqued my curiosity. It was for a job working for a test publishing company, although it did not say which one. They wanted someone who had psychological testing experience. I thought about it for a whole minute and decided that I was going to apply. I did. I got an interview. During the interview, it was decided that because of my computer experience, they would rewrite the job description to include duties as a software development editor along with the other duties from the ad, and I was hired on the spot. I gladly left Bechtel, as this new job brought me further into my true professional career path. I was ecstatic. I now had one more piece of my life and career puzzle back into the right place.

The career detour that I had taken with leaving my doctoral work at Northwestern University in 1979 had ended. I returned to my right path in 1985 with admission into the doctoral program at the University of San Francisco and continued when I accepted the job offer from Consulting Psychologists Press (CPP) in 1987. With Shahri's return to the United States, my life felt complete. What more could I ask for? Here I was at 35 with a perfect life. Little did I know that there would be some awful turns yet to travel.

In 1988, I was completing my doctorate at the University of San Francisco, and CPP was beginning the next revision of the Strong Interest Inventory. I was a rising star at CPP and actively involved in product development. Then another peak experience occurred, although negative this time. I was talking with the human resources consultant at CPP, and she asked me a hypothetical question about what would I do if there were a major problem at CPP and I was not able to go to a professional conference where I had major responsibilities. This was a question that I was not prepared for her to ask and my answer to her was obviously not acceptable, as I was called into the CPP president's office the next day and put on a six-month terminal contract. I had gone from the fair-haired boy of the company to not having a job in 24 hours. I was devastated. I even broke out in hives from the stress. I had never had this happen to me before. I had only been fired from one other job in my life, and that was when I was 18 and working a two-week temporary job to open the Wal-Mart store in Poplar Bluff, Missouri. This firing at CPP hurt very much because I thought everything was going very well. One wrong step and your life changes dramatically.

I had known what response the HR consultant wanted, but I had too much integrity to lie. I just could not imagine this type of scenario as real, whereas she was looking for my total commitment to the company. I had been confronted with the idea of competing commitments, but my overall responsibility to the profession was more important to me and that is what came through. They were committed to making a profit and wanted such singularly focused people around them. I was committed to the products (Strong Interest Inventory, MBTI, etc.) for the good they could do in the world.

I had been seeing some individual clients and doing some corporate consulting prior to my firing. This firing propelled me even more into my private practice—not that I wanted to rely solely on a private practice to pay my bills. I had completed my doctoral degree by this time and really wanted to move into a full-time tenure track position in academia. I had been enjoying my teaching as an adjunct faculty member at various universities in the San Francisco Bay Area, including Stanford University, University of San Francisco, Golden Gate University, San Francisco State University, and John F. Kennedy University, but felt rooted to the San Francisco area because of the health problems of my partner Shahri and the expertise in HIV and its complications in the Bay Area.

Subsequently, I started my business, Career Decisions, out of my house in San Francisco. We had a separate bedroom with a separate front entrance. It was perfect for an office. I could see clients and work out of my house. Every morning I would get up, take a shower and dress and go into my office at the house. I was quite focused and would basically stay there the entire day working. I had my couch for clients to sit on and my desk with a phone and computer. I did not need much more than that. The basic rule of thumb in starting a business is not to expect your income to exceed your expenses in less than two years, but in only six months I was making a profit—a small one, but a profit nonetheless.

In two years, I decided that in order to make the business grow, I needed to move into a new and separate office with a business phone number. This was a huge commitment financially, but I was clear that this was required to move to the next level. You don't have a real business until your mortgage or rent payment depends on your business income. So I got a one-room office in a building on Market Street in downtown San Francisco near parking and public transit. My business grew even more, and I had to get a suite of offices in downtown San Francisco with two counseling rooms, a group room, and even a reception room. I recruited 10 other associates to work with me and hired a full-time assistant.

Everything was going perfectly, and then my partner Shahri died in 1994. I was at the California Career Development Association Board of Directors meeting in San Diego when I received the phone call from Shahri. He had just visited our family physician who had told him that he had cytomegalovirus (CMV), the first opportunistic infection that Shahri had contracted. I got on a plane and returned to San Francisco immediately. Shahri had been HIV positive since his return from Malaysia. I had first been tested and was HIV negative, and so I told him that he should go because, since I was HIV negative, I was sure that he would be too. He acceded to my request, took the test, and came out from the results ashen. I just remember holding him and leaning up against the outside of the clinic saying, "It can't be." But it was, and we lived with that knowledge for the last eight years of our lives together. The diagnosis of CMV was, however, the first sign of this new reality in our lives.

So much more happened with his illness, and we lived every day knowing that it could be his last. When he died in the early morning of April 30, 1994, he died in my arms at home. He had Kaposi's sarcoma and CMV, and his immune system was so damaged and compromised that he just could not go on. I heard the sound of his last breaths, the death rattle. I saw his chest stop moving. I just laid there with him quietly for a long time.

I remember his last words—words that haunt me: "I miss my Mom." My Mom had come to San Francisco from her little town in southeast Missouri to help care for Shahri during his last six weeks. She stayed with Shahri in the hospital while I saw clients during the day in order to pay the bills. I went to the hospital at night to be with him and to take care of him while my mother went to our home to rest for the next day. He had his best day a week before he died, and I was not there to see him that day. I was the treasurer of NCDA and the NCDA board meeting was occurring before the ACA annual convention in Minneapolis. I decided that I would go for the board meeting and return quickly to San Francisco without attending the ACA convention. His best day was the day that I was gone. He was active and talking and asked my Mom where I was. She told him and he said, "I'm glad he went," and she told me later that he smiled very knowingly and understandingly. A few days after I returned, our family physician talked to me and said that whole systems of Shahri's were failing and asked if we would like to have Shahri taken home for his last days. Shahri came home and then died in two days.

I'm pretty sure that he was waiting for me to be okay with his death before he let go. We had gone to Malaysia to see his family, and this was when he first got very ill. He was ready to die there with his Mom and the rest of his family all around him, but I was not ready. I did not know that was why we were there. I got angry with him for giving up and asked him to come back to San

Francisco where our physicians were and where everything would be all right, I thought. He did it for me, because he knew that I was not ready. He was in pain and very sick, and he went from the airplane directly to the hospital upon our return to San Francisco. He was only out of the hospital for a very few and precious days in the six weeks before he died. But he gave me the greatest gift that any person can have: time. Time for me to get ready for him to die. He came back from Malaysia only because he knew that I was not ready. When I finally understood his terrible pain and suffering, I knew that it was time and that he was ready. When he saw that I understood, he let go and he died. I miss him. And I designed the memorial service that was held at the San Francisco Airport Marriott where he worked as a restaurant manager. Then I returned with Shahri's body to his family in Malaysia where he was buried beside his grandfather in the Muslim cemetery in his *kampung* (village). I visit his grave to bring water with flower petals in it. His family treats me like one of their family.

With Shahri's death, I was truly in mourning. I continued with my work, which was my salvation in so many ways. Being able to go to work every day gave me a routine and normalcy that I could cling to. I cried a lot then and some even now. I think I always will, for Shahri will never leave me. His death affected me in profound ways, for when you have survived the death of the one you love, you can truly survive anything. We were together for 13 years, and I cherished each day with him, for I never knew when the last one would be.

The first year after a loved one dies is always the toughest: the first anniversary, the first birthday, the first Thanksgiving, the first Christmas. It was a difficult time for me. I had the most painful time at the first Thanksgiving after Shahri's death. We usually had a big Thanksgiving Day feast with our friends. We had a big potluck dinner where we all gathered and ate and drank and spent the day together. It was always a marvelous time. Thanksgiving Day of 1994, however, was the worst of my life. I did not invite any friends over, nor did I accept any invitations. I had a frozen turkey dinner and pitied myself.

After that type of scene, I realized that I needed to do something different and decided that this particular Christmas was an opportunity to make a change. I decided that I needed to get out to some social events, and I started with the annual Pacific Friends Christmas party. Pacific Friends is a social group of gay Asian men and their partners and friends. I knew that I would have some acquaintances there. I went alone. As I walked in the door, I saw my friend Tee Lim, who was from Singapore and was at the door selling tickets for the event. That was nice. Then I went inside and walked over to the bar to get a drink. The place was relatively empty except for a few who were there to set up the event. As I had a drink, I met a man named Mario, who was a very handsome Filipino man (I'm good with recognizing nationalities). We began talking and he asked me if I was here with anyone and invited me to sit with his friends at a table for the dinner. I accepted his gracious invitation (hey, he was very cute), and we began talking with each other.

I liked this guy. He was the first person since Shahri that I had really liked.

There was an instant spark. I have always believed that you know very early in a relationship if a person is right for you and vice versa. If there is a spark, it is important to pay attention. It is an opportunity in your life, and such opportunities don't always come around again. We talked several times over the next few days and had our first date. It was an effortless date. Well, to abbreviate a long story, we became quite close. In fact, we are together now.

I think that it is quite special to have one great relationship in a lifetime, but to have two . . . Well, let's just say I am very blessed. Mario and I have been together since 1995, and he is a wonderful person. We have a strong, loving relationship.

A short time after I met Mario, I confronted him with a question. I had been considering leaving my successful private practice for a faculty position. I had not previously considered leaving the San Francisco Bay Area because of Shahri's health care needs. That reason was absent now, and I felt a strong need to pursue that previous path. I asked him if he would be willing to move with me if I had a job offer in another city. He thought about it for exactly 10 seconds and said, "Of course I will. I love you."

I then started looking for faculty positions in earnest in September 1996. I applied for three positions. Eventually, I was offered a position at the University of Missouri-St. Louis, but before accepting, I brought Mario here to meet my Mom and to experience St. Louis. It was the end of October, and the autumn is the most beautiful time in Missouri. We went to three gay bars to check out the gay scene. We went to the Central West End for a Halloween party. And Mario met my Mom. They fell in love with each other. I have always accused my Mom of liking my partners more than she likes me. Obviously, it is a joke, but she seems to accept them as just one of her sons (she has four sons already; hey, what's one more?).

Taking a faculty position in St. Louis met several needs of my own. I could work at a doctoral-degree-granting institution. I could be closer to my mother (although not too close), my brothers, and my nieces and nephews. I could be closer to my Cherokee tribe and participate more in our traditions. St. Louis also has some truly outstanding art education programs, and as Mario is an artist, it was a natural fit.

We moved to St. Louis in December 1996, and I started my position at the university in January 1997. And although I had never had a full-time position in academia, I had over 10 years of adjunct experience as well as several publications. I asked to come into my position as an associate professor rather than an assistant professor. With my publications and professional service, the university acceded to my request.

As you can see from these events in my life, I have had several career detours, but each has made me a better counseling professional, for I have learned about myself and our common humanity. After my hiatus from counseling in the late 1970s and early 1980s, I was glad to return to our profession, but I was also quite grateful for my sojourns outside of counseling. I learned that being a counselor was a better career fit for me than being a pipe fitter or a computer programmer and that although I could do both of these jobs, my passion was and is for helping people. After these detours, I have never questioned my career choice.

What Drives Me

People who know me know that I am driven. Driven is not bad in my worldview. When you find something that is important to you, then you want to make it continue. Driven to me is the nexus of passion and action. I asked my closest friends to describe me recently, and these are the adjectives they used: focused, passionate, driven, loving, sensitive, caring deeply, emotional, smart, a problem-solver, worldly, genuine, and a person of integrity. I think they could only think of some of my more positive characteristics. So, what drives me?

First, I knew that I did not want to be poor. I grew up lower middle class, eating beans and cornbread for supper and mayonnaise sandwiches for lunch (really Miracle Whip sandwich spread, which we always called mayonnaise in our family). And I have always known that I did not want to be poor—not necessarily rich, just not poor. After college and before my doctoral work, I was even on food stamps for a while. And if you knew my family and the way that we were raised, you'd know that being on food stamps was not acceptable. I allowed it because I had nowhere else to turn (so it seemed at the time), and I refused to ask my family and others for help because I was embarrassed by my poverty. I had made decisions that created the situation, and I was responsible for it. So I suffered emotionally and physically, but I appreciated the safety net that the government provided. It was short term for me, but I saw many others for whom it was permanent. And I wondered why. I learned that they had no hope left. That they were surviving the best way they could. It was merely a pragmatic choice. I rationalized it by saying that I had paid into the government for such a time in my life, kind of like a savings account for difficult times. But I never liked it, and I was ashamed of having to use it.

I am a passionate person. The plaque that I received from my service as NCDA president states it is awarded for "his passionate dedication to our profession." I believe passionately about our role in society and the good that we do every day in our profession. I cannot imagine living in a world that did not have counselors. In my career counseling, I help my clients find their passion in life and pursue it. Further, if you love your work, the lines between work and play are blurred. Work seems like play. You get lost in the moment.

When I am working on a manuscript, I am consumed by it. I love the creativity in writing. I love the focus and flow of the moment. My most creative moments are at some of the oddest times, like in the middle of the night. I wake up with a phrase or action that may be fleeting and therefore requires that I get out of bed and write it down before it evaporates into the darkness. When I am working on a manuscript, I will get up in the middle of the night and write for hours.

What I Believe

Finally, in an article titled "The Hidden Minority: Issues and Challenges in Working With Lesbian Women and Gay Men," one of my heroes, Ruth Fassinger (1991), spoke eloquently for so many of us who have chosen counseling over other kinds of applied psychology:

> Inherent in our philosophy is an approach that frames problems in terms of normalcy and day-to-day problems in living, and eschews a singular focus on pathology and diagnosis. We emphasize positive mental health and focus on strengths and adaptive strategies in our clients. We see ourselves as educators and advocates for clients, and we emphasize the empowerment of individuals. We value preventive as well as ameliorative intervention efforts, and we work toward enhanced functioning of all people. Our scope of vision includes environmental as well as individual interventions, promotion of mental health at the level of groups and systems, the effective use of community resources, and political involvement where relevant. We see ourselves as versatile, able to function in a variety of settings and to work collegially with other diverse professionals. We emphasize developmental approaches to working with people, including attention to their cultural context and the influence of gender, race, age, ethnicity, sexual orientation, (dis)ability, and sociohistory. (p. 159)

This is what I too believe about our profession, and this is why I am here.

References

American Psychiatric Association. (1968). *Diagnostic and statistical manual of mental disorders* (2nd ed.). Washington, DC: Author.

Bull, C. (2003, December 9). A big step for mental health. *The Advocate*, p. 25.

Fassinger, R. E. (1991). The hidden minority: Issues and challenges in working with lesbian women and gay men. *The Counseling Psychologist, 19*(2), 157–176.

Pope, M., & Schulz, R. (1990). Sexual behavior and attitudes in midlife and aging homosexual males. *Journal of Homosexuality, 20*(3–4), 169–178.

Chapter 17

Reflections on the Writing of
Journeys to Professional Excellence
●●●●●●●●●●●●●●●●●●●●●●●●●●●●●●●●●●●●●●

Fred Bemak and Robert K. Conyne

The development, planning, and editing of this book were profound experiences for both of us. Unlike many of the books, book chapters, and journal articles each of us has published, this book was very different from the start. As new chapters would arrive by e-mail, we would touch base. Our first comment was always on meeting timelines: "Got another," or "Five more to go," or "Should we prompt her or him?" and the like. These interactions were regularly centered on timelines, deadlines, and progress. As we progressed, however, we would inevitably have second comments about our amazement when we read the chapters: "This chapter is incredible!" or "I didn't know this about her or him!" or "What a powerful story!" or "This book is far more significant than we thought!" We were in full agreement throughout our process, believing we were creating a book that would be an important contribution to the field and one that far exceeded our initial expectations.

We were so moved by each of the chapters and our colleagues and friends' journeys that we began to wonder how to tie it all together in a way that was as meaningful as each chapter for you, the reader. We began to explore what would make sense, and finally decided to ask the contributing authors if they would be willing to share brief reflections derived from writing about their journey.

Request for Authors' Reflections

The letter we sent captures how we felt about the book and is copied below:

> April 9, 2004
>
> *Journeys* Book Authors
>
> Your chapters are terrific! We are just amazed by the depth of personal sharing. We think readers will be truly moved and gain both personally and professionally from your professional journey chapter. Thank you.

We noted an unusual amount of unsolicited comments from you about your experience in producing your chapter. You said things like, "It was really difficult to do this," "This was a meaningful experience for me," "Thanks for giving me this opportunity," and "I struggled with this."

As we (Bob and Fred) have reflected on the experience, we thought about adding a very short section about your writing process, believing that this would add an unusual and interesting aspect to the book. Thus, we are following up with each of you to ask you to write up to two pages (maximum, please!), double-spaced, about what you would like readers to know of your personal experience in writing your chapter, and what that experience has meant to you. We will edit and combine these into a final chapter of the book and encourage readers to examine their own lives in a similar fashion. We are hopeful that a discussion about your experiences of reviewing your journey will facilitate others to engage in self-reflection.

We hope each of you are willing and able to do this, even though it was not part of the original agreement. If agreeable, here is an outline of what would be most helpful in these two pages:

Reflections of the experience of writing your book chapter: What it was like and what you learned.

Please contact either of us for any questions or assistance.

Thanks!
Bob and Fred

We wanted to try to summarize what happened for our authors in writing such intimate and personal stories, and present themes, commonalities, and their experiences as a means for you, the reader, to further examine your own professional journey. Our hope and intent in this last chapter is to stimulate your own self-reflection as you think about where you are now in your own personal and professional development, imagine where you are going, and reach for your dreams. Nine authors found the time to share their reflections.

A good place to start our summary is with the following quotation often attributed to Socrates: "The unexamined life is not worth living." So how do we, some of the most prominent and well-known counselors in the field, examine our lives? What is this experience like?

Themes Emerging From Authors' Reflections

What follows are four themes we culled from the authors' reflections. These themes not only illustrate the effects of sharing publicly about one's personal and professional life but also provide additional insight into how professional lives are created and sustained.

Emotional Intensity

It was fascinating to us that one predominant theme was the emotional intensity that came along with the writing. One author said that writing this chapter was "personally therapeutic . . . opening up emotion." This author and others were surprised about still feeling so much emotional intensity. Fear of exposure, or anxiety about expressing too deeply, also was expressed by some authors, as the following example shows: "Even as someone who prefers extraversion, there are issues in my narrative that I have never discussed with anyone. . . . I was afraid of being judged negatively and having those negative judgments get in the way. . . ." Another author commented, "It was more difficult than I imagined, and more meaningful. I wandered into worlds I had not visited for a long time." One writer talked about strong emotions and "finding myself laughing and crying, remembering connections." Another said, "I cherished the opportunity to think (and feel) about my professional life, to put my intellectual affairs in order, as it were." In retrospect, as editors, we were both deeply touched by the chapters and did not anticipate their depth and emotional intensity nor the strong feelings in our colleagues that writing about their journeys would evoke. As we look back on the guidelines for authors, however, we realize that we set up this book to be different, to be deep, and to tap into this level of emotional depth. So in another way, it is no surprise.

Meaningfulness

Another significant theme that emerged was tied in with existential themes of meaningfulness. One person spoke about how "striving to make a difference has been a primary motivator in what I do." Another author, who is internationally acclaimed for numerous publications, shared that, "I'd done this [life review] in bits and pieces before, but this was my first experience with a more thorough approach." Authors reflected on the "remarkable" events in their lives, which was echoed in a comment that the experience "reaffirmed that life is a gift." One author expressed a view for many by remarking, "It felt good to reflect on my accomplishments and to recognize publicly how lucky I have been in my mentors and friends." Authors appreciated others around them, as this comment reveals: "I have realized through my disclosures in this chapter how important surrounding myself with optimistic and well-meaning people is. I eschew those who are negative and demeaning of others because I think they dehumanize our existence." Remarkably, the writing about one's life and journey provided a moment to reflect in the busy schedule of a number of the authors, and was uniformly felt to be important to them.

Significance of External Events

A few of the authors keyed into important national and world events that shaped their lives and carried great significance as they wrote their chapters. Michael Hutchins, who was a teacher years ago in Baghdad, spoke about the current events in Iraq as having great significance and bringing back feelings of joy and sorrow. Courtland C. Lee talked about JFK's assassination, the Civil Rights Movement, the moon landing, and the popularization of the Internet as defining moments. The force and movement of the surrounding world had importance for some of the authors.

Standing for Something of Value

Some authors wrote about the value of taking stands in their lives and about personal commitments to make changes in the world. As one example, an author wrote, "It has been central to me to make a difference. . . . The struggle is far from over, but I hope that I can say that I have indeed made a difference." In another case, an author shared, "My father's ability to stand up for right becomes more important (to me) every year. . . . He never hesitated, and I find myself relying on his spirit when things become rough."

Personal Traits

There also was a reconnection to personal traits that was shared by some. Writing was easier than talking for a few of the authors because modesty was an important cultural and personal trait. Another person spoke about the importance of maintaining humility in writing their chapter, while someone else talked about not "bragging or being egocentric." One author spoke about important values like "hard work, honesty, faith, helpfulness, kindness, friendliness, and civility." Another said, "I have told aspects of my career story on many occasions but have never put them together from an analytic perspective, as I did answering the questions provided to us by the editors of this volume." Humor was also identified as important by a number of authors who talked about the joy in writing their stories. One author stated, "I laughed out loud in recalling some of the times I have written about in this chapter." Tied in with the happiness in recalling one's story is the freedom that one author felt. "When I finished writing the autobiography, it was as if an unconscious psychological burden had been lifted from my soul. I was relieved of imperceptible negative emotions that must have impeded unknowingly my sense of completeness and satisfaction throughout life."

Conclusion

The richness of the authors' professional journeys, we think, is beautifully shared in this book. Each chapter is its own story. In turn, each story possesses a depth of disclosure that generates profound meaning for those of us who are fortunate enough to read them. As one author said, "Indeed, the self-examination was liberating."

We hope that you also will experience the joys, pains, struggles, and successes of our colleagues throughout this book and move toward your own liberation. Understanding the lives of others is certainly important in helping us realize our own unique gifts. This kind of understanding also can help us to develop greater personal meaning and the courage to reach for our dreams and to live life more fully.

We wish you all a wonderful personal and professional journey.

—Fred and Bob